Building a Comprehensive IT Security Program

Practical Guidelines and Best Practices

Jeremy Wittkop

Apress®

Building a Comprehensive IT Security Program: Practical Guidelines and Best Practices

Jeremy Wittkop
Boulder, Colorado, USA

ISBN-13 (pbk): 978-1-4842-2052-8   ISBN-13 (electronic): 978-1-4842-2053-5
DOI 10.1007/978-1-4842-2053-5

Library of Congress Control Number: 2016947953

Managing Director: Welmoed Spahr
Acquisitions Editor: Susan McDermott
Developmental Editor: Douglas Pundick, Laura Berendson
Technical Reviewer: Graham Laird
Editorial Board: Steve Anglin, Pramila Balen, Laura Berendson, Aaron Black, Louise Corrigan, Jonathan Gennick, Robert Hutchinson, Celestin Suresh John, Nikhil Karkal, James Markham, Susan McDermott, Matthew Moodie, Natalie Pao, Gwenan Spearing
Coordinating Editor: Rita Fernando
Copy Editor: Karen Jameson
Compositor: SPi Global
Indexer: SPi Global
Cover image designed by FreePik

Distributed to the book trade worldwide by Springer Science+Business Media New York, 233 Spring Street, 6th Floor, New York, NY 10013. Phone 1-800-SPRINGER, fax (201) 348-4505, e-mail orders-ny@springer-sbm.com, or visit www.springer.com. Apress Media, LLC is a California LLC and the sole member (owner) is Springer Science + Business Media Finance Inc (SSBM Finance Inc). SSBM Finance Inc is a Delaware corporation.

For information on translations, please e-mail rights@apress.com, or visit www.apress.com.

Apress and friends of ED books may be purchased in bulk for academic, corporate, or promotional use. eBook versions and licenses are also available for most titles. For more information, reference our Special Bulk Sales–eBook Licensing web page at www.apress.com/bulk-sales.

Any source code or other supplementary materials referenced by the author in this text is available to readers at www.apress.com. For detailed information about how to locate your book's source code, go to www.apress.com/source-code/.

Printed on acid-free paper

To my Mom and Dad who never gave up on me when they probably should've, Rob and Chuck who gave me opportunities few would've, and my wife who loved me through the entire crazy journey.

A special thanks to Graham Laird and the Apress publishing team who made it all possible.

Contents at a Glance

Contents

About the Author

Jeremy Wittkop is a leader in the Information Security industry, specifically as it relates to content and context protection. Jeremy brings insights from a variety of industries, including military and defense, logistics, entertainment, as well as Information Security services.

Jeremy started with InteliSecure as the leader of the Managed Services department and has overseen 1000% growth of that department by helping to solve complex Information Security challenges for organizations spanning the globe. Jeremy now leads InteliSecure's Sales Engineering team, which is responsible for architecting solution packages that include creative approaches to people, process, and technology.

About the Technical Reviewer

Graham C. Laird, CISA, has over eight years of experience in the cyber-security industry in a variety of positions as a Security Analyst, Project Manager, Financial Analyst, and Managed Security Service (MSS) Senior Team Manager. He has worked at InteliSecure, Inc. since 2007, helping the company grow from a startup with five employees to a global organization of two hundred employees. Throughout his tenure Graham has helped InteliSecure innovate the MSS offering for corporate Critical Asset Protection. These services support companies across many industries and include small enterprises to international Fortune 100 corporations. As the security industry has evolved, Graham has been on the forefront of analyzing how new technologies can integrate with existing corporate security portfolios.

Graham is a Certified Information Security Auditor (CISA) with ISACA and holds a Bachelor of Science in Finance from the University of Nebraska–Lincoln. He currently resides in Denver, Colorado.

Introduction

I have undertaken an incredible journey to get to a place where I would be writing a book about Information Security. My journey really started with my time in the United States Army. During that time, I discovered a passion for protecting those who cannot protect themselves from threats that mean them harm. During my time in the Army, I witnessed significant amounts of information that were benign, as well as information that, if compromised, could cause harm up to and including death for my fellow service members. The idea of Critical Asset Protection that we will discuss in this book was very applicable then, although I did not know how to describe it or what to do about it at the time. Additionally, around that time, unmanned aircraft, or drones, were making their debut on the battlefield. The early versions of drones were sending information in an unencrypted fashion from the actual drone to the drone operators and the operators on the ground. Obviously, these transmissions could be intercepted. How could this happen?

After I left the military, I went to college and pursued a career in the music industry. The industry was not right for me for a variety of reasons, but it was during that time that I became fascinated with Intellectual Property law and saw firsthand the economic harm that can be inflicted on individuals and organizations when Intellectual Property is not properly protected.

Ultimately, my journey led me through the defense contract space and eventually to a small building in Castle Rock, Colorado, where a meeting with Robert Eggebrecht changed my life forever. At the time, Rob ran a small company known as BEW Global, which then became InteliSecure, and I found my true passion in life, which was to protect those who could not protect themselves, specific to the information that is most important to them, in the rapidly evolving ever-changing cyber-world.

I wrote this book to help people understand the problem we are facing and to inspire hope that we can solve these problems should we choose to face these challenges head-on. It is my sincere hope that everyone reading this book will understand the global struggle that is pitting legitimate businesses around the globe against a multitude of threats that have the potential to cause significant financial damage to their organizations as well as their economies. I also endeavor to provide each reader with information that they can use inside their own organizations to build a comprehensive program to protect their information. Finally, the goal is to help security professionals and business leaders communicate better and work together on a foundation of mutual respect in order to solve complex problems together.

The process of learning all of these lessons has been one of the most rewarding experiences of my life. It has also been an amazing experience to write this book. I want to take a moment to thank you for reading and to express my hope that you find these insights as valuable as I have and you enjoy reading this book as much as I have enjoyed writing it.

CHAPTER 1

■ ■ ■

The Problem We Are Facing

A problem clearly stated is a problem half solved.

—Dorothea Brande

Have you ever sat in a boardroom directly after a cyber-attack? I have, and it is a terrible experience. Chief Executive Officers (CEOs), Chief Information Security Officers (CISOs), and Chief Information Officers (CIOs) silently shake their heads and stare out the window, wondering if their lives have been destroyed by this attack. What will happen to their organization in the following months? How many people will be laid off as a result? Too many hold their head in their hands contemplating the damage to the organization they have dedicated their lives to building after a cyber-attack. As they think about the families that will be affected by the inevitable layoffs that will follow, if the organization even survives the incident, there is a central question that they ask themselves, and it is a question I have endeavored to answer over the last few years. The pursuit of the answer to this question has driven me down a path that is culminating in sharing my experiences, ideas, observations, and research in this book. Why are we failing to secure our most sensitive data?

At one time, the case could be made that there was not enough attention being paid at the highest levels of organizations in the private sector, or that not enough money was being spent by organizations to protect themselves. However, simply browsing the risk factors section of Form 10-K reports for publicly traded companies, or simply looking at the volume and profitability of cyber-security companies and products make it apparent that the challenges we face are not due to a lack of spending or awareness that danger posted by cyber-threats are clear and present. Many executives I have spoken with tell me that they continue to spend money on the problem, but attacks continue to grow in scope and prevalence. For many companies, the threat of a significant cyber-attack is nothing short of existential. If the shortcomings in Information Security initiatives are not driven by resources or will, why do our efforts continue to fall short? What can we do as a business community to protect our most critical information, convince others of the importance of Information Security initiatives, and protect executives from the electronic jungle in which so many have been maimed and mauled – some to never return? As with any other problem we endeavor to solve, we must begin with a clear definition.

ThreatCon

"According to the Associated Press, U.S. intelligence officials have said that cyber-crime currently trumps terrorism as the biggest threat to the country's security." (http://blog.trendmicro.com/cyber-attacks-considered-top-national-security-threat/) Take a moment to let that statement sink in. While news reports are dominated by Al Qaeda, ISIS, Hamas, and countless other terrorist groups, the largest threat to U.S. national security is cyber-crime. The problem is not limited to the United States either. In fact, the World Wide Web has removed the proximity requirement from crime. Before the globe was truly connected, if I wanted to steal your credit card, I would have to be physically close enough to you to remove the said

© Jeremy Wittkop 2016
J. Wittkop, *Building a Comprehensive IT Security Program*, DOI 10.1007/978-1-4842-2053-5_1

card from your possession. Not only did that significantly limit the people that could attempt to steal that credit card, but it also limited each criminal to attempting to steal a single card at a time. Now, criminals can steal millions of credit cards and attack thousands of organizations while drinking a cup of coffee in their pajamas. Further, there is an entire illicit marketplace that exists on a part of the Internet that most people do not even know exists. This side of the Internet is sometimes referred to as the "Dark Web." The Dark Web is a digital black market where all manners of illicit activity take place and stolen goods, services, and information are bought and sold. The anonymity provided by the Dark Web is one of the many ways that hackers, crackers, and programmers leverage the significant knowledge gap between them and the general public for their own personal gain. These technically savvy individuals may be operating independently or as part of a group.

Removing proximity and simultaneous attack limitations presents a major opportunity for countries, groups, or individuals who possess superior technical skills to transfer wealth from less skillful individuals who have access to financial instruments, identities, and other pieces of information that may be of value on the Dark Web. When information is stolen from a business in a certain country, it impacts every individual in that country, as individuals inside economies are interconnected.

According to McAfee's Net Losses: Estimating the Global Cost of Cybercrime (http://www.mcafee.com/us/resources/reports/rp-economic-impact-cybercrime2.pdf) report, the United States loses about .64 percent of GDP annually to cyber-crime. In 2013, the U.S. Gross Domestic Product was $16.77 trillion, which means that approximately $107 billion dollars was lost to cyber-crime in the United States alone during that year. As a percentage of GDP, that corresponds to roughly 400,000 of the roughly 150 million jobs (According to Current Employment Statistics) that are occupied currently would be lost in a single year using the same percentage. Cyber-crime is a global problem, but there is no doubt that it affects more developed countries disproportionately. Terrorism, like the events of September 11, 2001, has a significant and lasting effect on the U.S. economy and captures attention due to the loss of life and shock value of the images of death and destruction. However, cyber-crime is far more prevalent and far more likely to directly impact an individual or organization than violent extremism or terrorism. Additionally, there is very little that individuals can do to protect themselves from a terrorist attack. With respect to terrorism, I am reminded of a saying I used to repeat to my mother when I was deployed to Iraq: "Worrying is like a rocking chair, it will give you something to do, but it won't get you anywhere." This is not to say that terrorism shouldn't be a concern to the average individual, as I'm sure my time in Iraq was concerning to my mother, but spending significant time worrying about circumstances outside of your control is not necessarily helpful, and can be destructive to both individuals and organizations. However, for business leaders, cyber-security *is* something that they can realistically defend against. As such, it is important to understand the threat landscape and take measures to protect themselves and their organizations from harm, which can be catastrophic.

From a macroeconomic perspective, the growing prevalence of cyber-crime leads to a reduction in the rewards and therefore motivation for innovation on the supply side, and a reduction in consumer confidence that results in a reduction in the demand side of the economic equation. In short, a reduction in consumer spending and a reduction in the amount of Intellectual Property generated translate to a major indirect impact to the American economy that is much more difficult to measure than the easily measurable direct impact of breaches as compared to Gross Domestic Product. Similar stories can be told about other prosperous economies and wealthy individuals throughout the world. Developing nations such as many of the growing economies in South America and portions of Africa risk emigration to other countries if they fail to protect the ideas and ability to profit from those ideas of their citizens. Such failures result in stunted economic growth and a lower quality of life for all of their citizens.

There is an ever-increasing amount of research available for those who would like to study the economic impact of cyber-crime on a global or regional basis. The important point for the purposes of this discussion is to understand the magnitude of the impact that cyber-crime, cyber-terrorism, and industrial espionage has on American national security and to extrapolate that impact to other developed countries across the globe. The purpose of understanding the magnitude of the threat is not to make the situation appear hopeless; conversely, it is to open the conversation about the appropriate levels of spending for organizations and governments to protect themselves against threats with appropriate countermeasures.

Individual businesses facing targeted attacks from well-funded and sophisticated attackers are unlikely to possess the resources necessary to successfully defend against these types of attacks. The silver lining in this dark cloud is that there is often a cost-benefit analysis of some kind performed when evaluating an attack target. If you are camping with four friends in a forest and you are attacked by a bear, you do not have to outrun the bear; you simply need to outrun the slowest of your four friends. Similarly, organizations don't need to build defenses that are impervious to cyber-attack; many would argue doing so is impossible anyway, but rather to ensure the work factor, or amount of time, money, and effort an attacker must expend to successfully attack a target, are high enough to make the cost-benefit analysis more attractive to attack a different organization.

What then is an appropriate countermeasure for an organization? The first step in answering that question is to define the different types of threat actors that exist and what types of information they are targeting. Richard A. McFeely, executive assistant director of criminal, cyber, response, and services branch of the FBI7 division of the Federal Bureau of Investigation said, "Our adversaries in the cyber realm include spies from nation-states who seek our secrets and intellectual property; organized criminals who want to steal our identities and money; terrorists who aspire to attack our power grid, water supply, or other infrastructure; and hacktivist groups who are trying to make a political or social statement."

▓ **Note**   An argument can be made that there are also criminals acting independently who would like to leverage their technical skills to make an illicit profit. For the purpose of this discussion, we will classify such individuals as Organized Criminals, even if they are acting independently, are as they are most closely related to the Organized Crime group in terms of resources, skill, and motivation.

Each of these actors has different profiles, targets, motives, tactics, techniques, and protocols that they use to attack organizations. Further, the appropriate protections and responses to each of these threat actors vary based on their unique motivators and techniques. It is a vital step in the process of building a comprehensive Information Security program to define what types of assets an organization has that are valuable and vulnerable to attack, and to match those assets to a threat actor or several threat actors that may target that type of information.

Prior to exploring the threat actor categories, it is important to note that these actors and what they are targeting does not remain static and is subject to change. It is incumbent upon Information Security teams and professionals to remain current on changes in the threat actor community, and the information they may be targeting. In general, the threat actor categories remain relatively constant, while the types of information they target may change. For example, in the three years between Richard McFeely's quote and the writing of this book, there were no categories of organized groups of actors added or subtracted, but some of the threat actors changed their focus: in some cases multiple times, over the same time period.

A Question of Motive

Each of the threat actor groups has different tactics, techniques, protocols, and targets that characterize the attacks and allow an effective forensics investigation to determine the likely culprit after a breach is discovered and investigated. However, it is the motive that is most important to consider with respect to classifying the threats an organization may face before a breach occurs. There are no absolutes with respect to motives per group, but enough evidence exists to suggest that there are motivational patterns that can be attributed to each of the four groups.

Spies and Nation-States

Spies and nation-states are generally motivated by two primary objectives. First is the ability to compete with their targets more effectively, or to gain access to Intellectual Property and secrets more quickly than if they were to develop the property independently. The second objective is traditional espionage activity. There are many examples of nation-states being responsible for breaches of information from cases of the United States gaining information about Iran's nuclear program or cases involving the Chinese government gaining information about U.S. government employees. It would be a relatively safe assumption that countless other successful and unsuccessful cyber-espionage attacks every day throughout the world. Leon Panetta, the former director of the U.S. Central Intelligence Agency (CIA) stated at the RSA Security Conference in 2015 that there were roughly one million daily attempts to compromise the CIA while he was the director.

It stands to reason that the majority of the cyber-espionage activity would be directed at world governments and their agencies or ministries. There have been cases, however, where private enterprise has been targeted for the suspected purpose of gaining information on government employees. One of the most common examples of this dynamic is compromising health insurance companies because they often have records of individuals as well as their employers. Nation-state actors are often well-funded and employ creative and intelligent individuals, so it is likely that they would continue to find creative ways to gather the information they seek with high probabilities of success and low work factors.

Organized Criminals

Organized criminals and, for that matter, individual criminal actors are motivated by profit. Regardless of whether they are using cyber-attacks or more traditional methods of accomplishing their objectives, the profit motive is relatively universal for criminals of all stripes. It is a relatively simple motive and one that is easily recognizable by the fact that the majority of the information they steal will likely be sold at some point on the Dark Web. Organized criminals also generally operate their organizations in a similar fashion to legitimate business. As a result, they endeavor to maximize profits while minimizing expenses both in terms of human and capital resources.

Terrorists

Many people are confused between nation-state attacks and state-sponsored terrorist attacks. They key differentiator between the two categories is motive and intent. Terrorists, state-sponsored and otherwise, are not concerned with the theft of information, but generally with the destruction of information, systems, or creating scenarios through technological means that could lead to destruction of property or loss of life. Also, terrorists generally take credit for what they do after they do it, while nation-state actors who are conducting espionage activities or stealing Intellectual Property endeavor to do so covertly before, during, and after the attack takes place. Therefore, attacks that are intentionally publicized or conducted with the intention of causing harm to the target rather than stealing information are classified as terror attacks for the purpose of this book, whether or not they originate from a nation-state.

Hacktivist Groups

Hacktivist groups, or individuals with similar aims, are motivated by making a statement. The motivation for the attack is often to expose information their target holds as secret in order to embarrass their target or to expose something about their target to the general public. Often, their attacks don't target information at all, but rather deface, degrade, or destroy an asset belonging to the target organization. Examples of this behavior include defacing a web site or launching a Denial of Service (DOS) attack. The motive is not for profit or to use the information for the groups' own purposes; they almost always make the information publicly available as proof that they successfully conducted their attack or operation.

Electronic Espionage

The first category of threat actors is the one that represents the vast minority of the threats encountered on a daily basis. Yet, they are the most adept, skilled, and talked about in the news media and many Information Security circles because of their ability to cause massive amounts of damage in comparatively short amounts of time. Advanced Persistent Threats (APTs), state sponsored and otherwise, are the spies and nation-states that McFeely discussed as targeting Intellectual Property. These threats always have a motive, goal, and have premeditated plans of action. Often, when private industry is the intended victim, it is Intellectual Property that is targeted. However, the connotation of Intellectual Property that is limited to product designs, copyrights, trademarks, and patents is far too narrow a view of Intellectual Property in this context.

The most valuable types of Intellectual Property for the actors in this category are business intelligence. What is business intelligence? Business intelligence from this perspective is defined as plans, processes, and procedures that allow one organization to deliver higher quality, cheaper goods to their customers at a higher profit margin than their competitors. Simply put, business intelligence is defined as anything that an organization would use to gain and maintain a competitive advantage.

Far too often, I have sat in war rooms helping organizations that fail to answer a simple question: "What types of Intellectual Property do you have?" The unacceptable answer that comes back is "We don't have any Intellectual Property." Additionally, this response is not limited to the executive level, but is a consistent response from employees at all levels of organizations. Let me assure you, if you do business in a developed country with a high cost and standard of living, and you do so profitably, you or your company has Intellectual Property that allows you to operate profitably. If you did not have Intellectual Property and everything you did was completely repeatable through publicly available information, I can guarantee you that a company would form in a less-developed country that would be able to provide the same goods and services you provide at a lower price point.

In my experience, I would expand the definition of what state-sponsored and industrial espionage actors are targeting inside of organizations to include all types of information that can expand their knowledge of their adversaries. For example, advanced espionage groups do not steal credit card data, Protected Health Information (PHI), or other types of regulated information, as their attacks are far beyond the purpose of stealing sensitive information for resale value. I attended a research presentation by Jon DiMaggio from Symantec's Security Technology and Response team detailing extensive research showing a Chinese-sponsored group named Black Vine by Symantec's research team that began to attack the health care industry. It is thought that this Black Vine group is responsible for the widely publicized Anthem [Blue Cross Blue Shield] breach. Why would China attack the health care industry? Theories abound, but the most credible theory that has been put forth, in my opinion, is the idea that they were attacking Anthem and other large health care providers that provide health insurance specifically to government employees and their families, so they can build databases of U.S. government employees. The thought process is that if they can build a comprehensive database of U.S. government employees, and someone comes into the country that is not in the database, there is a good chance that individual is involved in U.S. intelligence and using an assumed name. This statement is simply a theory, but we know that state-sponsored attacks are far too complex and forward thinking to steal health record information and try to sell it on the Dark Web. Additionally, there is reliable intelligence that says in these attacks no PHI was stolen. Instead, only the identity and employer information was stolen.

There are many sources of espionage-based attacks. The attacks originating in China get the most media coverage, likely because China has a formidable force of individuals that aim to attack governments and business that may have information that could be of benefit to them. However, China is far from the only sponsor of these attacks. Many countries have use for various business information for a variety of reasons. One example is when foreign companies want to do business in a country that controls all of the property inside their borders, they must purchase the land to fulfill their plans from the government. Prior knowledge of business plans or research such as Oil and Gas exploration data can allow for real estate price manipulation that can be quite lucrative for such countries.

Conducting cyber-espionage activities is in the interest of every country that has an intelligence agency. The United States has a documented history of offering skilled hackers reduced sentences in exchange for their service to the U.S. government. Many militaries also employ specialists, which are sometimes referred to as cyber-warriors, whose entire purpose is to facilitate offensive, defensive, and counterattacks that are deemed to be in their county's interest.

Furthermore, non-state actors may commission or develop teams of attackers to gain competitive advantages over their competition or gain the secrets necessary to overcome significant barriers to entry in certain industries. In short, the financial backing for these types of attacks can vary wildly, but there are some common threads between them with respect to types of attacks, tactics techniques and protocols, as well as their desire to stay covert.

The aspect of these actors that makes them the most recognizable and difficult to defend against is that they are sophisticated, well-funded, adaptable, and determined. It is likely that the term "Advanced Persistent Threat" originated with these types of threat actors, but at this point, that term has become cliché and using it has become counterproductive in that it is no longer specific and descriptive. The term "Advanced Persistent Threat" has come to be used by an organization to describe any attacker that was successful in attacking them.

One of the aspects that make these attacks so difficult to defend against and give them such a high success rate is that they often begin with Social Engineering. Social Engineering refers broadly to the practice of gathering information from individuals through social means. These types of activities come in a variety of forms, such as calling a user and asking for their credentials while posing as a member of the Information Security team, very advanced spear phishing campaigns in which very legitimate looking e-mails are sent with the purpose of tricking the recipient, or compromising legitimate web sites with malicious software in order to harvest credentials, among many others.

It is key to recognize that these threats are adaptable and sophisticated because it means that stopping these types of threats will require adaptable and sophisticated teams of individuals to defend against their attacks. Despite grandiose claims often made by technology vendors, there is no technology that can protect against a sophisticated and adaptable attacker with technology alone. The fact that the attacker is sophisticated and adaptable means, by its very definition, that the attacker will be able to identify and take the necessary steps to circumvent an organization's technology solutions. Vigilant and well-trained teams are necessary to recognize that something is amiss in the environment and investigate the issues in order to contain, eradicate, and recover from the attack.

Another critical piece of information to understand about these actors is that they do not want to be discovered. Not only do they not want to be discovered while the attack is in process, but they also make considerable efforts to cover their tracks while they are attacking and once they are finished. Impressively, they will actually fix security weaknesses while they are attacking to make it harder for others to detect their presence and to solidify their ability to control an environment.

Spies and Nation-States Modus Operandi

So how exactly do cyber-spies attack organizations? As with any of the threat actors, the attack profile varies significantly between groups, but there are some common threads. The attacks almost always begin with some type of Social Engineering campaign. Social Engineering practices range from phishing attacks, in which an attacker will send an e-mail that looks like it originates from a legitimate source, like a bank, and attempts to trick a user to log into a fake portal for the purpose of stealing their credentials, to phone calls from people pretending to be from Internet Technology (IT) groups or executive teams asking a user to divulge their password. These efforts may also include watering hole attacks, which are attacks in which legitimate sites are infected with malicious software that allows attackers to harvest the credentials of all users logging into the web page. The attackers will then use the credentials they have harvested in order to move throughout the network and gather the information they need. While Social Engineering attacks can vary wildly, they are generally characterized by an attempt by a nefarious party to trick a user into divulging a piece of personal or corporate information. In most cases, those credentials are used to compromise a system that will allow the attacker to gather information about the users of an organization. This is the first step of what is known as the reconnaissance phase.

The second step in the reconnaissance phase centers around probing defenses for vulnerabilities. Commonly available vulnerability scanners are relatively inexpensive to use, and generally do not require the customer to prove they own the IP addresses they are scanning. These factors create an inexpensive, relatively anonymous, and readily accessible method for would-be attackers to gain large volumes of information on the security gaps of their targets. Spies and nation-states are far from the only groups to use these scans either. Due to their availability and ease of use, I often advise my clients that anyone who seeks to attack them will likely run a vulnerability scan first. Consequently, it is imperative for each organization to also perform scanning exercises, if only to predict likely avenues of attack.

When the attack is actually executed, true zero-day attacks are often used. A zero-day exploit describes an exploit that is deployed during the period of time between when the exploit is discovered by someone and the time there is a patch made available to address that exploit. The use of a zero-day exploit is a reliable indicator that an attacker is well-funded, because zero-day exploits must be either developed or purchased, both of which require significant resources in terms of capital or manpower. As a frame of reference, in late 2015, a zero-day exploit for Apple's mobile iOS Operating System, was being marketed for one million US dollars. Since zero-day exploits are, by their definition, unknown exploits, the only defense against them is a well-defined program that can determine deviations from normal behavior and a vigilant team of security experts who can recognize subtle signs of abnormality in an environment. Also, since they desire to remain undetected, it is very likely that the majority of breaches perpetrated by these threat actors are never known.

Espionage Use Case Example: Anthem

The breach of health records associated with the Blue Cross Blue Shield company Anthem generated headlines around the world. Originally, the headlines were due to the size of the breach at around 80 million records. The headlines rapidly changed due to the group thought to be responsible. Anthem quickly released a statement after the breach was detected informing the general public of the attack and claimed the attack against them was sophisticated. In nearly every case of a breach, companies claim the attacks were sophisticated in an effort to convince the general public that the breach was due to skill on the part of the attacker and not a lack of vigilance on the part of the victim. However, this attack was different. It was highly sophisticated and it did not seem to fit the profile of Organized Criminals attempting to steal identities that could subsequently be sold for profit. Additionally, it was claimed by Anthem that no credit card data or health information was stolen, although that type of information was certainly present in the systems that were compromised. It was immediately widely suspected in the security industry that this was not an attack for profit at all, which was quickly confirmed by the fact that none of the stolen information appeared to be for sale. Given the sophistication of the attack and the lack of capitalization on the stolen information in the marketplace, the attack fit the profile of a nation-state more than that of an organized criminal enterprise. Was this in fact the case? (www.anthem.com/health-insurance/about-us/pressreleasedetails/WI/2015/1813/statement-regarding-cyber-attack-against-anthem)

At the end of July, *PC World* reported that the same group of hackers, dubbed Black Vine by Symantec, breached both the U.S. Office of Personnel Management and Anthem. The article also insinuated the same group may have breached information from United Airlines. Black Vine is a group that is believed to have ties to the Chinese government and has a history of targeting airlines, so why would they suddenly target health insurance? I have heard many theories and it is impossible to know for sure, but the most plausible theory in my mind, given the Office of Personnel Management breach by the same group in proximity to the Anthem breach, is that the Chinese are trying to build extensive databases on US government personnel. Anthem is a major health insurance provider for U.S. government employees. The theory surmises that if the Chinese can build databases of everyone who is employed by the U.S. government, then they can compare the U.S. government employees coming into China against their database and the people who do not match are likely spies using a false name. Again, it would be impossible to confirm or deny this theory, but it has been confirmed that Black Vine is responsible for the attack. So, who is Black Vine? (www.pcworld.com/article/2954872/opm-anthem-hackers-reportedly-also-breached-united-airlines)

Symantec's Security Response team member Jon DiMaggio released a white paper about the group after the Anthem breach and has tracked their activities back to 2012. He also linked them to the Chinese government and the use of a framework of zero-day exploits developed by the Chinese dubbed the Elderwood Framework. There is significant research into what types of attacks they have carried out and who they have targeted, and if this information is of interest, I would recommend reading more about them. The details that the Symantec team has been able to gather are fascinating. (www.symantec.com/content/en/us/enterprise/media/security_response/whitepapers/the-black-vine-cyberespionage-group.pdf)

The main point for the purpose of this example is to reinforce the profile of nation-state espionage threat actors. They can originate from anywhere in the world, but are often associated with world powers. China is the most well-known, but there are others. Essentially those countries are trying to become competitive with the developed world as quickly as possible, and they have found it to be more cost effective to develop exploits and steal Intellectual Property than to develop the Intellectual Property themselves. Also, as appears to be the case in the Anthem breach, there is a concerted effort to perform traditional global espionage efforts utilizing cyber technology.

The threat actors in this category usually are utilizing sophisticated attack methods and zero-day threats. The attack generally starts with some type of Social Engineering or phishing campaign designed to harvest credentials.

Many people who are not familiar with Information Security make the assumption that when something is stolen it was because the victim organization did something wrong. In the case of Anthem, the opposite is true. The Anthem Information Security team discovered the breach in progress due to their vigilance in monitoring their environment, which likely prevented further data theft. In fact, when a true zero-day attack is used, it is unlikely that any commercially available technologies will be of much use to the victim organization. When discussing attacks from the spies and nation-states group, the most vigilant and best-built programs are the ones that discover the breach. Organizations that do not have well-built Information Security programs might very well have been breached, and they never discovered that the breach happened. Some cynics would say there are two types of organizations, those that have been breached, and those that don't know they've been breached. Those that don't know they've been breached are likely currently being breached, and will likely be breached again. The true tragedy in the way the general public views breaches and the fact that breaches that are never discovered are never reported, is the organizations with the best programs are thought to be negligent when they report a breach, and the organizations that are truly negligent are largely assumed to be secure because they do not discover the breaches. In order to fairly assess the security of an organization, the general populace needs to understand that an organization that never reports of breach is not necessarily secure. We should be asking how they know they haven't been breached.

Nation-states are one of the most difficult threat actor groups to protect against due to their funding and their access to zero-day exploits. As such, traditional signature-based technologies such as Intrusion Prevention Systems and traditional anti-malware products are often useless against these actors. The most effective detection and protection methodologies utilize whitelisting technology that only allows programs that are specifically approved to run, and also programs to monitor deviations from normal system and user behavior. It is a harsh reality that it is very unlikely that an organization being targeted by a well-funded and sophisticated nation-state group will be able to resist the attack completely and keep the attackers out of the environment. Mean time to Detection (MttD) and Mean time to Response (MttR) are the metrics that matter with respect to limiting the impact of these types of attacks. The critical element is the ability to detect that an unauthorized actor is inside an environment. In order to do so, a program has to be well-defined and comprehensive in order to closely monitor the movement, storage, and access to Critical Information Assets as well as defining normal system behavior in an environment so that abnormal behavior of any kind can be quickly detected. There is hope in catching nation-state actors in the act of breaching an organization by performing both systematic and user-centric behavioral analysis and baselining. The other key element in responding quickly and appropriately to these types of threats is to build, test, and rehearse an effective Incident Response Plan. The specific methods of building programs that have the capability to detect and respond to these types of activities is the focus of the rest of this book.

In the case of very sophisticated attackers like Black Vine, the malicious programs are named exactly the same as programs that are authorized to run as part of the Operating Systems, which make whitelisting technologies less effective, but in all cases, there is a change in user or system behavior when data begins to be exfiltrated and stolen credentials are utilized. This is true of all threat actor groups who have a motive to actually exfiltrate data rather than destroy systems while they are inside a network. Behavior analysis and anomaly detection should be at the core of any security program that is designed to protect Critical Information Assets.

If Al Capone Owned a Computer

Organized Crime is changing significantly in the Information Age. In many ways it is difficult to be a traditional criminal. In the last century, it has become significantly more difficult for criminals to engage in traditional criminal activity. Walking into a bank and leaving with significant amounts of money at gunpoint is a rare occurrence, trafficking narcotics with the advancements in military and law enforcement technologies has become very difficult, and the advent of tracking technologies and unmanned surveillance vehicles makes it much more difficult to move people and things around the planet undetected. For example, after the Boston Marathon bombing, Dzhokhar Tsarnaev hid inside a boat in a suburban backyard. There was a time where that hiding place would be relatively effective, but with helicopters and thermal imaging technology, it was relatively easy for the authorities to determine someone was hiding inside the boat. However, for enterprising and intellectual Organized Criminals, advancements in IT have presented a wealth of opportunity. Consider the dream scenario presented to bank robbers in a globally connected world when proximity is removed as a requirement. Previously, in order to rob a bank, I would need to go to the bank, and I could only rob one at a time. Now, an organized criminal can deploy exploits against thousands of banks or other institutions simultaneously from the comfort of their own home. Further, consider the difficulty of selling stolen goods of traditional crimes. If I robbed a jewelry store, I would need to find an intermediate party that I could trust, meet to sell the goods, and hope if they were caught in possession of those stolen goods, that they would not inform on me to the police in order to reduce their sentence. Now there is an entire portion of the Internet dedicated to buying and selling illicit goods and information, and participants can buy and sell these goods and services in a largely anonymous fashion.

So who are these people? They aren't much different from the Organized Criminals that have operated throughout history. They primary difference is that the removal of the proximity element from the criminal equation exposes organizations to global cyber-crime groups. Additionally, the ability to transfer information globally allows attackers to physically locate themselves in territories that will not extradite them or that lack the criminal justice infrastructure to track, capture, and prosecute them, while attacking people or companies in far more developed countries with far more lucrative targets. The democratization of crime that results from the conditions described is a major contributing factor to the growing prevalence of global cyber-crime. The good news for organizations that may harbor information that can be sold by Organized Criminals on the open market is that Organized Crime is run much like a for-profit business. As such, attacks are subject to a cost-benefit analysis, and increasing the work factor to attack your organization can tip the scales in such a way that the criminals may choose a softer target with similar potential upside for the group. In other words, your defenses do not have to be impenetrable to defend against attacks launched by these threat actors, organizations simply need to have enough protections in place to make it not worth the effort for the attackers. There is a saying that says if you are camping with four friends and you are attacked by a bear, you do not need to outrun the bear; you simply must outrun the slowest of your four friends. This saying is applicable to defending against cyber-attacks from Organized Criminals, and since many of these attacks originate from Russia and other Eastern European countries, the imagery of outrunning the bear is comically ironic.

What do Organized Criminals want? Both their motives and their targets are relatively simple. As it has always been, Organized Crime is a for-profit enterprise, meaning their motive is profit and they target any information they can sell for a profit. Most people immediately think of credit card numbers stolen from retail organizations because these attacks are prevalent and widely publicized. Contrary to popular belief, credit card information and other financial instruments are far less valuable than identity-related information on the black market due to a concept that I like to call the persistence of information. Most consumers have become accustomed to fraud alerts from their financial institutions. If it is determined that an abnormal purchase is in fact, fraudulent, the consumer is often not liable for any of the unauthorized charges and within moments, the account can be closed and a new one opened. Additionally, many financial institutions have developed programs that are similar in nature to the ones explored in the remainder of this book that analyze usage against behavioral patterns in order to quickly identify potentially anomalous activity. For example, if I travel someone I have never visited before and begin making purchases, I may get a phone call, e-mail, or text message from my bank asking for confirmation that this transaction is valid before allowing the charge. They are essentially detecting potential risky behaviour and effectively requiring two-factor authentication before allowing the user to continue. This is an example of adaptive security, which we will explore in depth later in the book. As a result, there is a very small time window to profit from stolen credit cards, and a valid credit card often sells for less than a dollar per record.

Compare the very low persistence of credit card information with information related to identity such as a Social Security Number, or other national identity numbers. If it is discovered someone is fraudulently using my Social Security Number, what is my recourse to change it? Due to the prevalence of the theft of Personally Identifiable Information, a mechanism may need to be developed in the future to make such changes, but those changes to long-standing infrastructure will not be trivial. For example, what effect would allowing a person to change their Social Security Number on the credit reporting industry? What about tracking individuals for tax purposes? The challenges with making identity-related information less persistent dictate that there is not likely to be significant progress in this regard in the short to medium term, so for the foreseeable future, identity-related information will continue to be sold for twenty-five to one hundred times the price of nonpersistent information such as credit cards.

If identity-related information is so much more profitable than financial instruments, why do we see so many retail organizations continue to be targeted and successfully breached? One short answer is that the retail industry operates on relatively thin profit margins and are required to limit overhead costs as much as possible to remain profitable and competitive. Consequently, they tend to implement the minimum controls required to be compliant with the Payment Card Industry Data Security Standards, completely ignoring building a security program. As a result, it is relatively easy and cheap to target and compromise these organizations in general. There are certainly exceptions to this broad generalization, but despite the lower reward per record for compromising retail organizations, they generally have enough volume of information that is easily compromised to make the return on investment for a retail attack to make sense. Additionally, attackers can often deploy the same exploit to several retail organizations simultaneously or serially and experience high success rates. In subsequent chapters, we will explore the difference between compliance and security in much greater detail, but they are not the same thing. If compliance with published regulations and standards is the totality of an organization's Information Security Program, attackers have access to a complete detailing of the security controls they will face when attempting to compromise sensitive data. Additionally, once an attacker has successfully compromised one organization, the attack can be successfully repeated across an industry and any organization that uses compliance as the guidepost for their security program will be subject to the exact same attacks. Standards are rarely updated more than two or three times every ten years and cannot keep pace with changing exploits, tactics, techniques, and protocols.

A good analogy of this type of approach is to imagine an American football team. If one team were to declare exactly which play they intended to run prior to running it, how successful would they be? No team could be successful doing that, but that's exactly what happens to organizations that use compliance requirements to form the basis of their Information Security programs.

Once criminals have stolen information, how do they capitalize on it? There is a side to the Internet that most people are not aware of. It is called the Dark Web, the Tor network, and several other names. This is the wild west of the World Wide Web. You cannot access it using normal web browsers such as Firefox, Internet Explorer, Safari, or Google Chrome, so it is out of sight and out of mind for most users. In fact, since it is a very dangerous place full of criminal elements and of great interest to global law enforcement agencies, it is generally inadvisable for law-abiding citizens to access this side of the Internet unless there is an official reason to do so. Simply accessing this network may expose a user to increased scrutiny from law enforcement. So what goes on there? In short, all kinds of illegal activity. This side of the Internet is essentially the world's largest global black market where stolen identities and financial instruments are advertised, bought and sold. There are words used to advertise stolen information that would be completely unrecognizable to uneducated users used to describe how complete the information is, whether it has been verified, and even guarantees for buyers that the information will work as advertised. Criminals also buy and sell malicious software and exploits on this network as well as other illicit digital content such as child pornography. The dark side of the web is a dark, seedy, and in some cases very disturbing place. I do not recommend visiting the Dark Web, but is important to be aware of its existence. Literally anything can be bought and sold on the Internet. If the goods and services are legal, they are generally traded on the light side of the Internet, and if they are illegal, they are generally traded on the dark side. Often, when information is breached, they do not discover the breach themselves, but are made aware by law enforcement agencies. Many people wonder how the FBI would know about it when the organization does not. Essentially, the FBI is monitoring the Dark Web, and when they see information that can be confirmed to have originated from a specific source, they will notify the victim. The major difference between Organized Crime and spies that results in far more knowledge of Organized Crime attacks is that Organized Criminals intend to profit from the information by selling it and spies generally do not as their work is commissioned for a specific purpose and the stolen information is rarely placed on the open market.

I often tell my clients if you are not testing your networks for vulnerabilities, you are the only one who does not know your weaknesses. It is relatively inexpensive and anonymous to scan for vulnerabilities, which makes it easy for organizations to identify whether they are vulnerable to known exploits. Similarly, it is easy for attackers to do the same through reconnaissance activities. Mature security programs not only contain a Security Assessment program, but also have mechanisms to identify when unauthorized scans for weaknesses are taking place. Sadly, as we will highlight in our Case Study Examples, many organizations are not taking the necessary and basic steps to ensure they are not vulnerable to widely known exploits that have patches that can be obtained for free and implemented with little effort. Second, unlike spies and nation-states, once Organized Criminals have stolen the information they need, they do not care if their attacks are discovered. In fact, they often welcome the attention from a successful attack so they can repackage and sell their exploits to less sophisticated attackers for use. This is often referred to as "commoditized malware" or "commoditized exploits".

There are also sometimes similarities in attack profiles between Organized Crime and Espionage organizations, especially when dealing with the more sophisticated Organized Crime syndactes. The key in differentiating well-funded and sophisticated Organized Crime organizations from spies and nation-states is specific to the type of information they are targeting, what they plan to do with the information when they find it, and the overall cost of the attack to the attacker. For example, advanced syndicates often utilize a reconnaissance and Social Engineering aspect to the attack in order to increase the chances of success against organization that are determined likely to be a high-value target, but it is unlikely that they would dedicate the necessary resources to developing or purchasing a true zero-day attack as is common with spies and nation-states.

When Organized Crime activities begin with Social Engineering exercises, the majority of the attacks use email and often target less savvy users since Organized Crime attacks usually do not require the level of access that spies and nation-states require in order for their attacks to be successful. Sometimes, they will not target employees of their intended victim at all, but will focus on partners that may be smaller with less mature security programs, who likely have access to network and resources belonging to their intended target. Spies and nation-states target specific information that they will relentlessly attempt to compromise regardless of the cost, whereas Organized Criminals are far more likely to target general categories of information that can be sold for a profit, and will generally take the path of least resistance and cost available to get the type of information they are targeting. Therefore, it is very important for organizations who have identified themselves as potential targets for Organized Crime to have a mature third party management and auditing program. Many standards such as NIST and ISO 27001 establish guidelines for how third parties should be managed at a minimum, and can be used as a starting point for organizations to build their programs. When discussing the security continuum in subsequent chapters, we will explore how some organizations have built third party management programs that have resulted in systemic security that increases the security posture of everyone that interacts with them.

Once credentials are harvested, the attack itself often starts from a single factor authentication server that allows the attacker to move freely throughout the environment and deliver malicious packages or manually begin the exfiltration of data. Simply implementing multi-factor authentication significantly increases the level of effort necessary for Organized Criminals to successfully exploit systems, and may result in the criminals choosing a softer target. Given unlimited time and unlimited resources, most security controls could be defeated, but in the case of Organized Crime, we do not need to outrun the bear, just the slowest of our peer group. In military counter-terrorism operations involving kinetic combat, it is a best practice to project strength to reduce the likelihood of an attack or to increase the risk factor for an attacking force. This does not mean an ambush would not be successful, it simply means the terrorist organization will likely look for a softer target in order to increase the likelihood of success with limited loss of life. In cyber warfare, when dealing with a for-profit criminal enterprise as an adversary, projecting strength can be similarly effective.

Organized Crime Example Case Study: Target

Perhaps the best example of a textbook Organized Crime attack is the Target case. Besides the specific tactics, techniques, and protocols used in the attack itself, it follows the typical food chain. An advanced organization compromises the initial victim, in this case Target, and then packages the successful attack for sale and reuse by less sophisticated criminal organizations, which subsequently used a similar attack against similar organizations, which we saw in the subsequent attacks against Neiman Marcus and Home Depot. Target is also a good case study due to the fact that there were periods of time when the damage could have been mitigated, but due to poor decisions or gaps in the program, the damage was multiplied. This is a common theme in very large Organized Crime breaches. Often, conscious decisions to procrastinate in responding to the threat result in large increases in the damage caused by the attack. I have been fortunate in my career to have very good leadership, and one of those leaders during my time in the U.S. Army, Bill Burford, used to say "Bad news does not get better with time." This is especially true in the cyber-security world as dwell time, or the amount of time the attacker has in the network or system prior to a response, is a key contributor to the overall cost of the breach. The longer an organization waits to implement the proper response to a threat, the worse the overall outcome will be. Additionally, from a reputational perspective, it is far better to tell the world you have been breached, rather than to have a government or other organization notify you that you have been breached (and subsequently, to discover that you knew about the breach and did not notify as obligated).

Many people have heard portions of the story of what happened at Target, and most people have at least the foundational knowledge that Target suffered a large-scale data breach during the holiday shopping season of 2013. The breach was, at the time, the largest retail breach in history. There have been conflicting reports about the timelines as well as who knew what and when, but I will attempt to tell the story using facts that are not in dispute at the time of this writing. Shortly before Thanksgiving 2013, malicious software was installed on Target payment systems with the intent of stealing credit card information while a customer was actively making a purchase. It is an important distinction that this attack was not designed to harvest stored information, but to attack information at the point it was provided to Target. The reason this is important is that it means that the length of time the attack lasts before it is detected and mitigated is directly related to the amount of data that is compromised. The stolen information was to be initially stored on a compromised server inside Target's environment. From there, the intent was to exfiltrate the data to computers in Russia.

▓ **Note** According to a recent white paper released by Raytheon (`http://www.raytheon.com/capabilities/rtnwcm/groups/cyber/documents/content/rtn_269210.pdf`), the dwell time, or average amount of time an attacker is inside of a network before being eradicated, is 200 days. In many cases, meaningful reduction in dwell time is likely to equate to meaningful reduction in the financial damage caused by breaches.

The real tragedy of this breach is that Target had deployed a technology as well as a company to manage the technology in India. The specific technology, FireEye in this case, detected the breach and escalated it to the Security Operations Center in Bangalore, India. What happened next is the subject of debate. There are essentially two versions of events. The first states that the Managed Services provider in India did not appropriately respond to and escalate the threat as they were contracted to do. The second says that the alerts were escalated to the proper Target resources, who chose not to respond appropriately in fear of interfering with the holiday shopping rush. Regardless of who was responsible for the lack of appropriate action, appropriate action was not taken at the time, where appropriate action could have significantly limited the number of users affected, or prevented any customer information being breached, depending on who you ask. The central lesson from this portion of the story is that the proper technology was deployed, and someone was "managing" it. It is obvious from the result, however, that a proper program and Incident Response Plan was not built and/or executed. What is universally acknowledged, based on post-breach investigations, is that the technology alerted the correct resources as it was supposed to in real or near real time.

If it is true that Target was notified and did nothing, or if it is true that the management company did not properly notify Target, there was a failure of a person in either case. However, if a single person's failure can result in the failure of an entire program, the process has also failed. Human beings are fallible by nature. Any process or program should have mechanisms in place to identify and mitigate damage from human error.

The breach was finally discovered and reported by an agency that was not part of Target. To people unfamiliar with IT Security, it is often surprising that someone else would discover the breach before the victim. However, according to Bloomberg News, "A three-year study by Verizon Enterprise Solutions (VZ) found that companies discover breaches through their own monitoring in only 31 percent of cases. For retailers, it's 5 percent." (`http://www.bloomberg.com/bw/articles/2014-03-13/target-missed-alarms-in-epic-hack-of-credit-card-data`) There are many reasons for this which will be explored in later chapters, but this is an essential statistic that must be changed in order for organizations to begin to be more successful in protecting Critical Information Assets.

There are a few characteristics of the Target breach that makes it a textbook Organized Crime cyber-attack. First, it was a relatively unsophisticated attack that utilized a type of malicious software that could be easily recognized by commercially available tools with little tuning if managed properly. These are normally not well-funded or well-planned attacks. Had Target acted quickly and actually thwarted the breach before it happened, which may or may not have been possible, depending on which side of the story you think is more credible, the attacker group would have likely tried to execute the same attack on a different target, pardon the pun. These attacks are generally high in volume and low in individual cost, which is precisely the opposite of the Espionage group. Second, the attackers had a profit motive, and always intended to sell the stolen information on the black market. That is also opposite of the patterns exhibited by espionage actors.

Terrorism 2.0

Intelligence Officials tell us that cyber-security now trumps terrorism as the number one threat to the security of the United States, according to the Associated Press, but what happens when the two converge? Leon Panetta participated in a panel at the 2015 RSA cyber-security conference with Tom Ridge and shared some very interesting insights from his time on the front lines of the global cyber-war as the head of the U.S. CIA. Obviously, many of the insights Panetta had were classified, but he did share that the CIA was attacked more than one million times daily. Undoubtedly, many of those attacks were related to espionage activity, but some for them were likely originating from terrorist organizations. It is widely accepted that a contributing factor to the rise of ISIS as the dominant terrorist threat in the world is their technical and digital savvy. It would be naïve to assume that they would limit their technological efforts to simply producing and distributing propaganda on social media. Due to the sensitive nature of publicizing successful and unsuccessful terrorist attacks, there is likely much happening in this area that the general public is blissfully unaware of, but it is important to understand what could happen digitally that would result in significant loss of life or major harm to the U.S. economy. Further, many emerging terrorist organizations have created a decentralized model where people are radicalized and trained where they are, making it much more difficult to positively identify a terror attack based on origin, or to track the movement of the terrorists themselves. As the San Bernandino terror attack made painfully clear, there may be radicalized individuals who mean us harm anywhere among us, including inside our neighborhoods and organizations. Some may already have access to our networks, which eliminates the need for terrorist organizations to breach network perimeters or conduct Social Engineering activity.

One World Labs founder and CTO Chris Roberts caused significant problems for himself and his company by exposing security vulnerabilities in airplane systems. As Americans and more recently, Russians, are painfully aware, aircraft continue to present an irresistible target for terrorist organizations. There are a few reasons for this. Taking down an aircraft results in a powerful image that scares people and harms economies as travel is often a significant revenue generator in developed countries. Additionally, the casualties of such attacks are generally much higher. If a terrorist wants to kill people on a bus or a train, the device they use to attack said vehicle must actually harm the victim, whereas with an aircraft, destroying or catastrophically degrading the intended function of the vessel itself will kill all of its occupants. While governments around the world have taken significant precautions to prevent weapons and explosives from being brought onboard aircraft, if the catastrophic event could be caused by an exploit launched from a cellular device or tablet, it would be extraordinarily difficult to prevent those devices from being brought onboard. Instead, the systems themselves would need to be hardened to avoid this type of attack.

Self-driving cars are in development by several companies around the world, and there seems to be significant interest in such technologies at least at a superficial level. Unsurprisingly, there have been a plethora of reports detailing the vulnerability of self-driving cars to hacking through all kinds of methods, including the ability to modify the behavior of a self-driving car with something as simple as a laser pointer. These types of emerging technologies are often developed with functionality in mind, rather than security. However, when computers are control of life and death decisions, such as the decisions the driver of a car makes, a threat to the security of the software is essentially a threat to life and limb. These types of technologies would prove to be attractive targets to technology-savvy terrorist organizations.

In the Oil and Gas industry, there was a cyber-attack from what could be classified either as a terrorist or a hacktivist organization against Saudi Aramco. The attack itself erased several thousand hard drives, but the attack vector highlighted the ability of attackers to pivot from oil companies' IT networks to Operational Technology networks. According to the Dark Reading article written about the attack entitled "How Hackers can Attack the Oil and Gas Industry Using ERP systems" (`http://www.darkreading.com/vulnerabilities---threats/how-hackers-can-hack-the-oil-and-gas-industry-via-erp-systems/d/d-id/1322877`), 90% of Oil and Gas companies have systems that are vulnerable to these types of exploits that could result in oil spills, overflows, or explosions. Large-scale explosions or gas leaks in urban areas could cause significant damage, fear, and insecurity and may, at some point become a target for terrorists.

Similarly, Intelligence Officials are concerned terrorists could electronically manipulate the chemicals used to treat water supplies to poison large portions of the populations. Many of the chemicals used to treat water to make it suitable for drinking like Chlorine and Fluoride are potentially lethal in sufficient amounts. It must be a national security priority to secure these networks properly in order to protect the population.

The power grid is another high-value target for attackers. The optics of a terrorist organization having the capability to cut power to American, European, or Russian homes in and of itself would further many terrorist organizations' agenda, but in conjunction with the economic harm that would be caused, attacks on the power grid represent a high-value target for terrorists.

While terrorists do not use a traditional cost-benefit analysis like Organized Criminals, there is an element of Opportunity Cost associated with their choices of what attacks to attempt. For example, suicide attacks have historically been used by insurgencies and terrorists globally since the advent of asymmetrical warfare. Willingness to die for the cause is the great equalizer for organizations that lack the capability to compete with their adversaries in conventional warfare. When I was deployed to Iraq, I was frustrated by the American Military's doctrine of using shows of force in an attempt to dissuade attacks. How would the threat of violence be a deterrent to an individual who plans to die as a part of his or her operation? However, whenever possible, whether we're examining the insurgency in Vietnam, Northern Ireland, the Russian invasion of Afghanistan, or the American counterinsurgency operations in Iraq, when these organizations have the opportunity to inflict damage on their enemies without loss of life on their side, these types of attacks were widely preferable. For example, when the Iraqi insurgency discovered they could cause just as much if not more damage by remotely detonated Improvised Explosive Devices triggered by commonly available cellular phones, these types of attacks became highly preferable to suicide bombings. Why is this important? There is a similar opportunity presented by technology vulnerabilities in critical infrastructure that if exploited effectively, allows terrorists to cause economic and physical harm to their enemies without the need to sacrifice the lives of their followers in the process. This is not to predict that cyber-terrorism stands poised to replace more widely recognized forms of terrorism in the foreseeable future, suicide bombings still take place in Iraq, Syria, Israel, etc., but simply to say that these types of attacks will likely grow in prevalence with the rise of more technically savvy terrorist organizations.

Tactics Techniques and Protocols in use by terrorists are often closely guarded government secrets, so little publicly available research and case studies exist. Shortly, we will examine the case of Sony, which is very close to a terrorist attack, if it would not be officially classified as such, as the sole purpose of the attack was to cause harm to Sony and send a message to other organizations that refuse to bow to pressures to restrict their free speech by actors with a political agenda. However, if you find yourself charged with the protection of any of the above types of systems or networks, it is prudent to partner with law enforcement and intelligence officials to ensure the program is built to withstand attacks from terrorist threat actors.

Live Free or Die Hard, an American movie released in 2007, details a hypothetical use of IT by terrorists to cause extensive damage and mayhem in Washington, D.C. Essentially, the villain in the movie is a cyber-terrorist using computer-based attacks to cause mayhem and Bruce Willis teams with a young hacker in an effort to stop them. One memorable scene has the cyber-terrorist turning all of the lights in all directions at a busy intersection green at the same time causing a major crash. How feasible are these types of attacks? Could these events really take place? It should come as no surprise that a movie has taken certain creative liberties with the capabilities of some of its characters, but reality is quickly catching up with Hollywood's vision of a world that can be brought to its knees by cyber-terrorists. With the increase of smart technology and the rise of the Internet of Things (IoT), things such as televisions, washing machines, refrigerators, and even medical devices like insulin pumps and pacemakers are accessible over the Internet. As is often the case, these technologies are developed to be highly functional at the lowest possible price point, which means these types of devices are often built with nonspecific computer chips. This means that the chip has capabilities beyond what is necessary for the intended function of the machine. An excellent illustration of this point is the fact that there have been botnets discovered with smart refrigerators, washing machines, and televisions among the compromised machines on the network. There are many potential benefits to various professional and domestic applications of such advancements, but the security implications are staggering. For example, what if someone held your pacemaker for ransom, threatening to literally stop your heart if you did not pay them? That very scenario is rapidly becoming more feasible.

Terrorism itself has also evolved. Al Qaeda and similar groups that have long targeted Western interests have always had the intent of causing harm to Western citizens and economies, but their capabilities required infiltration into a population and the execution of an attack, which was logistically very challenging and was also very expensive to execute. The interconnectivity of all things, especially financial systems, has created opportunities for terrorists to cause great harm to countries without ever crossing the border. This changing reality has resulted in an emerging attack surface and one that is waiting to be exploited by a savvy terrorist organization. The very nature of programming, computers and the Internet – created from rudimentary knowledge that has evolved very quickly over time – allows for new and creative ways for inventive people to take advantage of problems that are extremely difficult to predict and prevent. Consequently, the digital battlefield is rapidly evolving and changing, rendering defensive technologies and tactics obsolete on a daily basis. An effective security program must be nimble enough to evolve to the rapidly changing security landscape. Enter the Islamic State of Iraq and Syria (ISIS), which is also known by several other names. Whenever I hear ISIS mentioned, which seems to be very frequently, there is almost always an accompanying message about how "technology savvy" or "social media savvy" they are. What I haven't heard talked about enough is what implications that has on the world beyond the terrorists' ability to spread fear through professionally produced and gruesome execution videos, and radicalization efforts on Facebook and Twitter. A far more sinister threat exists, one that is not getting enough attention.

The case studies of Saudi Aramco and Sony will highlight the types of damage that can be done when a cyber-attack is designed to cause harm to an organization rather than to steal data. While cyber-crime is far more prevalent than cyber-terrorism, the implications of these types of attacks on individual business or even national and regional economic interests are too serious to be ignored.

Example Case Study: Saudi Aramco

The Saudi Aramco attack is one of the most important attacks to have taken place at the time of this writing, and of the case studies, it has garnered the least media attention, at least in the United States and Europe. Perhaps the fact that the victim organization is in the Middle East skews the coverage, but nevertheless, what happened to Aramco is extremely important to understand. Far more interesting than what the attackers did is what they could have done with the access they gained, had they been so inclined.

Saudi Aramco supplies roughly 10% of the world's oil. Many people outside of the Oil and Gas industry do not know the name of the company, but they are a significant player in the global energy market. In 2012, they were attacked by an organization calling themselves "Cutting Sword of Justice" in protest of Saudi Aramco's support of the Al Saud royal family. The attack took place while most people were on holiday for the holy month of Ramadan, and the attack destroyed the data on roughly 35,000 workstations. The response was frantic, and the containment of the threat involved taking the majority of the company's infrastructure offline. Global operations were disrupted in quite a significant way. According to *CNN Money*, "When it comes to sheer cost, the recent cyberattacks on Sony Pictures and the American government pale in comparison." (www.money.com/2015/08/05/technology/aramco-hack) Everything that happened in this case was bad, but what could have happened is far worse. In order to support that claim, let us first examine what happened.

The attack, by most accounts, originated with the compromise of the organization's Enterprise Resource Planning (ERP) system. The method of entry is important because most energy companies make a concerted effort to completely separate the networks responsible for IT like e-mail and shared files, and the networks responsible for Operational Technology (OT) such as pipes, drills, power distribution, etc. Enterprise Resource Planning, by its very nature, needs to have connectivity to both networks in order to be effective. Therefore, ERP systems in Oil and Gas companies present major risks to the organization that should be defined and treated appropriately. During the attack, the attackers used connectivity afforded to them by the ERP system to pivot from the IT network to the OT network. Essentially, they were able to compromise a server remotely and then use that intrusion to gain access to the machines that control things like pipes and drills. What they did with their access, wiping the hard drives of thousands of computers, was damaging, but rather pedestrian compared to what they could have done. Imagine if a terrorist organization was able to cause a pipe to burst on an offshore rig, or cause a fracking well to poison the water supply of an even moderately populated area. The point is not to scare everyone or to condemn Oil and Gas as an industry asleep at the wheel, but to say that the world has a vicious, ruthless, well-funded enemy operating with reportedly sophisticated technological capabilities. Recent events in Eastern Europe, specifically between Russia and Ukraine have highlighted the fact that state-sponsored organizations with significant equipment and capabilities can be deployed to cause havoc. The prospect of similar attacks being used to manipulate power grids and services like natural gas is a clear and present danger that could have far-reaching economic and humanitarian consequences. Understanding that threat and preparing appropriate countermeasures is critical to protecting companies, nations, and even, to an extent, the global economy from groups that promote fundamentalist views and rejoice in creating suffering and chaos.

Example Case Study: Sony

Monday, November 24, 2014, a devastating cyber-attack was launched on Sony Pictures by a group calling itself the Guardians of Peace. There are conflicting reports about the reasons behind the attack, but it is a relatively consensus opinion that the group had warned Sony Pictures against doing certain things, and launched the attack in retaliation for what it considered a failure to heed those warnings. The Sony attack is significant for two reasons. First, the attack was enormously damaging to Sony. There was a period of time where Sony employees were communicating with paper and pen due to the massive damage to the network and the lack of assurance that any electronic transmissions were secure. This attack represented a major disruption to operations, which was also the case for Saudi Aramco, and is a major indicator of cyber-terrorism rather than a profit or espionage motive. Second, the type of attack is significant in that it was definitely a terrorist attack, an attack by a group that was intended to cause harm to the victim due to ideological reasons, but it was an attack on an international enterprise and not on a specific government or populace. Most terrorist attacks are launched on governments and their populations for political reasons. So what happened at Sony?

The attackers first stole everything they thought could be of value to their cause, including Sony's Intellectual Property, employee information, and anything they deemed might be embarrassing to the company if disclosed publicly. Second, malware was deployed with the express purpose of causing damage. This malware was sophisticated and lethal, rendering thousands of machines useless, and erasing massive amounts of data on the hard drives using methodologies intended for the secure deletion of data for government applications. All told, the attack brought down about half of Sony Pictures' infrastructure. (www.fortune.com/sony-hack-part-1)

Many people were quick to condemn Sony after the attack, saying that they had failed to implement a variety of safeguards that should have been in place. In some cases, that may be true, but by all accounts, Sony was not less secure than the average organization. Therein lies the problem, not with Sony specifically, but with organizations in general having a weak overall security posture. These types of attacks highlight the need to build a more effective and comprehensive IT Security program. Some would argue it is impossible to keep a highly skilled and well-funded attacker out of an organization with currently available technologies and processes. This may or may not be true, but even if it is, a well-built security program can quickly identify the anomoulous activity, isolate it, and eradicate it, before the attack has the opportunity to cause the type of damage observed in the Sony case.

Corporate Terrorism, or terrorism aimed at causing financial harm and embarrassment to an organization, is a relatively new phenomenon, but is one that I predict will grow in popularity. Ransomware is an example of a type of malicious software that utilizes this concept. The basic premise is the malicious software affects a machine and threatens to disable some or all of its functions unless a ransom is paid. What happened to Sony is similar to ransomware on a grander scale, with the exception that the attackers were demanding capitulation with demands rather than a ransom. In many cases, it was very similar to the airline hijackings that were popular with terrorist groups in the 1980s. If the country complied with the terrorist demands, the airplane and the passengers would be returned unharmed. If they failed to comply, the airplane would be destroyed and the passengers would be killed. The growing capabilities of organizations around the world to carry out these specific threats means that organizations that are unprepared to defend themselves against these types of sophisticated attacks may need to begin considering a policy for responding to these types of ransom demands. Response to ransom demands should definitely be a part of every organization's Incident Response Plan.

Shades of Gray

Fill in the blank: The enemy of my enemy is my _____. Hacktivist groups like Anonymous often count enemies of the state such as ISIS or the Ku Klux Klan as their enemies, while simultaneously targeting government groups and organizations. So should we aim to stop and disband groups like Anonymous? The answer is never black or white, it is most definitely constantly shifting shades of gray. For example, if Anonymous attacks ISIS and exposes their membership online, exposing their identities to world governments so they may be more effectively targeted and their assets can be frozen, that would be generally accepted as a good thing. However, Anonymous is an anti-government, largely anarchist organization. The majority of global citizens do not want to live in a world with no order, regulations, or laws, so in that sense, Anonymous conducts many operations against the will of the people. Adding to the complexity is that Anonymous is very appropriately named. The group likely counts neighbors, coworkers, friends, and possibly family among its membership. They are everywhere, and they are amorphous and headless with no overall directional leadership. Essentially members decide whether or not to unite behind a cause solo or in groups on a cause-by-cause basis. Are there common threads among such an amorphous group, let alone when we expand the question to include other hacktivist groups that are less well-known? It turns out there are some commonalities in tactics techniques and protocols that can assist organizations that suspect they are or may be targets for hacktivist groups.

So what are they after? Types of information or target organizations for hacktivist groups shift with the winds. It is generally a good practice to assume at some point, any organization may find themselves the target of one of these organizations. An important fact to consider is that hacktivist groups occupy a different area of cyber-crime than the other groups of threat actors, in that hacktivist groups are far more likely to be engaged in cyber-mischief intended to embarrass or expose an organization, rather than cyber-theft or cyber-terrorism.

Anatomy of an Anonymous Attack

Since Anonymous is by far the most prevalent hacktivist group, this section will focus specifically on how this specific group operates. First, it is important to note that Anonymous often uses Distributed Denial of Service (DDOS) attacks as part of their signature. DDOS attacks do not yield stolen information, but they do cause harm to the targeted organization. Since DDOS attacks are part of the equation, Anonymous employs laypeople as well as skilled hackers. In fact, the ratio of laypeople to skilled hackers is often 10:1.

Stage 1: Recruiting and Communication

The first stage of an attack is to essentially campaign about what is going to be done and why. It is common for these groups to use social media or Twitter to rally sympathetic users to their cause. Videos are often made and released. Since hacktivist attacks are usually crowdsourced, and not funded, this stage is necessary. As such, effective monitoring of the proper channels can give organizations advanced warning they are going to be a target. Since laypeople must be recruited to the cause as well as technical experts, these messages are often visible to the general public to people who know where to look. Campaigns are often characterized by propaganda in the form of meme's or videos designed to champion the cause, create a mystique and sense of belonging for anyone who joins the group, and to demonize the adversary as much as possible. The idea for hacktivist recruiting is similar to terrorist recruiting. Essentially, the appeal is to disenfranchised people that they can be powerful and they can be heroes setting right the world's wrongs.

Stage 2: Reconnaissance and Application Attack

The second phase is generally performed by the more skilled technical resources. Stage 2 consists of gathering information that can be helpful in the attack and identifying any countermeasures in place that will need to be defeated in order for the attack to be successful. A key to this stage is that the attackers prefer to remain undetected. The second part of phase 2 is for the attackers to actually compromise an application server. In order to do so, the hacking team will utilize any tools that are available to them in order to identify and exploit vulnerabilities.

After the application, most often a public facing web server, has been compromised, the attackers will often replace the legitimate page with their own page making it clear they have compromised the server and will spread their message for why they are doing what they are doing. This propaganda shows the power and efficacy of the group and often serves as a final recruiting effort to rally more people to their cause prior to entering the final phase of the attack.

Stage 3: DDOS Attack

As mentioned before, DDOS stands for Distributed Denial of Service. This type of attack consists of many machines making requests of the same target simultaneously in order to prevent the legitimate users from gaining access to the server. These types of attacks can be especially devastating for online merchants or service providers because it results in customers not having the ability to purchase goods or services, or results in breach of Service Level Agreements for providers. Distributed DDOS attacks are not particularly difficult to perform successfully, especially if there are enough machines recruited to the cause. A DOS from a single target is relatively easy to defeat with certain countermeasures, but it is much more difficult to distinguish a DDOS attack from very high volumes of legitimate traffic until it is too late. (`http://resources.infosecinstitute.com/weapon-of-anonymous/`)

There are many more groups than Anonymous, and even Anonymous employs different tactics, techniques, and protocols in different situations. The main identifying characteristic of a hacktivist attack is the propaganda before the attack to rally people to the side of the attackers, as well as the propaganda after the attack to take credit for what they did and use the successful attack to recruit for their next attack.

Hacktavist Example Case Study: Federal Reserve

Anonymous has long considered the U.S. government its enemy and an enemy of the world. Anonymous stands firmly against secrecy and censorship, and accuses the U.S. government of trying to operate in secrecy in an effort to censor all voices they disagree with. The anger reached a boiling point with the suicide of Aaron Schwartz. Schwartz was the founder of Reddit and was prosecuted by the U.S. government for wire fraud and computer fraud, among other charges related to his obtaining copyrighted material he believed should be available free of charge. Schwartz believed he was facing a long prison sentence and committed suicide rather than face the sentence.

Anonymous was angered by Schwartz's death and launched what they called Operation Last Resort. In the Recruiting and Communication phase, Anonymous broadened the message to be not only about this specific prosecution, but a larger backlash against the government in response to high-ranking bankers and officials not being held accountable for the 2008 financial crisis. It was the opinion of the group that the people responsible for the crash faced relatively little hardship, while the people bore the burden for their misdeeds. As a result of the broadened scope, Operation Last Resort targeted the Federal Reserve Bank, and specifically high-ranking bankers inside of the bank.

The attack exploited a "vulnerability in a website vendor's product," according to a Federal Reserve statement. On Super Bowl Sunday, Anonymous revealed that they had compromised four thousand bankers' credentials and had gained the capability to disrupt a major emergency communication system used in case of financial emergency. The federal government acknowledged the attack but disputed Anonymous's claims regarding the depth of the compromise.

As is typical for a hacktavist attack, the actual damage caused by the attack was far less than the perceived value of the attack in terms of publicity, in the collective opinion of the group. There was very little actual harm that can be quantified in the attack, but the attack did serve to embarrass the Federal Reserve and call their security measures into question. When Anonymous attacks other groups like the Ku Klux Klan (KKK) or ISIS, it is questionable whether embarrassing these groups truly matters, since they are not concerned with their public reputation in most cases. Organizations such as Anonymous could cause significant harm to these organizations and dissuade potential recruits however, by publishing their names or identities or working with law enforcement in order to bring them to justice. The question becomes, in that scenario, which side would they be on? Would they be willing to work with one perceived enemy to degrade another? The answers to moral questions for these types of amorphous groups are often difficult to determine. As a result, truly understanding where these groups loyalties lie or trying to predict their behavior when faced with complex decisions involving competing interests is extremely difficult. Additionally, determining whether they are good or bad is a matter of opinion given the situation. At a minimum, all Information Security professionals should be familiar with their tactics and prepare for the possibility their organization may one day be targeted by one of these groups.

Conclusion

Each of these types of actors and each of these breaches highlighted could have been mitigated or prevented in some way, which we will explain in the subsequent chapters of this book. Just like there is no such thing as impenetrable defenses, there is also no such thing as an undetectable attack. Locard's exchange principle is as relevant in the digital world as it is in the physical world. Every time a crime takes place, the attacker takes something from the crime scene and leaves something behind that wasn't there. Becoming experts in detecting those changes is a key element of building a comprehensive IT Security program.

Throughout the remaining chapters of this book, we will explore a number of different principles and best practices that could be implemented to prevent these types of attacks, and mitigate the damage posed by them should they occur.

■ ■ ■

CHAPTER 2

Protecting Critical Assets

If you think technology can solve your security problems, then you don't understand the problems, and you don't understand the technology.

—Bruce Schneier

Throughout the remainder of this book, we will operate under the central premise that every organization across the globe has too much information flowing throughout their environment for it to be feasible to monitor the content and context of everything that is transferred. Due to the volume of electronic information, should an organization choose to attempt monitoring of every transmission, half or more of the organization's staff would be dedicated to the effort. If it is, in fact, infeasible to monitor everything, how do we separate the wheat from the chaff? Content and content aware tools have become indispensable for organizations to identify, monitor, and protect what is most important to them, but many struggle to use them effectively.

Since 2002, three wise men have used their vast and varied experiences to converge on a single idea that has advanced the cause of Information Security into a new era. The idea of identifying assets critical to an organization through an extensive interview process with business stakeholders and translating that information into operational processes that allow Information Security teams to efficiently and effectively execute the vision and strategy of business leaders has proven extraordinarily potent and effective for organizations across the globe who have chosen to embrace it.

Three Wise Men

Industries are built and advances are made when clear vision and the right blend of experiences are combined with tenacity and relentless drive to solve a problem that presents challenges to organizations around the globe. Such circumstances existed in 2002 when Robert Eggebrecht and Chuck Bloomquist came together to found a company called BEW Global, which was the first company dedicated to content- and context-based security products and programs. The two subsequently met Ryan Coleman, who had founded a consulting company called Dayspring Technologies, a consulting firm focused on ISO 27000 and effective Business Process Design, and was able to contribute his perspective to Rob and Chuck's vision. The result was the origins of the Critical Asset Protection methodology we are exploring in this chapter.

Each of these individuals had a different background that led them to develop the skills and perspectives necessary to allow them to effectively execute complex programs. They also all possessed the vision to realize, far ahead of the rest of the marketplace, the future of Information Security. It has been my pleasure to have personally known each of these visionaries and shared enough time with them to be able to share their stories with you, in hopes that it provides the insight necessary to understand these ideas and concepts and their implications for building next-generation Information Security programs.

© Jeremy Wittkop 2016
J. Wittkop, *Building a Comprehensive IT Security Program*, DOI 10.1007/978-1-4842-2053-5_2

Rob Eggebrecht

Rob Eggebrecht is the cofounder of InteliSecure, formerly BEW Global. Rob has been heavily influenced by his father, Lewis Eggebrecht, who "rose from the roots of a dirt-poor dairy farmer in Michigan to board member at Avago." Lew, as most people call him, is an extraordinarily humble and soft-spoken man, but he has offered incredible insights to Rob throughout his life, which have served him well in business.

Rob gained his first degree from the University of Denver Daniels College of Business in International Management. After graduating with his degree, Rob was faced with the choice many young people are faced with after college: now what? If you ask him, Rob will tell you he is an overeducated ski bum. Rob's first love is the mountains and specifically skiing. This passion almost drove him to open a ski shop. Had he done so, the Information Security landscape would be very different than it is today, and many young Information Security professionals would have been robbed of a phenomenal opportunity to learn from one of the greatest minds in the industry.

Rob instead chose to pursue roles in Business Development and international opportunities for large organizations including Level 3 Communications, Virtela, and Qwest Communications. It was during his time at Gemplex that he and Chuck Bloomquist decided that there was a better way to do business than they had experienced, and there was also a coming challenge with respect to securing Critical Information Assets that the general marketplace was unprepared for. These two central ideas formed the genesis of what would later become BEW Global, and subsequently InteliSecure.

Culture was always important to Rob. He was an early adopter of the philosophy that people do their best work when they love what they do and they enjoy their lives thoroughly outside of work. Regardless of what the business would be doing, creating a fun, engaging, enjoyable culture that offered an outstanding quality of life was always going to be at the forefront of the company's mission. This dedication to creating a positive work environment and a stimulating corporate culture created a passionate and fiercely loyal working environment that contributed to the overall success of the organization.

Second, Rob saw a fundamental truth in the way corporations were changing throughout the 1990s and into the new millennium. He didn't see cities and buildings as cold stone, steel, and brick structures anymore, but electronic nervous systems pulsating with information. This information was the lifeblood of these organizations, and protecting the information was going to change many companies' fortunes in the coming years. At this time, many organizations were perimeter-driven in terms of their approach to their security programs, and were oblivious to the central truth that some data was more valuable than other data. Rob played a central role in the coming years in helping to educate the marketplace and shift this paradigm.

Rob was uniquely positioned to understand the challenges these organizations faced with his experience in business development and business process optimization gained from his experience, as well as his background in technology. He was one of the first visionaries to make the connection that in order to truly solve the challenges posed by cyber-crime, it would take an unprecedented cooperation between the business and the technologies they chose to deploy. The year was 2002, and BEW Global, along with what would be come to be known in the industry as a Critical Asset Protection Program was born.

Chuck Bloomquist

Chuck Bloomquist has been working with technology in the defense and telecommunications industries for most of his adult life. He has been involved with various projects ranging from developing and implementing weapons systems for the U.S. military to building the necessary infrastructure to provide Internet service to rural communities in New Mexico.

Chuck Bloomquist and Rob Eggebrecht crossed paths a few times in their career, specifically at Ticketmaster and Gemplex. After the turn of the millennium, many people in the technology field found themselves evaluating their futures. The Y2K hysteria had passed without any major dire problems and the tech employment bubble had burst, giving way to what Chuck refers to as the "IT depression." Many people were turning to non-technology-related career paths like mortgage loans, real estate, insurance sales, etc. Chuck and Rob had no interest in moving away from the technology field, and they began thinking about their futures as a team.

In addition to their shared love of skiing, Chuck and Rob had been meeting socially consistently between 2000 and 2002. They spoke at length about the value system inside of the organizations they had been involved with and how those values did not match their own. They shared the belief that there had to be a better way to run a company and earn a living. The entrepreneurial seeds inside them both were beginning to germinate; they simply needed to determine what they were going to do.

Chuck had begun hearing an increased desire from clients to have security be incorporated in their networks. At the time, firewalls were an emerging technology and the idea of Information Security was still in its infancy. The technologies that did exist were perimeter-based technologies that focused on building virtual walls to keep unauthorized users outside of the network. Technology did not yet exist to allow users to determine what they wanted to protect and stop it from leaving the organizational perimeter. Rob and Chuck both agreed that it was really about the data and not about keeping people out of a network.

Chuck understood that a network, by its very nature, required porosity, or the ability for information to flow in and out, to be effective at transferring information between networks. As long as that porosity existed, there would be the potential for unauthorized users and actors to gain access to the network through the holes that were required to be there. When telling the story of his vision back then, Chuck likes to talk about the Bank of London. If thieves spent all their resources trying to get into the vault by tunneling under the bank from across the street, given enough time and resources, they would likely get in. If they got inside and were unable to get anything out, what harm did they cause? Certainly there would be physical damage that must be repaired in order for the bank to resume normal operations, but the thieves were unable to take anything of value and the bank did not lose any money. In a virtual world, there are far less repair costs, and the harm is greatly diminished.

It all leads to a central idea that has been a cornerstone of BEW Global since its inception. In order for an attacker to gain value from an attack, they have to not only infiltrate a network, but also exfiltrate data. The same is true for harm to be realized for the victim: data has to be exfiltrated from the environment. Regardless of the presence of unauthorized personnel, so long as the data resides where it is intended to reside, no harm comes to the victim and no benefit is realized by the attacker. Therefore, building programs to keep unauthorized actors out is not only likely to fail, but misses the mark even with respect to what they are trying to accomplish. Keeping critical data out of unauthorized hands must be the intent of an effective security program. That idea seems obvious now, but at that time, it was truly revolutionary.

Ryan Coleman

Ryan Coleman's journey in Critical Asset Protection started around the 2005 time frame while he was the manager of technology for a pharmaceutical firm, in Philadelphia, Pennsylvania. It was at PMRS that Ryan began to develop methodologies for applying the Software Development Life Cycle (SDLC) to business process. Ryan was charged with a variety of duties including technology, compliance, innovation, and process improvement. His approach was unique and would form the basis for his subsequent contributions to the evolution of the Critical Asset Protection Program and the work the BEW Global team was doing to marry business process and technology for the express purpose of protecting critical information.

In 2009, Ryan left PMRS to start his own consulting practice called Dayspring Technologies. It was at this point when he began to collaborate with BEW Global to bring his approach to process design and improvement to BEW Global's Critical Asset Protection Programs. It was also around this time that BEW Global was creating the first Managed Security Services Practice (MSSP) specifically designed to protect Critical Information Assets using content- and context-aware technologies. Ryan's Quality Management System approach was incorporated into the idea of protecting Critical Assets to form a mechanism and methodology to continually improve programs throughout their life cycle.

The combination of Rob's vision, Chuck's technical expertise, and Ryan's proficiency at building and improving processes created the foundational elements for the explosion of growth that InteliSecure experienced between 2009 and 2016. The core ideas InteliSecure pioneered have become widely accepted and are now recognized and practiced by a variety of organizations, including some of the largest consulting practices in the world. Rob, Chuck, and Ryan are visionaries that have made significant contributions the evolution of Information Security over the years. They are the rare professionals that have the vision and the foresight to leverage their experiences to accurately predict the problems of tomorrow, and the courage to take great personal and financial risks to solve those problems. Simply put, without the contributions and visions of these three, I would not be writing this book, and the world would be an even-more dangerous place for business than it is today. The work they have done is an example of the evolution of the business community to begin to take cyber-threats seriously and take tangible steps to improve the security landscape.

What Is a Critical Information Asset?

What is a Critical Information Asset? Simply defined, a Critical Information Asset is any piece of information that could cause irreparable harm to an organization should it be lost, stolen, improperly shared, or improperly exposed. Some types of Critical Assets are well-known and regulated pieces of information such as Protected Health Information (PHI); Personally Identifiable Information (PII) such as U.S. Social Security Numbers; Canadian Social Insurance Numbers, and the like; and Payment Card Industry Information (PCI) or Credit Card Numbers (CCNs). Other Critical Information Assets aren't regulated but are very important to an organization, such as Intellectual Property, Business Research and Planning Information, and financial information such as financial statements, price lists, and Merger and Acquisition (M and A) information. Similarly, some types of harm that can come to an organization from the loss of Critical Information Assets are well-documented and well-known, such as loss of brand reputation, as in the case study of the Target breach, or fines from regulation agencies as detailed in the case study of the Community Health Systems breach. Other lesser recognized harm caused by failing to protect Critical Information Assets are things like operational impact and a periodic loss of organizational efficiency, as detailed in the Sony case; or the untold consequences in the form of lost revenue and diminished competitive advantage as a result of state-sponsored and industrial espionage. Any information that when lost or stolen could result in those outcomes are Critical Information Assets.

What constitutes a Critical Information Asset varies by organization and is generally tied to balance sheets, revenue forecasts, operational budgets, and risk models. Theoretically, given unlimited resources and manpower, all of the assets determined to be important could likely be protected comprehensively and in perpetuity. However, most Information Security teams do not have unlimited resources, so assets must be prioritized. In the next chapter, we will explore a methodology for prioritizing Critical Assets, but one-size-fits-all approaches to protecting Critical Information Assets are simply ineffective. As Chuck Bloomquist has said repeatedly to business leaders throughout the world, "There is no easy button" to solve the complex and evolving threats presented by threat actors.

Some Critical Information Assets can easily be determined by asking executives questions like "What keeps you up at night?" and by reading the risk factors section of a publicly traded company's Form 10-K Report. Other times, it takes an in-depth mapping of key business processes that are projected to drive important revenue streams in order to truly identify what is important. Most often, it requires the aggregate of discussions with key executives, business unit owners, and the employees closest to the processes themselves to identify what is most critical to the organization. The most important factor in determining what is critical and what is not is to rely on facts rather than opinion; tie the assets back to the company's financials, goals, and vision; and to ensure input is gathered from as broad a group of key business stakeholders and subject matter experts as possible. Often, it is necessary to have these conversations be mediated by a neutral third party, such as a consultant who is experienced in creating these types of programs, especially when it comes to prioritizing the assets. Many times, there is little debate about what is critical, but which assets are most important can often be the subject of fierce debate. I personally prefer tying prioritization to a tangible calculation of risk to an asset expressed in financial terms, but there are other ways to effectively prioritize assets. The key is that the methodology used is as objective as possible and is established prior to undertaking the exercise. In cases where there is still disagreement, it is often best to involve the highest-ranking executive sponsor of the program.

Data Life Cycle Elements

It is critical to take the content, community, and channel into account when building a Comprehensive Information Security Program. Many breaches are indicated by anomalous behavior in one of the three categories, so the lack of comprehensive monitoring and response programs that take all three into account significantly increases the risk of undetected breaches of sensitive information.

What was previously outlined is a business-centric approach to defining what is critical and what is authorized with respect to those Critical Information Assets. Programs designed to monitor system-driven events and that employ context analytics technologies are built on a concept of data life cycles, which are designed to define baseline behavior in an environment and detect deviations from that baseline, ideally highlighting anomalous behavior as it relates to the most critical data in the environment. There are four technocentric categories that can define the life cycle of a Critical Information Asset: Creation, Storage, Usage, and Transmission. Figure 2-1 illustrates the life cycle of a critical asset inside an organization.

Figure 2-1. *Data Life Cycle Elements*

Creation

In order to protect a Critical Information Asset throughout its life cycle, it is important to understand the creation or "birth" of an asset inside your infrastructure. Intellectual Property often is actually created inside the organization, but what about PHI: we do not actually create it? Creation in that sense is related to when the asset begins to exist in the environment. In the case of PHI, that might be a patient filling out a form or another physician or insurance company referring a patient. The importance of understanding the creation of a Critical Information Asset is best illustrated by the breach involving Specs.

Specs is a wine and liquor retailer primarily operating in Texas. They experienced a breach that exposed a treasure trove of PII belonging to roughly 550,000 customers over a period of 17 months. The actual tactics techniques and protocols used to attack Specs have not been made public, but given the fact the breach affected 34 of 165 stores instead of the entire infrastructure, and that the number of customers affected seems to be directly tied to the length of time the breach took place, it is reasonable to surmise, based on public information, that the breach was not an attack on centralized infrastructure, but rather making a copy of data at the point of creation, in this case the stores, therefore bypassing many of the centralized security controls around their regulated Card Data Environment. The lesson to be learned from this breach, in my opinion, is that protecting data from the moment it is entrusted in an organization's care is extraordinarily important to prevent long-term, large, and undetected breaches.

Storage

Once an asset exists in an environment, it must be stored somewhere. The proper method of storage and the appropriate community along with levels of access for privileged users are important considerations for comprehensive protection. Improperly stored information along with overly permissive accounts are a centralized theme in many high-profile breaches. A good example of this trend is the eBay breach.

In 2014, eBay had a small number of employees' credentials compromised, which resulted in the potential for unauthorized access to information relating to all 145 million eBay user accounts. It is very unlikely that this small community of users required access to such a large population of user accounts for performance of critical business duties. It is very likely that the information was not vetted with respect to need to know of Concept of Least Privilege, or that there was no separation between the need for administrative rights to make changes to systems, and the need to have access to all information in the environment. This lack of separation is very common based on my experience, and should be revisited by organizations that endeavor to protect themselves from the majority of cyber-attacks, which involve either an indiscriminate phishing campaign to probe a network, or a more targeted and advanced spear phishing campaign targeting privileged users followed by the use of overly permissive accounts to gain access to whatever information they deem to have value to them.

Usage

It is generally inadvisable to store information that has no intended business use. There must be a balance with the human tendency to store everything in perpetuity with the increased exposure that doing so creates. There are times when storage of certain types of information is mandated by law or corporate policy. In other cases, storage should be tied directly to business use. Storing everything in perpetuity is considered overretention, which has a corresponding increase in risk exposure. If all information has an intended use, it is important to define the users that will use the information and what is the acceptable usage of said information. Doing so allows for the building of controls to allow critical business processes while preventing unauthorized use of Critical Information Assets.

It is important to make a distinction between a user who has a business need to access and use certain types of critical information, and a user given unfettered access to such information. Many organizations that apply the Concept of Least Privilege, do so related to whether or not a user may access the information. This determination has historically been a binary yes or no decision. It is my opinion that the Concept of Least Privilege should evolve to not only determine what information an individual must have access to in order to perform essential functions, but also what types of specific activities the individual must complete in order to perform those functions. It should also be deployed with other best practices such as job rotation and separation of duties in order to make fraud and improper activities less likely to occur.

For example, an administrative employee in a hospital that is responsible for billing insurance companies and patients must access PHI in order to perform those functions. However, should that same employee have the ability to save sensitive patient information to removable storage devices or send the information to their personal e-mail accounts so he or she can work from home on an unsecured personal device? The answer may vary based on organizational risk tolerance, but the question should be posed with respect to an organization's most Critical Information Assets.

There are countless examples of organizations I have worked with that were able to identify anomalous behavior by defining how critical information was authorized to be used. Defining authorized behavior patterns allows for the immediate recognition of unauthorized behavior with respect to the assets. Further, by defining and documenting the communication plan that informs employees of what is and is not authorized helps to categorize unauthorized behavior based on apparent intent by the user. It is important for the purpose of appropriate response to identify whether the behavior is accidental, the result of a broken or poorly communicated business process, or suspicious behavior on the part of the user.

Transmission

Some assets should never leave the organizational infrastructure. However, most have an authorized method of transmission and authorized destinations for the data. For example, customer PHI may be shared via encrypted e-mail with patients. On the other hand, it would be considered a breach if that information was shared in an encrypted format with the wrong person, or shared with the appropriate person in an unencrypted format. These nuances and specifics form the cornerstones of effective Information Security Programs. It is generally the specifics that sophisticated attackers will target rather than the generalized protections that almost all organizations will employ at a minimum. This is not only logical, but has also been proven through thorough examination of breaches that have been thoroughly examined and publicized.

A good example of the importance of defining authorized transmission methods is a manufacturing organization with operations in China. It is certainly risky to send Intellectual Property to China. When doing so, it is important to ensure the information is protected in transit, and only shared with proper recipients. Further, it is often a best practice to ensure that no single person holds all of the information necessary to create a product. It is far more secure to send pieces of information to different recipients so interception of the information and reassembly is much more difficult. Choosing to prevent the information from being sent would be detrimental to the organization. Choosing the proper strategy to protect the data in transit, documenting the strategy, and setting up a program to monitor for deviations from the strategy can protect the information while allowing key business processes to continue unimpeded.

Vertical Challenges

While broad generalizations are dangerous, there are common threads and assets that serve as good examples of the types of information often deemed critical to protect in different verticals. These examples are not to be taken as comprehensive lists, but rather to serve as a starting point for business analysis and vigorous debate, as well as to illustrate some of the reasons that securing Critical Information Assets is important in each vertical, and also to illustrate the types of threats that may target each vertical. Many times throughout my career, I have heard organizations argue that they are not subject to regulations, and therefore did not have Critical Information Assets that needed to be protected. I have never seen an organization where that is the case. The section below is designed to stimulate thought about what is critical to each of the below verticals as well as to stimulate thought about assets that may be critical to organizations in verticals that are not specifically mentioned.

Law Firms and Other Service Providers

Law firms and other providers of professional services have a very interesting problem when it comes to protecting Critical Assets. Since the most critical types of information for these organizations tend to be information entrusted to them by their customers and clients, the content of the assets could be anything. Additionally, there are often very specific, client-driven requirements with respect to the confidentiality of specific documents and ongoing access management. Many times law firms are a treasure trove for potential attackers of all types. For spies and nation-states, law firms often house information about research and patents before they are filed. Organized Criminals are likely to find PII related to litigation, especially cases involving insurance companies. For terrorists and activist groups, law firms may have information that would be embarrassing or potentially harmful to their clients if it were to be improperly accessed and publicized. To exacerbate the problem, many times customers may have competing interests with each other and ethical walls often need to be built and maintained in order to prevent the service provider from bringing harm to their customers, and by extension, the service provider's reputation. It is difficult to define the form and function of the types of information that should be protected by these enterprises, but identifying and protecting the assets is possible.

Often the key to protection of customer data is the process in which information is provided by the customer and client. Building a program to properly identify and track what has been submitted by whom is the first key to effectively protecting the data. Applying human readable and machine readable digital markings is also critical for these types of providers to build and maintain ethical walls. For example, all documents inside of the infrastructure that contains PII should be protected and only shared with the authorized community of users, but the authorized community of users will vary based on which client supplied the information. Clearly identifying the information to both users and protection systems is critical to solving the challenges presented by this use case.

Oil and Gas

Oil and Gas is the industry that has inexplicably been cautious to adopt and build comprehensive Information Security programs, especially in light of the quantity and breadth of the threats they face. Of all of the verticals that I have encountered in my career, Oil and Gas, and the broader energy sector, is the vertical that is most likely to be targeted by all four of the threat actor groups that have been identified by the FBI, in my opinion. Each of the threat actor groups has different reasons for targeting Oil and Gas, and the reasons along with the commonly targeted information are explained in detail below.

Spies and Nation-States

Spies and Nation-States have been known to target a variety of Critical Information Assets in the Oil and Gas industry. Product formulas used to refine gasoline and create petroleum products for sale to consumers for the purpose of competitive advantage either on the open market in the case of industrial espionage actors, or for production by a nation-state entity in state-sponsored cases can cause an increase in domestic product and a decrease in imports. This scenario can lead to great economic harm done to the victim organization. There are also documented cases of totalitarian governments stealing research information and business planning information for the purpose of manipulating real estate prices for pieces of property foreign business deem critical to their expansion plans or mining and drilling activity. Finally, developing or expanding countries and competitive industrial actors often target methodologies and business processes that can be used to improve the attacker's ability to execute similar activities that have been refined and sometimes perfected by the target organization

Organized Crime

Organized Criminals target information that is likely to generate a profit. Often Oil and Gas companies employ large numbers of people, and have reason to maintain databases of PII for their employees. While this type of information is maintained by most employers, the size of the organization dictates the benefit to the attacker for compromising the system; so larger organizations are more lucrative targets. Additionally, research on commodities markets and price projections that are maintained by the Oil and Gas industry along with prereleased financial performance information can be utilized by organized criminals for the purpose of using insider information to profit from investment activity in global markets. While financial performance information is able to be exploited in all verticals for publicly traded companies, the speculative research with respect to the commodities market offers another avenue for Organized Crime to profit from stealing financial information and projections from the Oil and Gas industry.

Terrorism

Terrorists can use attacks on Oil and Gas companies to create very high-profile disasters. The successful attack on Saudi Aramco showed the potential for attackers to pivot from Information Technology systems to Operational Technology systems using ERP systems. The Saudi Aramco attackers stopped short of causing a major disaster and simply destroyed computer equipment, but the potential for causing oil spills through cyber-attacks is a very real and credible threat that will be discussed in further depth throughout the book.

Hacktivism

Hacktavist Groups are motivated by many things, but most tend to be anarchist and outside the mainstream in ideology, meaning many of the groups have an anticorporate, anti-Oil Producing and Exporting Countries (OPEC), anticorporate greed and profits, antistate control of resources, or anti-fossil fuel agenda. There are certainly a variety of reasons hacktavists choose to attack a corporation, but many of the hacktivist groups find themselves at odds with Oil and Gas corporations for a variety of reasons.

Given all of the potential attacks against the industry, the relatively weak security posture of the industry is perplexing. I have personally made an effort to speak to the community as much as I can, operating under the assumption that the lack of protection is related to a lack of understanding of the threats the industry faces.

Health Care

The most obvious Critical Information Assets in health care are related to PHI and PII. For most health care organizations, these heavily regulated assets are at the top of the list of assets that need protection, but for most, there are other assets that are to be protected as well. Many hospitals also perform research, which needs to be protected in order for the Return on Investment for that research to be realized. Additionally, many health care enterprises grow by acquisition, so Merger and Acquisition documentation may be very important. Each individual health care organization will have different concerns, but it is important to expand the thoughts of what protections are necessary beyond PHI regulated by the Health Insurance Portability and Accountability Act in the United States or similar regulations and consumer protections around the world. It is interesting that many healthcare organizations I have encountered allow regulations to dictate their security posture, primarily concerning themselves with regulatory information and not Intellectual Property, Merger and Acquisition information, or the other Critical Information Assets that are likely to exist in a health care environment. Further, many are concerned more with compliance than security, even when referencing regulated information, which leads to a weak overall security posture in many cases. There are some shining examples of health care organizations I have worked with, however, that have demonstrated a commitment to securing their corporate information as well as their patient information, far beyond the extent in which they are required to. Those organizations should be applauded for their vigilance.

Manufacturing

Critical Assets in Manufacturing are primarily the process in which they manufacture their products and the plans and designs of the products themselves. These types of Intellectual Property are related to the core operations of the business, and often are directly related to current and future revenues for the organization. Often, security professionals inside these organizations mistakenly believe that simple products are not important. Regardless of how common a product may be, if the organization has a process to produce the product cheaper or of higher quality than their competitors, that product is critical to the business. The challenge of protecting manufacturing assets revolves around tightly controlling the community of users who access the information and clearly defining the authorized use of the information for the community of users. In the manufacturing industry, processes, designs, and formulas are very valuable and outsourcing is common, which leads to additional security concerns. Additionally, some of the risks must be accepted in order for business to continue in a profitable fashion, so close monitoring of authorized users and business processes in order to find minor deviations in those processes is required. Due to the global economy and lower operational costs and lower regulatory burdens abroad, many manufacturers are doing business in some very dangerous parts of the world from a cyber-security perspective. It is critical for those organizations to be vigilant to ensure the security costs in the form of breaches do not outweigh the operational benefits of the decisions that were made.

Financial Services

Financial Services firms are one of the most obvious targets for organized crime and one of the most heavily regulated industries in the world. As a result, the financial services industry has some of the most well-defined Critical Assets, and they are what you would expect: financial instruments such as CCNs, bank account numbers, PII, and credentials to accounts, as well as financial planning data and research that is the primary form of Intellectual Property in need of protection.

Essentially, all of these assets fall into two primary categories. The first category is customer information and is inclusive of both their financial information and their personal information. Protecting customer information is very important with respect to how the organization is perceived. Since trust is a major factor in most customers' decision-making process with respect to which financial services firms to do business with, the inappropriate disclosure of customer information could have a significant impact on revenue for a financial services firm. Financial services is one of the few industries where programs have to be built to monitor individual customer activity in an effort to detect fraud, as the financial services industry is often liable for the fraudulent use of financial instruments, and protecting customers from fraud is a central part of each firm's marketing strategy.

The second category of Critical Information Assets consists of corporate intelligence or business information. This type of information is often far more important to financial services firms, especially firms that rely on making investments as part of their business strategy. An example is a Real Estate Investment firm. Essentially, they are similar to a mutual fund in that they pool capital with investors in an effort to gain a generous return for both the investor and the organization. A long-term plan for such an organization is extremely sensitive since it details where they plan to invest and what characterizes a good and bad investment for them. Should that information get out to a competitor, it will be much easier for the competitor to compete effectively against the organization. Even if the recipient of the improperly disclosed information wasn't a competitor, the intelligence could be used by others to make investments, which could drive up the price of those investments and mandate that the organization adjust their strategy accordingly. Either scenario would cause significant damage in terms of opportunity cost.

Retail

The retail sector, similar to the financial sector, has assets, mostly in the form of CNNs, which can be easily and unimaginatively exploited by cyber-criminals. Unlike the financial services sector, the retail sector tends to have relatively weak security posture and often does not spend as much on security as other sectors of the global economy. The reduced spend can be attributed to the fact that most retail organizations operate on very thin profit margins and therefore have less to spend on security solutions and other solutions that may be seen as overhead expenses. Retail organizations are primarily focused on cutting costs and overhead, resulting in them being targeted as soft targets by cyber-criminals. Moreover, the string of publicized successful attacks on the retail sector has further emboldened the attackers to continue their activities.

At some point, there must be some change to the way retail organizations do business with respect to Information Security. The problem is that banks and credit card issuers have become so effective at protecting their customers from financial harm when breaches occur that there is little pressure from the consumer community for retailers to better protect their information as compared with health care providers, for example. Further, few customers would be willing to pay more to shop at a retailer that does a better job protecting their information, since there is little perceived personal harm that comes from these breaches. Simply put, consumers have become accustomed to breach notifications and there is less public outcry as a result.

When a retailer wants to accept credit cards at their location, they pay a fee per transaction or a percentage of each transaction to the credit card issuer. The Payment Card Industry (PCI) council is the regulating body for how card data is protected by organizations that store, process, or transmit payment card data. One possible scenario that could help increase the retail security posture is if the PCI council were to offer different rates to retailers based on their security posture. There is currently no indication that this is likely to happen, but if fraud becomes a large-enough problem for the credit card issuers, creative solutions may be put into place in order to reduce the impact of the problem. Essentially, retailers pay a percentage of their gross sales via credit card to the credit card issuers. If demonstrating a better security posture was shown to reduce risk to the card provider, and the card provider responded by providing the retailer a lower rate, retailers would be more incentivized to build effective programs to protect information.

Publicly Traded Companies

Although it is not a vertical, publicly traded companies face some unique challenges based on their need to report financial information accurately and at the right times. There are a variety of regulations that regulate the disclosure of financial statements prior to their official release dates, and other regulations that expressly prohibit trading based on insider information. However, there is often significant movement in stock price prior to the release of financial statements. This movement could be explained by pure speculation, but there also may be times where investors have been able to access information that indicates a stock may underperform or outperform market expectations. In order to ensure financial information is not improperly shared prior to its disclosure, protections must take the current date into account as an important input into the overall protection profile.

Needles in the Haystack

Now we've established what is critical to the organization and effectively mapped the threats against those assets. How do we protect those assets? The next logical step is to put people, process, and technologies in place that can effectively detect and analyze actions against the assets in progress. Among the myriad of technologies available, the foundation for protecting Critical Information Assets is built upon content- and context-aware monitoring tools.

Content Analytics

If we accept that some information is more critical than other information, we must have a method for distinguishing critical information in motion, in use, or at rest, from noncritical information traversing the same channels in the environment. Content analytics, therefore, is a cornerstone of any effective security program that is targeted at specific information assets. Data in motion, Data in Use, and Data at Rest are defined in detail in subsequent sections of this chapter. The most well-known and well-established content analytics technology is the Data Loss Prevention line of technologies. Data Loss Prevention experienced a surge in popularity at the beginning of its life cycle due to its ability to help organizations comply with regulations that were emerging at the time. The recent resurgence in the popularity of Data Loss Prevention is largely attributed to programs like InteliSecure's Critical Asset Protection Program, which is designed to help organizations prioritize and protect all assets that are critical to the organization, whether or not they are regulated. Although Data Loss Prevention is experiencing a resurgence, no line of technology will last forever. However, for the foreseeable future, programs will require an element with the ability to find the proverbial needles in the haystack and track the movement of that information throughout its life cycle. As mentioned previously, there are currently three areas of monitoring for content analytics systems: Data in Motion, Data in Use, and Data at Rest.

Data in Motion

Data in Motion refers to the ability to detect Critical Information Assets as they move throughout an environment or as they ingress or egress an environment. Common Data in Motion protocols are Simple Mail Transfer Protocol (SMTP) commonly known as e-mail; Hyper Text Transfer Protocol (HTTP), commonly known as the Internet, and the File Transfer Protocol (FTP). Due to increasing decentralization of Information Technology infrastructure and the growing prevalence of cloud technologies, Data in Motion monitoring systems and programs have undergone a transformation to integrate technologies like Cloud Access Service Brokers to ensure that an organization can establish and enforce rules with respect to where data is allowed to go and the methods in which it is allowed to be shared.

Acceptable use of data, especially critical data, has to be addressed at the executive or board level. To be clear, executives are not expected to participate in the day-to-day activities of the program. The executives and board members are responsible for providing guidance and a budget for the program. The vice president level should provide more specific guidance with respect to their business units, and assign responsibility to the levels below them. It is important to understand that security is everyone's responsibility, and there should be an organizational commitment to protecting Critical Information Assets. There is a role for all levels from the board down to the everyday user, and every level in between.

For example, in the case of sensitive data being transferred to cloud applications, if there is not an official and enforceable policy set forth by the executive team, users will follow the path of least resistance, which generally includes exposing Critical Information Assets to consumer cloud applications that carry with them undue risk. From a user perspective, there is very little difference in the way they access the consumer side of cloud technologies like Box.com, for example, and the corporate Box.com infrastructure. There are, however, significant security differences in the consumer and enterprise versions of the services, that are, by design, as close to imperceptible to end users as possible. In subsequent chapters of the book, we will explore in detail methods in which organizations can refine processes to be more secure while ensuring the end-user community accepts and supports the changes.

The growing prevalence of encryption for data transmissions has forced a change in how Data in Motion monitoring is performed as well. There was a time, not too long ago, where I could set up a passive monitoring device on a network that could monitor unencrypted traffic as it egresses a network and actually discover inappropriate behavior. At that time, popular Internet mail sites like Yahoo Mail and Gmail were not encrypted. Currently, very little is transmitted without HTTPS protection, meaning that it is difficult to monitor the transmissions without decrypting Data in Motion. Similarly, corporate e-mail was often transmitted over the unencrypted SMTP. Currently, many organizations wrap SMTP transmissions in Transport Layer Security (TLS) encryption to prevent unauthorized individuals from intercepting transmissions.

Many of the changes that have made it more difficult to monitor data transmissions are actually made in the interest of general security. It is a good thing that the majority of transmissions are encrypted from a security perspective. However, the changes dictate that Information Security programs integrate with the organizational infrastructure in order to monitor those transmissions. The prevalence of encryption technologies to secure Data in Motion highlights the need for the Information Security program to be comprehensive. If the encryption strategy is executed in concert with the rest of the program, the encryption technology will be centrally managed and deployed with the requirements for decrypting the information when appropriate in mind. If the program is disjointed and operates in silos, it will be extremely difficult for the team implementing content analytics capabilities to comprehensively monitor Data in Motion without completely breaking the encryption that has been deployed by another team.

Data in Use

Data in Use refers to the ability of a technology to monitor how information is used by end users, typically at the endpoint device level. This often includes not only how information is shared over the Internet and e-mail when not connected to the corporate network, but also things like what information is being printed and what types of information are being saved to removable storage. Traditionally, many organizations were forced to make binary decisions such as whether or not to allow a specific user to transfer anything to a USB removable storage device. With Data in Use technologies, organizations can implement and enforce rules governing what types of information can be transferred through these popular methods. Facilitating monitoring allows for organizations to relax restrictions on technologies that streamline process while protecting Critical Information Assets. This is one of the rare opportunities to allow a security program to increase business process efficiency rather than adding overhead to processes and slowing down business functions.

Monitoring Data in Use generally offers the greatest visibility into the usage of data in an environment, but it is also the most intrusive for the end user. There must be a proper balance between security and productivity whenever implementing Data in Use monitoring. In my experience, there is a fine line between acceptable monitoring that users understand the need for, and overmonitoring that is seen as an invasion of privacy by the end-user community. The acceptable of monitoring differs across different cultures, and can be difficult to manage both from a corporate culture and a regional law perspective. However, long-term planning and effective communication can create solutions that are acceptable to the user communities as well as regulatory bodies in various countries. There are also generally capabilities to interact with the end user in real time, such as pop-up messages asking users to confirm they intended to take a specific action, when certain conditions are met. This type of capability offers tremendous opportunities to reinforce security training and amend inappropriate behavior with on the spot corrections. It also presents unparalleled risk in terms of casting doubt on the program due to excessive False Positives or alienating the user community with improper messaging. The old saying "With great power comes great responsibility" is definitely applicable to Data in Use monitoring.

Data at Rest

Data at Rest refers to the ability to find critical information where it is stored. This capability often solves business problems for legal teams, records and information management, compliance teams, and Information Technology teams, as well as security teams. From a security perspective, improperly stored Critical Assets are exposed to unnecessary risk. Additionally, many breaches cause exponentially more harm when organizations fail to comply with concept of least privilege and separation of duties. Many Data Loss Prevention vendors are combining Data at Rest monitoring with permissions visualization capabilities to review appropriate access to the most critical information in the storage infrastructure. Additionally, as was the case with Sony, overretention of information that has no business value often presents a problem. Data classification and tagging programs play a significant role in preventing potentially harmful data from being stored when there is no business need to do so. Data at Rest portions of a content analytics program are often transparent to end users, so many large organizations that lack the political capital to complete a highly publicized rollout of monitoring capabilities will start with Data at Rest monitoring programs. There is invariably a process in which Critical Assets are created, stored, used, and transmitted. This is an example of an Information Life Cycle (ILC) and will be addressed in detail later in the chapter.

The Future of Content Analytics

Traditionally, content analytics engines have been restricted to text-based content, but research and advances are currently being made to allow for images and models to be analyzed as well. Forthcoming improvements in the content analytics arena allow for behavioral analytics to play a role in the appropriate response that should be taken in a given area. Additionally, data classification products are providing ways for people to become part of the Critical Asset Protection solution rather than part of the problem. The future of content analytics engines, in my opinion, will incorporate three central pillars: traditional Data Loss Prevention style content analytics engines; behavioral analytics through integrations with identity and access management products; as well as integrating user feedback via data classification and tagging components.

■ **Note**   Behavior Analytics refers to identifying and baselining individual human behavior in order to detect deviations from that normal behavior. This is similar to the idea of baselining systems in an effort to detect deviations from that baseline. Behavioral analytics requires profiles to be built of users based on factors such as location, work hours, job function, among many other things. These models, in order to be effective, may need to be quite complex.

The volume of events and transfers is ever expanding. While current technologies are heavily dependent on user monitoring in order to execute processes, future technologies will leverage technologies like automated user behavior analytics and automation workflows in order to reduce the burden on individual users. Additionally, it is likely machine learning will be increasingly leveraged in order to eliminate inconsequential alerts and reduce the workload on individuals. Increasing computing power and the presence of supercomputers like IBM's Watson have made calculations that were previously impossible a reality. For example, sequencing a human genome used to take weeks, but now several can be performed in a day. Similarly, complex behavioral analytics models can leverage increasing computing power in order to realistically build behavioral models and detect deviations from normal behavior in near real time.

There are some important aspects of content analytics currently available that make these technologies indispensable to comprehensive Information Security programs. However, there are also clear opportunities for improvement of these types of technologies. Today, content analytics is largely event based. What that means is that they collect records of individual transfers of information or behaviors by an end user. The next evolution requires contextual information to be taken into account to present risk profiles and possibly to make preliminary determinations with respect to whether the risk is a compromised system, a well-meaning insider, or a malicious insider threat. It will take time for the industry to fully realize this vision, but my prediction is that there will begin to be tangible steps taken in this direction within the next few years, and some steps may even be taken by a leading vendor between the time this book is written and the time it is published.

Some content analytics engines are now building adaptive or connected security models that allow changing behavioral risk profiles to drive real time and sometimes proactive responses to changing risk profiles. For example, if a user is deviating from normal behavior, the system could react by not allowing that user to transfer sensitive data off of their machine until an investigation was performed. These types of activities have long been performed by effective Information Security programs in a manual fashion, but driving these capabilities into the technologies can cut reaction time from hours and minutes to seconds, which has the potential when deployed well to stop some types of breaches before they occur, or at least limit the amount of data that is lost in such scenarios.

Additionally, further convergence of data classification technologies and content analytics will help to increase the efficacy and flexibility of content analytics programs. Data Classification has become an essential way to include the user community in solutions that protect Critical Information Assets. I expect these trends to continue and become even-more complementary as next-generation content analytics solutions utilize as many sources as possible to make qualitative behavioral analysis suggestions to Information Security teams. These advances will have a profound effect on the ability to respond to threats and breaches expediently and appropriately.

Context Analytics

Context analytics products, traditionally known as Security Incident and Event Management (SIEM) products, are a convergence of two ideas and original technologies, Security Event Monitoring (SEM) and Security Incident Management (SIM). SEM products are designed to collect logs and allow those logs to be analyzed and searched. There are many global regulations that require log collection and in many cases, some level of log review. SIM products are designed to allow an organization to correlate information from multiple sources in order to recognize patterns that may indicate a system or network is compromised. The original SIEM systems fell short of delivering on the promises they made because the technology was not fast enough to ingest very large volumes of information and correlate that volume of information in a useful time frame. For example, many times the complex correlations would take hours, triggering an alarm well after the damage was done. In order to be effective, SIEM systems need to be much more efficient and much faster. SIEM was developed in the 1990s in order to store logs, and it has been effective at doing so. Recent generations of SIEM systems represent the necessary quantum leap in technology necessary to deliver on the security promise of SIEM in large environments, which is the ability to correlate millions of logs in near real time in order to provide timely and useful alerts to systematic behavioral patterns that indicate an attack may be in progress. This technology change has been due to the change from relational databases to nonrelational databases with elastic search capabilities.

First-generation SIEM products have given way to next-generation SIEM products, which have significantly increased the real-time monitoring and detection capabilities. Many of the next-generation products are utilizing technologies designed to analyze very large volumes of information in near real time. The majority of products in the first generation of systems were using relational databases like Microsoft Structured Query Language (SQL) databases. Very few, if any, remaining next-generation systems leverage these types of databases.

The next natural evolution in the space is to allow for adaptive security modeling taking user behavior as well as Indicators of Compromise into account when deciding whether or not to allow a network transaction to take place. Many people overlook the importance of Context Monitoring systems, but they are vital, especially for organizations targeted by Industrial- and State-Sponsored spies. Since adaptable and well-funded adversaries employ zero-day exploits to attack their targets and often encapsulate and encrypt targeted data before making a transfer, in many cases the only indicator that something is happening in these attacks are deviations from the baseline of normal behavior in the environment. It requires comprehensive content analytics in order to baseline environments and alert on deviations from that baseline, which can then trigger a comprehensive Incident Response process.

Evolution of Context Analytics

Recently, there has been a growing prevalence of Context Monitoring capabilities being utilized on individual machines as a complement to or a replacement of signature-based anti-malware products. Technologies that allow organizations to define acceptable applications and whitelist them, generally also have a component monitoring the behavior of authorized applications to ensure they are behaving properly. For example, I may choose to allow Notepad in my environment, but if that Notepad program starts to launch PowerShell scripts, those scripts can safely be terminated since that is not normal behavior for a Notepad file inside the environment. This is an example of an endpoint-based context analytics technology.

The context analytics industry is beginning to move away from the SIEM label, and we have begun to see Security Intelligence Platforms become the new name for these types of systems. Regardless of what they are named, the key for context analytics systems with respect to protecting Critical Information Assets is that they ingest information from a comprehensive set of devices in an environment and can normalize and correlate disparate information in as close to real time as possible. It is often lamented in the security industry that programs are measured in mean time to detection, or the amount of time that elapses between when a breach happens and when a breach is detected rather than measuring success by the number of potential breaches that are thwarted by a security program. Another newer term used to describe a very similar metric is dwell time, or the amount of time an attacker has undetected inside an environment to exploit it. Dwell time can be inclusive of a period of time in which an attacker sits dormant inside of an environment in an effort to not draw attention to the breach. These attacks are known as "low and slow" attacks because the attackers keep a low profile and slowly move toward their objective in an effort to remain undetected. These attacks make it far more difficult to detect an attack in progress, but forensic evaluations after the fact can often re-create the elements of the attack, including the amount of time an attacker remains dormant prior to taking action on the attackers' objective.

While I agree with the sentiment expressed by my esteemed colleagues with respect to their disappointment that that attitude suggests we have conceded that breaches are inevitable, with the current state of the industry, the majority of technologies and programs lack proactive capabilities and are therefore reactive. As such, teams cannot react to incidents until they know an incident has taken place or is taking place. As the systems progress into the future, I expect a premium to be placed on proactive capabilities that prevent a breach from occurring in the first place rather than reacting to a breach in progress. At this point, programs and technologies have not yet advanced to the point to make these types of aspirations realistic.

Types of Events

When building a comprehensive program, there are essentially two categories of events that happen in an environment that must be identified and taken into account. First, there are user-driven events, which are actions taken by a user, and are generally monitored best by content analytics systems. Second, there are system-generated events, which help to identify compromised systems or anomalous behavior on a network. System-generated events are generally monitored by context analytics solutions.

Content, Community, and Channel

Programs designed to monitor user-driven events and that employ content analytics technologies are built on a foundational concept of content, community, and channel, which is a methodology to define acceptable user behavior and authorized business processes. If Acceptable Use Policies specific to the handling of Critical Information Assets do not exist, how do we work with the business to build effective content-specific security products without hampering critical business processes? This question is the central concern preventing many programs from being implemented, and many more from being expanded to the extent where they protect Critical Information Assets in a meaningful way. Secure Business Process Design is the best way to design processes to be secure from their inception, which we will discuss later. The majority of the time, it is not feasible to pause business operations in order to maximize the effectiveness of an Information Security Program. Instead, as the saying goes, we may need to remodel the car while driving down the road.

The first step in building a program that helps rather than hinders the business while improving organizational security posture with respect to Critical Information Assets is to identify the business processes that relate to those assets. Defining core business processes often results in analysis to paralysis if the parameters are not laid out in advance. For the purposes of building a program to protect Critical Information Assets, the primary three things that need to be gathered from all concerned parties are the "three 'C's" as they relate to the asset, the content, community, and channel. Figure 2-2 illustrates Content, Community, and Channel and what each of these programmatic elements refers to.

Figure 2-2. Content, Community, and Channel

Content

The content is simply the aspects of the Critical Information Asset that can be used to identify it. What is it that is unique to that specific asset or class of assets? What is it that distinguishes that asset from assets of average value inside the environment? The process of translating this business intelligence into technical programming that can be understood by technical systems, as well as all of the intervening steps necessary to build an effective program that bridges the significant gaps between business stakeholders and technologies and Information Security teams responsible for the day-to-day operations of the program will be discussed in detail when we review the Business Intelligence Model. The most important concept to take away from this section is the idea that when defining content with respect to Critical Information Assets, gathering as much detail, and ideally, as many examples, as possible is of paramount importance.

Content refers to what the program endeavors to protect. A violation of content rules would be if someone in the organization accesses content they should not be accessing as part of their responsibilities. For example, in a health care organization, there is likely not a business need for the IT department to access individual patient records. Many times detection of sensitive content in a behavior is not, by itself, indicative of an Incident. In order to determine the appropriate response, community and channel must also be applied. Many organizations that struggle to gain value from content analytics technologies and programs do so because they are only monitoring sensitive content, failing to take the other aspects of community and channel into account. The result is a large volume of Incidents that do not have business value and are not actionable. This creates a needle in the haystack scenario where the important Incidents become lost in the noise. The truth is if an asset is valuable and critical, it will be used by the organization, and many times will be used often. Defining acceptable use for these assets is a crucial step that cannot be overlooked. Failing to define acceptable use can result in ill-will from the user community as systems are built to inappropriately interfere with user activity. Additionally, if certain actions are prohibited, and users are not made aware, those users may feel the monitoring program is unfair.

Community

Community is an important element that is far too often overlooked. Time-tested and universally accepted best practices such as the Concept of Least Privilege and Separation of Duties are rooted in determining the community of authorized users who have both a business need to interact with a Critical Information Asset as well as the necessary training to understand how that asset is to be handled and whom it may be shared with. This is often as simple as defining authorized users of types of information and authorized recipients of the same. Sometimes it requires complex mapping, especially for service providers who wish to ensure ethical walls are established and maintained.

Community answers the question of who should have access to an asset and who the asset may be shared with. A classic example of a violation of community is if a service provider sends one organization's information to another organization they provide a service for. If you analyze the transmission of data, the content was appropriate, and the method of transfer was likely appropriate as well, but the information was shared with the wrong community of people, this can result in a breach and a significant loss of customer confidence.

Channel

Channel refers to the ways authorized users can utilize and transmit sensitive content. The simplest definition of channel deals with transmission, but in the context of creating a Comprehensive IT Security Program, the definition must be expanded to include the way an asset is utilized. Many organizations incorrectly assume that authorized users of sensitive content can do what they please with the content. For example, if I am allowed to access customer PII for the purposes of processing claims, am I also allowed to transfer that sensitive data to a USB device or send it to my personal Gmail account so I can work on it at my convenience? The answer often is, or should be, a resounding no; however many organizations continue to whitelist users rather than user actions.

■ **Note**   Whitelisting user behavior rather than user actions is especially popular for executives. This practice is excessively dangerous as executive users have a tendency to have access to the most sensitive and valuable assets in the organization. In order for a program to be effective, everyone, including the CEO, must be subjected to the controls. No one can be above the rules or the entire program will have a fundamental flaw. Executive credentials are often targeted because in most organizations they have the highest level of access and the least amount of restriction and monitoring.

This overly permissive stance not only opens the organization to risk related to disgruntled employees, or careless individual practices as they relate to security, but also increased risk as a result from trusted user accounts and machines being compromised.

Channel is designed to answer how an asset may be utilized, or transmitted. A classic example of a violation of channel affects the health care industry in the United States and elsewhere. In the United States, there is a regulation called the Health Insurance Portability and Accountability Act (HIPAA) which mandates, among many other things, that e-mails to patients containing health-related information must be encrypted in transit, unless the patient has written authorization on file for the organization to send their information unencrypted. If a hospital sends information to a patient in an unencrypted format, which could happen for a variety of reasons, that represents a violation and a breach. In this case the content was authorized, and the community was correct transferring from an authorized user to an authorized recipient, but the channel was not correct.

A Proper Response

For many organizations, Incident Response Planning is very similar to life insurance or creating a will for an individual: something unpleasant that few want to think about and fewer want to spend any length of time planning for. However, failure to plan for unfortunate events does not reduce the likelihood that they will happen; it only increases the negative consequences when they do. At the 2015 RSA conference, when asked what advice he had for America's CEOs as it relates to cyber-security, former U.S. Central Intelligence Agency director Leon Panetta said, "People can either choose to deal with these threats through leadership, or they will be forced to deal with them through crisis." With the ever-expanding volume of cyber-attacks, it is likely that every organization has been attacked whether they know it or not. Further, given the current trends, it is likely that everyone reading this book, will, at some point in their career, be involved in a breach situation, if they have not been already.

I often tell people that the worst time to teach someone how to fight a fire is in the midst of inferno. Similarly, it is very difficult to efficiently and effectively respond to an Incident without a clear well-thought-out plan. Often the hardest part of doing anything is getting started, and the same is true for Incident Response planning. Too often, organizations do not create a plan because they are intimidated by the herculean task of planning for every possible scenario and contingency.

Incident Response Planning will be discussed in detail in chapter 5. The central point to remember with respect to Critical Asset Protection is that a program must account for the proper response to an incident before implementing capabilities to identify such an incident. The only thing worse than experiencing a breach and being unaware of it in the context of Information Security is detecting a breach and being unprepared to respond appropriately.

Conclusion

Critical Assets are the key to an organization, both from an operational as well as a security perspective. Protecting Critical Assets is the goal of any security program whether or not the program explicitly defines those assets or acknowledges its true purpose. Think of where you live: everything inside of the structure is an asset. There are likely locks on the doors and windows. Those locked doors and windows are very similar to perimeter-based technologies. They are necessary, and very few people would forego them completely. For assets of average value, things like your television, your couch, coffee table, etc., these locked doors and windows are likely adequate protection. However, if you have assets of very high value, like rare and expensive jewelry, additional protection may be necessary; in this example, maybe it would be a safe. The safe is too small to fit everything you own, and expanding the capacity of the safe would be very expensive, so you must prioritize which of your assets belong in the safe and which do not. This is exactly the challenge facing today's organizations that are trying to build a security program.

Many organizations seek to harden their perimeter defenses and do not choose to build a program based on protecting their most Critical Assets. Doing so is like not having a safe and instead choosing to leave your Critical Assets in plain view, but adding bars to the windows and installing steel-reinforced doors. However, the doors and windows must be able to open in order to perform their function. Due to this fact, there will always be a risk that they may be forced open when they shouldn't be. Without that second layer of protection for the most Critical Assets, those assets would be exposed to undue risk. Everyone has locks on their doors and windows. We're here to talk about your safe.

CHAPTER 3

■ ■ ■

Monetizing Risk

In God we trust, all others bring data.

—W. Edwards Deming

■ **Note**   This chapter is specifically relevant to businesses that have a profit motive. Elements of this chapter may be applicable to not-for-profit organizations, but the concepts expressed in this chapter are specifically applicable to profit-driven enterprise.

The three most personally interesting subjects I have come across in my personal journey are history, politics, and business. I love history, in its truest form, because it is rooted in fact. Either things happened or they did not. Certainly, there are examples of revisionist history in which people twist the facts in order to support their position or view of the world, but history that can be proven by fact and does not rely on eyewitness accounts has an element of purity to it, in my opinion. There is also an element to history where we get to choose in what ways we would like to apply lessons in order to shape our current actions in an effort to achieve our desired outcomes. The convergence of indisputable fact with conjecture and opinion makes for very interesting discussions. I find politics fascinating because there are no universally accepted truths. Each side tends to be able to produce contrary facts and figures that should not be able to coexist in the natural world. The fact that the sides of an issue never tend to agree and yet accept their side of the argument as universally correct without exception is a fascinating journey through the human mind. Business is fascinating to me because the results of decisions present enormous consequences to those involved, and there are few things in business that can be qualitatively analyzed without also being quantified at some point. Businesses forecast many things based on assumption, but all things, at some point have an economic impact, which provides universal truths in business for those who know where to find it. When evaluating my options after leaving the military and beginning my college career, I chose business over political science and history because of not only its universal application, but also because of the fact that given enough time, there will be an inarguable result of efforts that can be quantified in terms of economic impact.

Many people have told me that it is impossible to quantify risk. They posit that certain elements may be quantified, but there are portions of risk that are impossible to quantify, and therefore, risk is intangible. This may be true for personal risk, as how does one place a value on life, limb, or eyesight? On the other hand, with respect to business risk, my opinion is that the preceding statement is categorically and indisputably false. Business risk is that essentially bad things can happen to a business combined with the likelihood that such things could happen. What bad things, or good things for that matter, could happen to a business that does not have an economic impact? Everything that happens to a business of consequence, whether positive or negative, by its very definition, has an economic impact. Economic impact is always

© Jeremy Wittkop 2016
J. Wittkop, *Building a Comprehensive IT Security Program*, DOI 10.1007/978-1-4842-2053-5_3

quantifiable. There is an entire industry devoted to allowing consumers to transfer their risk. We know this industry as insurance. If risk is inherently intangible, does that mean insurance organizations, which are some of the longest lasting organizations in the world, run through black magic and assumption rather than facts and science? Of course not. Insurance companies understand that everything that could happen will have an economic impact, and they must adjust their premiums to allow the company to pay out the costs incurred by things that are difficult to predict as well as make a profit. They do so through the use of models very similar to the model we will explore in depth in this chapter.

All business risk is quantifiable, even existential threats to the business. In order for a threat to be existential to a business, the economic impact of the risk must be greater than the economic resources the organization can bring to bear in order to address the risk, leading to insolvency, which is death for a profit-driven enterprise. Just as not all risks in the physical world are fatal, business risks include things like loss of market share, loss of customer confidence, and loss of brand reputation, which can be difficult to quantify at times and may not lead to bankruptcy, but cause real financial harm for an organization, its shareholders, and often its employees as well. There are widely accepted concepts and formulas utilized in the insurance industry for things like houses and cars, which can be used to accurately calculate risk against an asset. We will review these concepts first, and then discuss a methodology to quantify risk reduction as well as predict and report on Return on Investment (ROI) for Information Security Programs, which has historically been an elusive metric for Information Security professionals.

■ **Caution**   The contents of this chapter are not intended to be full-scale representations of insurance calculations. Insurance calculations are generally far more complex and involved than the examples in this chapter. The contents of this chapter have been formulated by simplifying calculations used in the insurance industry and combining them with generally accepted Information Security practices outlined in the CISSP common book of knowledge. The purpose of this chapter is to provide opportunities for Information Security professionals to create financial models for the cost-benefit analysis of their programs and proposals.

Quantifying business risk and the reduction of such is often thought of as impossible; but it is not. It is difficult at times and it requires skills many Information Security professionals do not possess or are uncomfortable applying. The importance of building this skill for Information Security professionals, however, cannot be overstated and is growing by the day. Information Security budgets are expanding and increasingly higher-level executives are asking questions about the programs in place. The level of attention being paid to security offers unprecedented opportunities for security teams in terms of the programs that can be built and the tools that can be purchased. The flip side of the coin is that the business stakeholders want to understand the returns on their investments in security, which is something that has not historically been expected. As we continue to build our teams, we must take the changing landscape into account and expand our skills to meet the evolving demands from organizations. Professionals who choose to embrace these concepts are generally very successful and well compensated. Those who do not must face shrinking job prospects as an increasing number of Information Security positions require certain levels of business literacy.

Calculating Annual Loss Expectancy

Annual Loss Expectancy is a concept that comes to us from the insurance industry. The basic premise is that an organization can complete a threat modeling exercise taking into account two factors. When the time came to select my major in college, and consequentially, my career path, I had a difficult decision to make. Majoring in history significantly limited my earning potential, so that choice was quickly eliminated. Deciding between business and politics was more difficult. After careful examination, I chose to focus on business because politics was based on opinion and trying to sway a person to one line of thinking or another; and business, at its core was based solely on fact, usually tied to financial profit or filling a market niche. There are many opinions in business, and some decisions are made based on opinion or emotion, but successful businesses and entrepreneurs invariably make decisions based on projected financial impact to the business. I would much rather bet my employment prospects on a largely scientific process of experimentation and analysis like business than to bet my future on public opinion and popularity contests like I would be doing had I chosen a career in politics. Therefore, business represented a far more stable and predictable career path for me than politics since business was based on universal truth and political fortunes shift, and many politicians spend their entire lives in public service without accomplishing the things they originally set out to accomplish.

In my experience, there are two types of security organizations inside of for-profit business: those that struggle to obtain funding, appropriate budgets, and are subject to frequent and seemingly arbitrary cuts; and those that have the funding that they need to run effective and efficient security programs. The former are generally intentionally or unintentionally disconnected from the rest of their business, make decisions in a vacuum, and operate solely inside the echo chamber of their own thoughts, ideas, and opinions. The latter are generally led by people who have learned to communicate effectively with the business by explaining security programs in financial modeling frameworks such as cost-benefit analysis and building ROI models. Businesses may spend discretionary funds on programs that are not well understood, but when times are more difficult, those are the first budgets to get cut. Security leaders that can effectively tie the security program to the bottom line of the business in a realistic and compelling way, however, rarely have to fight for the budget they need. Further, the value they provide and demonstrate generally results in positive personal consequences for them such as increased responsibility and compensation. In fact, during my business tenure, I have seen several examples of security programs based solely on "checking the regulatory box" that have met a quick demise or have achieved virtually no ROI for the business. This is a perfect example of how security programs should *not* be approached.

Many people comment on the fact that it is difficult to build financial models for security programs, and they are correct. However, it is also possible to create a model and it is essential to the overall health, success, and longevity of the program. The best-built security programs will fail if they are not appropriately funded, so failure to build effective financial models for security is an existential threat for many cyber-security programs and leaders.

First, we must calculate the cost of a single event from the threat modeling exercise expressed in a currency amount. This is known as a Single Loss Expectancy (SLE). In terms of data breaches, there are two types of costs that make up the SLE: direct costs and indirect costs. Direct costs are defined as costs that are paid by an organization as a direct result of a breach. Fines for regulatory violations and spending on public relation firms to help repair corporate image are good examples of direct costs. By their nature, direct costs are relatively easy to quantify, and could be covered by a cyber-insurance policy. Indirect costs are much more difficult to quantify and are unlikely to be covered by cyber-insurance policies. These types of costs are often associated with things like damage to brand reputation and reduction in sales. While sales can be compared to historical performance, a reduction in sales is difficult to attribute to a single factor. Often, there are many factors that contribute to success or failures in terms of sales, but how much of the reduction is due to the breach and how much is due to other unrelated factors is difficult to quantify. One could attempt to compare the potential reduction in sales to previous breach examples, but even then there are too many variables such as the product's market, the type of product, the type of consumer, competitor interactions (such as the creation of similar products), and the publicity of the event to truly forecast anything other than an estimated range.

It is often difficult for people with traditional Information Security training to build financial models, largely because Information Security curriculum rarely contains consequential amounts of business education. Conversely, business users rarely have education in security, so business people often lack the ability to correlate Information Security challenges to business risk. I have both an Information Security and a business background, so I can identify with the struggles of both sides. The primary reason that engineers struggle with building financial models is that they are looking for universal truth that can be proven and demonstrated. Results in the engineering world must be tangible and demonstrable. While financial impacts can be seen as universal truth, forecasting financial impact and attributing different portions of a measured impact appropriately to different factors often requires educated guesses and documented assumptions. Any financial model includes some amount of these elements, and developing comfort with these types of activities is crucial for one to become effective at building financial models and forecasts.

The second factor is the probability that an incident will occur expressed in a number of times per year. If it is anticipated the event will happen less than once per year, the number may be less than one, but it may not be a negative number. This second factor is known as the Annual Rate of Occurrence (ARO). This portion of the calculation, along with indirect costs of breaches, is often the subject of debate. Historical information is often helpful in estimating both numbers. Since both are an estimate, if consensus cannot be reached on a specific number, high and low estimates can be provided in order to complete the calculation. A final consideration is to look at information about the industry your organization is participating in, and ensuring that the estimates do not cast your organization as an outlier on either side of the equation, unless specific information exists to justify doing so.

If you multiply the SLE by the ARO, the output will be the Annual Loss Expectancy (ALE), expressed in economic impact on an annualized basis. ALE is the quantification of a specific risk against a specific asset. The risks against an asset can then be added together in order to provide a total amount of risk to that asset, and the risks against all assets that are identified can be totaled to provide a line item in the budget for risk against a department or the business as a whole.

It is imperative that Information Security professionals be cognizant of their relative position when presenting these models. It is generally the Information Security department's position that they are trying to retain or secure additional budget. Due to this fact, all estimates should err on the side of being conservative so if there is disagreement, their argument will only improve. A successful challenge to the model that results in the benefit of a measure being revised downward will damage the presenter's credibility. An upward revision of the benefit analysis will only help the presenter's case.

Example Case Study: Hurricane Katrina

According to About News (www.useconomy.about.com/od/grossdomesticproduct/f/katrina_damage.htm) Hurricane Katrina caused damage between $96–$125 billion USD with $40–$66 billion USD in insured losses. The hurricane hit the United States Gulf Coast, with its largest concentration of damage in New Orleans, Louisiana. For the purpose of this example, we are only concerned with insured losses, since the example is referring to how insurance companies use the ALE model to calculate risk exposure and help set premiums. Taking the conservative estimate of $40 billion USD should be crippling to the insurance industry, shouldn't it? After all, storms of this magnitude are far from common, and who could predict when they will hit? Keep in mind throughout this example that the risk of a catastrophic hurricane to an insurance company is very similar in terms of predictability and impact as a large-scale data breach to an organization.

Long before Hurricane Katrina ravaged the Gulf Coast of the United States, calculations were done by the insurance companies and the premiums paid by the insured in the area were already helping to prepare for the event of the disaster. Though the exact hurricane could not be accurately predicted with information such as size strength and location until about 24 hours before the storm, the United States Gulf Coast is prone to hurricane activity. The insurance companies can, and likely did, look at historical models of how often hurricanes make landfall and which cities were most at risk. They may have surmised that a major hurricane will hit a population center in Louisiana once every 40 years. That is the Rate of Occurrence. To turn that number into an ARO, it would be converted into the number of times per year in a decimal form, which would be .025.

The SLE would be gathered by averaging the inflation-adjusted economic impact data from hurricanes affecting all population centers, so there was more data to use in the calculation. For the sake of argument, let's say that calculation for the SLE came out to $70 billion USD. When calculating the ALE, the ARO would be multiplied by the SLE, which would tell the insurance company that they needed to collect greater than or equal to $1.75 billion USD annually across their entire premium base to cover the risk. This money could be raised through underwriting, premium management, and other activities. Also, there is far more nuance involved in the insurance industry and how they calculate risk, but the high-level exercise follows a similar model to the one detailed above. These numbers are used only for the sake of example, but the point remains the same. Organizations can, and must, quantify their risk and take measures to either treat it, or keep capital on hand to cover their losses if the risk is to materialize. Insurance companies have been doing so successfully for many years, proving that doing so is far from impossible.

Additionally, modeling must be carefully completed with proper assessment of all risks, minor to catastrophic. Did the insurance companies properly plan for the risk of a hurricane and the related disaster in the Gulf Coast region? Did they ever take into account the possibility of so much rainfall that the levees would break, leaving the city under feet upon feet of water? When building models, it is important to be comprehensive and thorough. All risks should be identified, so they can be treated, based on whichever treatment strategies are best for the business. Going through the motions of building a model can do more harm than good by creating a false sense of security for the organization.

Risk Treatment Strategies

It is very important to understand Risk Treatment strategies and choose to apply the most appropriate one any time risks are identified inside an organization. Even if the risk is not identified, a Risk Treatment strategy is being unwittingly applied. The four Risk Treatment strategies are risk acceptance, risk avoidance, risk mitigation, and risk transference. Since every risk is treated in one of the four manners, it is in the organization's best interest to identify risks and apply treatment strategies to these risks consciously rather than having the risks be treated by default means.

Risk Acceptance

Sometimes risks are accepted because there is no viable alternative. Often, when a viable alternative is subsequently available, the original risky practice isn't necessarily reviewed and eliminated. A good example of this is a Data Loss Prevention Proof of Concept that I did for an independent hospital that had been around for many years and was still relatively small. The practice of replicating patient records to a third party via an unencrypted File Transfer Protocol (FTP) was common and accepted during the 1980s and 1990s. As encryption technologies became more prevalent and less expensive, most organizations moved to a more secure method of transferring records to their offsite storage locations. When health care became a more strictly regulated industry, most of the global regulations, including the regulations governing this hospital, required any transmission of patient data to be encrypted. The hospital was attempting to be compliant and implemented a process for secure file transfer. When a Data Loss Prevention System and program to monitor all outbound unencrypted network traffic was implemented, curious activity involving unencrypted records being transferred via FTP daily at the close of the administration team's workday was observed. This was a risk that was easily avoided by shutting down the server. It was discovered that there was turnover in the networking team during the time the new system was set up. The new employees tested and certified the new system, but were unaware the old system still existed. This was a risk with no business value that was simply a liability. It also highlights another key point to building a comprehensive Information Security program. If you do not have the ability to monitor what is happening inside the environment, you do not truly know what is and is not happening, and if you do not plan appropriately you will unwittingly counteract any well-intentioned plans. Another key point is that implementing a monitoring program that monitors authorized behavior is relatively useless. It is far more useful to define what is authorized with respect to Critical Information Assets and set up monitoring programs to identify any behavior that is outside the defined authorized process. Doing so will simultaneously highlight improper behavior as well as identify business processes that are simply not working as desired. Countless times when implementing a new content aware system, the results of how users are circumventing approved processes is shocking. Many of them are well-meaning insiders, but human beings are like electricity: we generally take the path of least resistance. Therefore, when an approved process is onerous or time consuming, users simply find an easier way that is not expressly forbidden rather than escalating their concern to their management teams, and rarely report this circumvention to management. This dynamic is the result of a culture in which feedback from management is not actively sought, which can have negative consequences across the business in far more areas than just security.

Risk Acceptance is the default Risk Treatment Strategy in which the risk is treated by continuing to maintain the status quo. There are times where Risk Acceptance is the best strategy, specifically when the cost of implementing any of the available countermeasures has a cost that outweighs the benefit of the countermeasure, based on a differential analysis of the ALE model compared with the Total Cost of Ownership associated with the countermeasure. Acceptance also occurs if the cost of a loss is negligible. In most cases, it is not appropriate to choose Risk Acceptance as a Risk Treatment Strategy unless that risk is quantified and all available alternatives are explored. How can you accept a risk if you do not know the impact of the risk you are accepting? It is often necessary for an organization to accept risks as a cost of doing business. However, accepting the wrong risks or accepting risks without understanding the impact often has catastrophic consequences, not only in the context of Information Security, but also in the context of business in general. Business is a series of risks that must be taken in order to achieve results such as profitability. People who are successful in business consistently are generally methodical in the evaluation of risk and take risks in a calculating manner when the reward outweighs the risk with probability of positive and negative outcomes taken into account. This is the same in the context of Information Security. It is important to remember that while Risk Acceptance is the default strategy if an organization does not address or identify the risk, it is only the appropriate strategy when the other strategies have been evaluated for their efficacy as compared to the Risk Acceptance strategy.

Risk Mitigation

Risk Mitigation is the Risk Treatment Strategy that is explored in the most detail in this book and is the strategy that should be employed for the majority of identified risks to Critical Information Assets, often because the risks to those assets have such a large financial impact; so the benefits of an effective countermeasure generally outweigh the costs of implementation and ownership. Risk Mitigation can take many forms, but any form of Risk Mitigation should involve people, process, technology, and the full support of the entire organization.

Risk Transference

Risk Transference is a popular strategy for a many business and financial people. The strategy on its surface is very appealing; rather than accepting, avoiding, or mitigating the risk, why not pool it with the marketplace and make others responsible for it? This is a tried and true approach that is most commonly used in the insurance industry, although it often may appear in other forms such as pricing for warranties. It is popular and very effective for risks to assets that have clearly defined values, like cars and homes. There are very few indirect costs associated with these risks, and there is very little debate with respect to the value of the assets as there are legitimate and well-established marketplaces for these items. Assets that have values that are harder to quantify are much more difficult to insure.

Risk Avoidance

Risk Avoidance is a strategy that appears to be better than it is in many cases. Most of the time, simply stopping a risky behavior is not feasible. If it were, often the behavior would rarely be taking place. That said, there are behaviors that are no longer necessary as a business evolves and changes, but the organization either does not realize the behavior still exists or is unaware of the alternatives.

Real-World Example

For example, when doing a security evaluation for an organization, I discovered that employees in their accounts receivable department were writing down credit card numbers on a notepad prior to entering the numbers into the system for processing. Upon further investigation, our team determined that the primary reason that individuals were writing down the credit card numbers was that they needed their customer information screen available while talking to the customer; and in order to enter the credit card numbers, they would need to close out the application in order to open the secure portal in which they were supposed to enter credit card numbers. This is a good example of a risky behavior the organization was not aware of. There are a few inherent risks. First, the risk of accepting credit cards over the phone was accepted by the organization. The second risk was writing the credit card number down, for which the decision was made to avoid the risky behavior, as there was no desire on the organization's part to manage and dispose of the numbers that were written down. In order to ensure the risk was truly avoided though, the organization had to remove the barrier to productivity that was the genesis of the risky behavior. It was determined that adding a second monitor to each system the payment processing team was using effectively allowed them to view their customer information screens while they were entering their information into the processing system. This is an example of a solution that allows an organization to avoid risky behavior while not only avoiding interference with existing business practices, but actually making the process more efficient. Types of scenarios that both improve risk while improving processes and avoid introducing additional problems are significant to discover not only in the business world, but in situations that occur throughout daily life. It is often believed that security slows process down and is an inhibitor to productivity. When a process can be made more secure and more efficient simultaneously, the result is often an increased willingness to engage with the security program on the part of business unit leadership.

A Different Approach

Of the Risk Treatment strategies, the human mind tends to gravitate first toward risk acceptance, second toward risk transference, third to risk avoidance, and finally toward risk mitigation. This is due to the perceived level of effort and inconvenience. The principal of inertia's general application states that the easiest path is to simply continue what you are already doing if it is not broken. Second, if something must be done, most people prefer to make it someone else's problem, which is best suited toward Risk Transference. If the risk cannot be transferred, people generally would like to avoid the risk if feasible. If none of the other strategies work, the human tendency is to begrudgingly explore the more difficult, expensive, and time-consuming strategy of Risk Mitigation.

My argument is that the opposite approach is best. The first strategy that should be explored is Risk Mitigation, because that is the only strategy that actually reduces the risk. If it is not cost effective to mitigate the risk, Risk Avoidance should be evaluated to the extent it is feasible. If it is not, the organization can reduce the risk to them in some cases by transferring a portion of the risk. As we will explore, the risk associated with the indirect cost of data breaches may not be transferred, and those risks often outweigh the insurable and direct costs of breaches. Finally, if no other strategy is appropriate, Risk Acceptance can be employed. By taking this opposite approach, an organization can limit the amount of risk that is accepted, and therefore significantly reduce the probability that risk to Critical Information Assets will result in catastrophic and unrecoverable financial damage to the organization.

■ **Note**   The above represents my personal opinion. There is no right or wrong way to apply the Risk Treatment strategies, so long as the risks are identified and consciously treated.

Regardless of which strategy is chosen, it is most important that risk is identified, critically analyzed, and that a treatment strategy is selected. Simply completing a Risk Assessment and a Risk Treatment Plan can have a major positive impact on the amount of organizational exposure.

Indirect Costs of Breaches

Many organizations have a strong desire to make Risk Transference a central part of their Information Security strategy, so why can't they? The answer lies in a concept called the indirect cost of breaches and the largely undefined value of Information Assets. These two factors result in many cases in which the cost of litigation to agree on a sum of money that should be awarded sometimes even exceeds the award itself. This problem will likely be settled at some point as case law sets precedents with respect to what should and should not be accounted for in a cyber-insurance settlement. The bigger problem is related to the indirect cost of breaches, because that problem will not be resolved in the foreseeable future. Direct costs of breaches are defined as capital outlays directly related to the breach. Examples of direct costs include regulatory fines or the credit protection services offered to the consumer that have become prevalent in breach response, especially as it relates to public relations. Indirect costs of breaches are much more difficult to quantify including the loss of brand reputation or the public trust, and resultant long-term loss of revenue. How are those effects measured? As indicated in Figure 3-1 below, the indirect costs of breaches either constitute a significant amount of the overall financial burden of the breach, or in some cases, the majority of the associated cost, categorized by the country of the breach. There are many possible reasons for the variance in indirect costs of breaches between countries, but factors such as the importance of positive brand association, and the degree to which the society is litigious, certainly play a role. So how do we calculate the indirect costs of breaches in order to complete the Risk Modeling exercise? There are two approaches we will explore: the first is a simple calculation and the second is a more in-depth evaluation of what may happen.

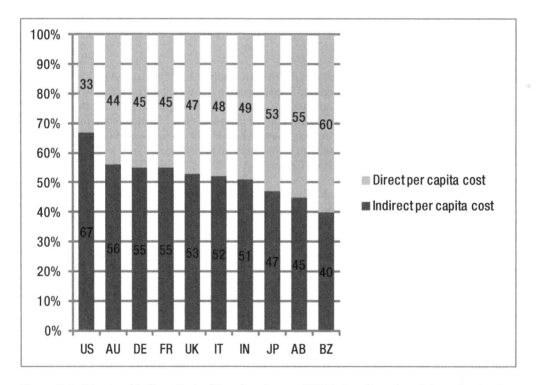

Figure 3-1. *Direct and Indirect Costs of Breaches. Source: 2015 Verizon Data Breach Investigation Report*

The first way to calculate the indirect costs of breaches is the simpler to complete, but less accurate methodology. It simply consists of taking the country the anticipated risk affects and using the ratios of direct to indirect costs to estimate the indirect costs once the direct costs are quantified based on historical data. For example, a company in the United States that has calculated the direct costs of a specific risk should it be exploited is going to be $1 million USD. In the United States, indirect costs constitute 66% of the overall costs, or a 2:1 ratio to the direct costs. Therefore, the total estimated cost of that breach would be $3 million USD, with $1 million being attributed to direct costs, and $2 million USD being attributed to indirect costs. A company doing business in Japan with calculated direct costs equal to 100,000 Japanese Yen, would estimate indirect costs of about 113,000 Japanese Yen due to the fact that direct costs constitute about 47% of the cost in Japan while 53% is attributed to indirect costs, forming a ratio of about 1:1.13 direct to indirect costs.

The modeling approach outlined above works for a quick assessment or a rough order of magnitude for indirect costs, but there are a few problems with the approach. First, the statistics are broken down by country, but they do not take industry or type of asset into account. Across different industries in different countries it is conceivable that there may be major disparities in the figures and ratios. Second, the result is not specific to individual threats or other relevant inconsistencies from breach to breach. It is probable that a breach of strategy documents and plans would likely result in mostly indirect costs, whereas a breach of regulated information is far more likely to produce a heavy direct cost burden. Finally, this data does not model breach costs over time taking into account public knowledge, opinion, and regulatory impact, so without introducing more data we cannot see how these costs have varied over time. Overall, this data gives one a starting point and can prove useful as an initial starting point in a statistical analysis.

An alternative approach is to do what is called a Critical Asset Valuation and Risk Model. This exercise is much more involved and much more burdensome to internal resources, and far more expensive if the work is outsourced to a third party. This approach first defines the Critical Information Assets and then assigns value to the asset. The protections in place for each of the assets is taken into account, and a gap analysis is conducted. Then, a Risk Model is built and indirect and direct costs are estimated individually for each of the threats presented as part of the model. While far more expensive and time consuming, this approach is exponentially more likely to produce an accurate assessment of the potential impact.

Either approach is an exercise in predictive analysis, which is by its very nature an inexact science. For example, CIO Insight did some thorough research into the cost to brand reputation after a breach. They cited a range of between $184 million USD to $330 million USD. This information is enlightening to give Information Security professionals the ability to gain an idea of brand value impact, but it is a wide range of dollar figures with significant room for interpretation with respect to what is included. Are we only including the direct costs to the brand such as hiring a public relations firm and increased advertising to counter the negative effects of a breach, or are we including loss of potential revenue based on historical analysis of trends in the industry and market share before and after the breach? The safest assumptions with respect to indirect costs is that they will be significant and may outweigh the direct breach costs. Beyond that, the level of effort required for the calculations should be balanced with how accurate and specific the information needs to be in order to make an informed decision. For example, if the cost-benefit analysis of a countermeasure is yielding a borderline result, further investigation may be warranted. However, if the projected benefit is already 10 times the cost of a countermeasure, does it really matter if its 15 or 20 times the cost with more specific information? If that is the case, it is best to repurpose those resources toward implementing the countermeasure rather than continuing the analysis for analytics sake.

Modeling Risk

What goes into a Critical Asset Valuation and Risk Model? The steps to completion are actually in the name. First, you must determine what the Critical Assets are; second, you must apply a value to the overall asset; and finally, you must determine the risk profile for each asset within each scenario you would like to model.

The first step is evaluating Critical Assets. As discussed in the second chapter, Critical Information Assets are defined as assets whose loss or inappropriate exposure would cause irreparable harm to the business. By the time a Risk Modeling exercise has begun, the Critical Assets should have been identified and prioritized. It is very difficult to define Critical Assets universally at the organizational level, because the people who know most about the assets, are have a biased view of those assets' importance to the organization. It is important to involve a variety of business leaders in the process, and also to apply an objective priority to each of the assets. Most often, this is accomplished in financial terms if an organization has never gone through the process of identifying, quantifying, and prioritizing Critical Information Assets.

Valuation may have occurred in order to rank the priority of the Critical Information Assets after they were identified, but if the valuation has not occurred, valuation should be undertaken at this point. Valuation consists of assessing the overall value of an asset, which is easier in some cases than others. For example, a piece of Intellectual Property directly tied to a product or service can be valued in accordance with its overall contribution to the product or service compared against projected revenues for that service. Additionally, the loss of an asset may result in some indirect costs such as the loss of confidence of consumers, partners, or investors. These indirect costs are difficult to quantify, but may be more impactful than the direct costs of the breach. If a specific design makes up about 20% of a specific product and that product is projected to generate $5 million USD in revenue, the value of that asset is about $1 million USD. It is a bit more difficult to value regulated information or information that contributes to the value of the brand or the public trust. In those cases, the value is best determined by calculating the anticipated direct and indirect costs of a breach on a per-record basis in order to determine a per-record value. Then, by calculating how many records exist in an environment, the organization can determine the value of their entire database of information. For example, if a Spanish company has Personally Identifiable Information that results in a total cost of 85 EUR per record, and houses 10,000 records, the total value of those records is roughly 850,000 EUR. After the values of all of the assets are calculated, the priorities of those assets may change. It is important to remember that finance is often the primary driver in business decisions. Most decisions eventually come down to "bottom-line impact" or the projected impact of the decision on the organization's finances. Business consists of a lot of opinions and qualitative analysis of comparative importance based on frame of reference. It is very rare that one can approach business unit leaders and have them all agree on what is most important and what is least important. Whatever is most important to their specific tasks will get unequal weight in their minds. The best way to get an objective analysis is to assign a financial impact common denominator to each scenario and then rank them objectively based on projected financial impact. Doing so makes a largely subjective process far more objective and is often the most expedient path to consensus with respect to Critical Assets, so long as all of the participants agree on an equitable and realistic methodology prior to the beginning of the engagement.

Once Critical Assets are identified, an assessment must be done on each asset to assess its vulnerabilities. The vulnerabilities identified will be a critical component of the Risk Modeling exercise. The most common methodology for assessing vulnerabilities is called a CIA assessment, which will assess its Confidentiality, Integrity, and Availability. Vulnerabilities in terms of Confidentiality affect the capabilities of the organization to ensure the asset is not accessed in an unauthorized manner while it is being stored, while it is being used, or while it is being transmitted. These vulnerabilities are part of the majority of security programs. Vulnerabilities in terms of Integrity relate to the assurance that the asset going to an authorized party is from the source it appears to originate from. An ability to change an asset without detection is an Integrity vulnerability. For example, if you are reading a message, and that message could be modified between the time it was written and the time you read it, would you trust the contents of that message? Integrity refers to the level of trust the end user has that the message has been unaltered. Vulnerabilities to availability are directly related to attacks that make an asset unavailable to legitimate audiences. Denial of Service Attacks are the most common threats to availability. A Denial of Service Attack is an attack in which a service is overloaded so that legitimate users cannot access the service. For example, if a Denial of Service Attack was launched against a news web site, the site would be overloaded so that it would appear as down to users trying to access the site to retrieve content. Since a Denial of Service Attack is designed to make a resource unavailable to a legitimate user, it is an attack on availability. Some assets may be more vulnerable to one of the aspects of the CIA assessment than others, but understanding the vulnerabilities of these assets is an important step.

The next step in the process is to perform a Risk Modeling exercise. It is important to remember that the Risk Modeling exercise is designed to model the risk that exists at the present moment, not to project what the risk would be in an ideal scenario. This is an important point because many organizations actually harm their security programs by painting an overly optimistic picture of the current state in the environment. Doing so skews the results of the exercise to actually diminish the value proposition for the changes they are trying to implement. Think of it this way: if the environment is already secure, why would we continue to invest in change rather than simply trying to optimize what is already in place? The inverse is also true. Painting an overly pessimistic picture will result in the organization questioning why they already made the investments they have, including the investment in the individual presenting the findings, when they have gotten such dismal results. It is important in this step to be truthful and accurate. Skewing the result either way will often result in undesirable outcomes. Figure 3-2 below shows the flowchart for calculating risk.

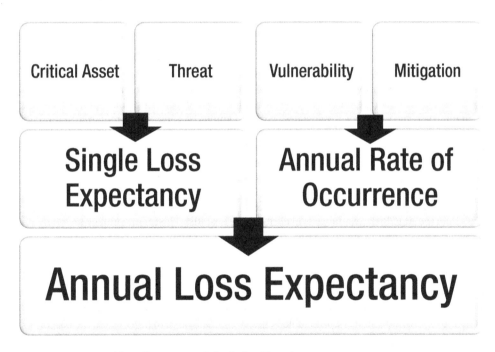

Figure 3-2. *Annual Loss Expectancy Calculation Flowchart*

Using the chart is relatively straightforward as each of these concepts has been identified and should be widely understood by this point in the process. Critical Assets are the assets in the organization that we are trying to protect. Threats are the identified scenarios that may cause harm to these assets. If you look at the Critical Asset in conjunction with what we are afraid my happen to that asset, we can project the financial impact of that event. That impact expressed quantitatively in financial terms produces the SLE. On the other side of the model, the vulnerabilities around Confidentiality, Integrity, and Availability with respect to the Critical Assets identified is compared to mitigation techniques currently in place. The result, expressed in a probability in decimal form of number of times the vulnerability could be expected to be exploited per year, is known as the ARO. SLE multiplied by the ARO will yield an ALE, or the specific annualized financial impact of a specific threat against a specific Critical Information Asset.

The model outlined above, while relatively simple, is fascinating in its many applications to bridge the gap between Information Security programs and business unit leaders, which is a critical component to building an effective Information Security program. The first application is the ability to calculate not only risk exposure but the benefits of treating risk. Any Risk Treatment Strategy has a cost-benefit analysis implication and we will explore each using the model to represent how they fit together and can be leveraged to provide the most benefit for the least cost.

Risk Mitigation deals with adding a new mitigating technique to the mitigation section of the model. If a new mitigation is added, the benefit can be calculated by calculating the ALE before and after the mitigation technique is applied. In terms of benefit, Risk Mitigation is the most impactful of all of the strategies, which is why it is often the preferred strategy for the most Critical Information Assets. These assets tend to have the largest ALEs, so the benefit side of the calculation by adding mitigation techniques is often quite impactful. These strategies also often have the largest Total Cost of Ownership (TCO) as well. TCO refers to all of the capital and operational expenditures associated with procuring, implementing, and operating a mitigation technique. To a lesser extent, TCO can be applied to other mitigation techniques. For example, the TCO of an Information Security technology deployed as a mitigation technique includes hardware costs, software costs, implementation costs, and the costs of ongoing care and management of the system. It is important to remember if an organization decides to perform the work associated with implementation or management, those activities are not without cost, and are not one-time expenditures. The most efficient and effective organizations in the world require accounting for internal resources as well as capital expenditures in order to evaluate the cost of internally sourcing resources against the cost of procuring services from a professional services organization. In the case of Information Security, it is often more beneficial to procure services externally due to the scarcity of expert resources and the efficiencies gained by having true experts deploying and managing systems. Also, due to the costs associated with mitigating risks, less-important information assets with lower ALEs are less likely to have a favorable cost-benefit analysis. Costs for low ALE assets are more difficult to treat to achieve a large cost benefit if the ALE before the measure applied is already relatively low. The focus of the discussion for the majority of this book is on Critical Information Assets, but in the case of other assets with a lower value to the organization, a strategy must still be applied. Risk Mitigation is unlikely to be the best strategy in those cases.

Any time an organization determines that the annualized value of a Critical Asset in the valuation stage of this model is less than the ALE, Risk Avoidance is likely to be the best Risk Treatment Strategy to deploy. The cost of a Risk Avoidance strategy is the loss of the use of the asset or activity. This strategy, however, is the only strategy that can result in a 100% removal of the risks associated. As such, the benefit is the totality of the risk. There are times, as highlighted in the Risk Avoidance definition section, where there is little or no business value associated with a risky behavior. In those cases, the cost-benefit analysis for a Risk Transference strategy looks very good because there is essentially zero cost in exchange for a large benefit. These occurrences are somewhat rare, but these opportunities should be aggressively seized whenever identified due to their overwhelming and demonstrable benefit to the business. In other cases, the cost of Risk Avoidance is high but the benefit is much larger due to the fact that the behavior is inherently risky. These cases often offer opportunities for Risk Avoidance coupled with an alternate activity that may provide some or all of the benefits of the behavior with a more acceptable risk level.

When no other strategy is determined to have a favorable cost-benefit analysis, the only strategy that makes sense is Risk Acceptance. Risk Acceptance has zero cost and zero benefit as it is maintaining the status quo with respect to risk to a specific asset. It is important to consider inertia in business organizations and the reasons why it exists. Far too many organizations use Risk Acceptance as their first option rather than their last option. This approach results in accepting far too many risks that would be better addressed by one of the other strategies. It is difficult to convince a business to make a change without a compelling Return on Investment (ROI).

The effective use of this model helps to facilitate objective large decisions for topics that are not widely understood across the business that are related to security. Too often, organizations try to come to agreement about the larger question of whether or not a countermeasure is appropriate based on qualitative analysis and subjectivity based on perceptions of the overall value of the control. This model allows organizations to apply subjectivity to smaller issues that are easier to form consensus on. The result is that the larger decision is turned into an objective evaluation of what is the best outcome for the business based on a cost-benefit analysis. This outcome essentially turns these decisions into a math problem that can take input from business leaders into account without those individuals needing to be experts in Information Security. It also allows Information Security professionals to take the business impacts of ideas into account without having to be experts in business process design or analysis. A committee can be formed that allows subject matter experts to make qualitative decisions about topics they are subject matter experts in while allowing for a quantitive assessment of the larger problems that the program is attempting to solve.

Conclusion

Risk is omnipresent in business. There simply is no business that is without risk. Truly understanding risks and applying the proper strategies to treat those risks is important to operating a profitable enterprise within tolerable risk levels. Regardless of whether an organization decides to consciously address the risks inherent in their activities, a strategy is being applied. Taking a proactive approach to risk allows the organization to select the proper strategy in a given scenario. Further, mastering risk models with respect to cyber-security helps Information Security professionals to communicate effectively with the business while justifying their staff, budgets, and their own position. Tom Ridge, who was the first secretary of the Department of Homeland Security, which included the cyber-security of the United States, said, "your cyber-security strategy must be part of your business strategy." This statement is being increasingly adopted by global business leaders. In support of this idea, Information Security professionals are expected to possess an increasing amount of business acumen. Tying business risk to cyber-security initiatives is a powerful method to demonstrate understanding of the business while simultaneously presenting business justification for current and future Information Security funding.

CHAPTER 4

■ ■ ■

Security Intelligence Model

Your cyber-security strategy must be built into your business strategy.

—Tom Ridge

The primary challenge facing executives and security leaders in businesses around the globe is integrating security teams and technologies with the business. It is often extremely difficult to integrate business strategies into cyber-security strategies. Over the years, I have worked with several solutions to bridge the gap between the business and the security teams, and successfully doing so has been a primary leading indicator of success for my clients. In order to explain and visualize the effective methodologies and communication structures necessary to accomplish this objective, I have created the model displayed in Figure 4-1, which we will explore in depth in this chapter.

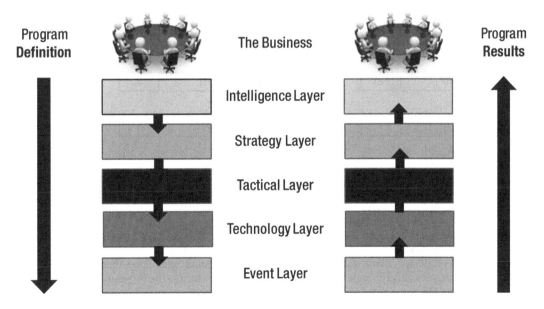

Figure 4-1. *Security Intelligence Layers*

© Jeremy Wittkop 2016

J. Wittkop, *Building a Comprehensive IT Security Program*, DOI 10.1007/978-1-4842-2053-5_4

How the Security Intelligence Model Works

This model was built in a similar fashion as the well-known Open System Interconnect model, which was developed in order to explain and structure the role of different types of technologies in network communications for the purpose of helping to assist with troubleshooting and to clearly explain exactly what role a device plays in the communications infrastructure. For people not familiar with the Open Systems Interconnect Model, the basic premise is that the user of the model begins in the upper left, works down to the bottom left, transfers to the bottom right, and then works upwards, finishing in the upper-right section of the model. The Open Systems Interconnect Model is illustrated below in Figure 4-2.

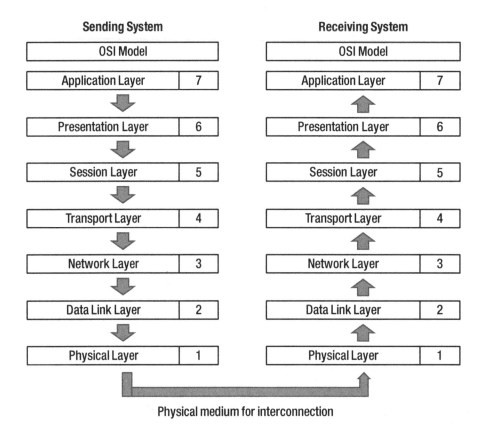

Figure 4-2. Open Systems Interconnect Model

The Security Intelligence Model is exactly the same. Simply put, in order to go from defining the program from a strategic perspective to gathering strategic results from a program, one must define the tactics for the program, select and operate a technology, and gather events. On the Program Results side, events must be gathered by some technology, analyzed in accordance with appropriate tactical processes, and applied to the Strategy that was defined on the Program Definition side. Unlike the Open Systems Interconnect Model, however, the Security Intelligence Model is designed to be operated in its entirety every time it is utilized in order to be optimally effective. While certain technologies only require operation up to a certain layer of the Open Systems Interconnect Model in order to be effective, gathering Security Intelligence should start with the business from a Program Definition side and should provide results up to, and including, the executive level representatives of the business from a Program Results perspective.

These layers have been identified through years of experience implementing effective programs and analysis of the failure of ineffective programs. Due to the sensitive nature of information that is gathered during the definition and operation of Information Security programs, detailed accounts of specific programmatic elements that did and didn't work would often be a violation of confidentiality agreements. However, some common themes have become apparent. Successful programs start with the business that yields Business Intelligence specific to the goals of the program. Intelligence can then be converted into a strategy that can be leveraged to set the parameters about what assets are going to be protected, why, and what the risks are against those assets. The strategy then can dictate the tactics necessary to support those strategic and business objectives. Once tactics have been developed and the strategy has been taken into account, the Program Definition will yield functional and business requirements for the selection of an appropriate technology or technologies that should be selected, deployed, integrated, or optimized in support of the program.

■ **Note**   Due to the proliferation of technologies in organizations, technologies that posses the necessary capabilities may already exist within the organization. In those cases, expanding the scope of those technologies or optimizing them to perform tasks more efficiently is also an effective use of the model.

The technology can then be appropriately deployed to monitor the events that flow throughout an organization's "electronic nervous system," which is a phrase coined by InteliSecure founder and CEO Robert Eggebrecht.

On the Program Results side, the process starts with the event layer or the "electronic nervous system." The technology then will collect the events, tactical processes will analyze and perform triage on the events, and the important events will then be filtered through the strategic perspective in order to yield Business Intelligence. Finally, the business intelligence is packaged for distribution to the business itself. The volume of information as the Program Results side of the model is traversed vertically should decrease in volume, the higher level that is achieved.

The model is very simple in its concept, but the effective operation of the model requires a disciplined and rigorous process and continuous process improvement. The benefit of effective operation of the model is business-centric results that are achieved more efficiently and effectively than any other methodology that I have encountered. Each layer of the model also consists of several key requirements and core concepts that must be understood in order to operate the model effectively.

The Business

Prior to discussing what "The Business" means and how this layer operates for the majority of organizations that have a profit motive, it is worthwhile to note that this model will also work for not-for-profit or government entities, but is often much more difficult and time consuming to determine what is most important to the organization if there is no profit motive to provide objective comparison and analysis. In these cases, the organization's mission is often a good place to start.

■ **Note**   The proper priority of Critical Information Assets in not-for-profit organizations often is the subject of extensive debate and disagreement. In my opinion, it is a best practice to establish a project charter in these types of organizations and define not only the key decision makers that have a vote, but also the conditions for ratification of a prioritized critical asset list. Alternatively, organizations can approach prioritization assets from a risk of loss perspective, prioritizing assets that could cause the most harm above all others.

In not-for-profit organizations, the level of effort required to complete the information required for the Program Definition "Business" layer is going to be directly related to the decisions made in the project charter. While project charters are important in all organizations, they can fulfill an expanded role in not-for-profit in helping define the way in which decisions are made and problems are resolved. For example, if a simple majority of stakeholders is required, it will require far less debate than if it is decided that a unanimous ratification is required. Other organizations may require two-thirds or three-quarters majority. I have seen organizations get creative and decide that it takes a simple majority to ratify the items on the list, but a two-thirds majority to ratify their ranking once the items are ratified. There is a myriad of options to solve this problem, but it is important to understand that this extra step may need to be taken for organizations that are not profit driven.

Many people ask me a simple question when I first present the model: what is "The Business"? Simply put, "The Business" refers to the people who are directly responsible for the profit and loss of a department or group in a for-profit enterprise, and any person who is responsible for a budget in any other organization. This designation generally starts at the director or vice president level and continues upward through the executive team and to the members of the board.

The next question is generally the following: do you really expect C-Level executives and board members to participate in the definition of an Information Security Program? Many times it is the delegates, and not the business stakeholders themselves, that participate at the Strategy level, and their delegates that participate at the Tactical level, but it is imperative that the mandate and the business requirements come from the board and/or executive teams. The good news is that the mandate inside many organizations already exists. For example, every Form 10-K report filed annually by every publicly traded company contains a section 1A, which is Risk Factors. I rarely come across a Form 10-K report that does not contain Risk Factors related to cyber-security. The information contained in this report is approved by the board, so any reference to cyber-security in this report may be a sufficient mandate and may also provide detail with what types of protections could alleviate the concerns of the board. This report and reports like it are often a very good place to start when looking at the desires of the business.

Another great place to gather Business Intelligence is at the individual Line of Business owners. Many times, the specific information related to anticipated revenue or the value of specific assets is better known by the resources that are directly responsible for each specific asset and not as high level as the senior executive and board levels. So long as there is an objective way to compare the relative criticality of Lines of Business against each other, the individual Line of Business owners is usually a fantastic source of information. Almost every organization operates within budgets, so it's often relatively easy to determine the relative importance of business units and Lines of Business by reviewing financial statements.

There are many instances that come to mind featuring situations in which the assets the Information Security teams considered critical were vastly different than the lists created by the business unit leaders. The reason for this is that while good Information Security professionals have a high-level knowledge of the workings of the business, they usually lack the nuances and details of the individual components of information that significantly impact the bottom line. A good visual analogy is that of a puzzle. The Information Security teams often understand what the puzzle looks like when it is completed, or get the "big picture," but the individual Lines of Business often have intimate knowledge of each puzzle piece, how they fit together, why they fit together, and how to most efficiently identify the proper location for each piece to get them out of the box and into their proper place with as little effort as possible.

While the big picture is likely enough for running antivirus systems or signature-base Intrusion Detection or Prevention Systems, protecting Critical Information Assets utilizing a content and context-aware approach requires the intimate knowledge that is rarely possessed by the Information Security teams. There have been many instances I have personally witnessed in which Information Security leadership tried to demand that we build a program by only speaking with them and getting only their perspective. I personally believe that this simply cannot be done well, and have actually refused to complete contracts under these conditions. In my opinion, it was simply not worth the risk to my reputation to build a failed program due to inappropriate constraints being placed on me by the customer. I encourage all Information Security professionals to take their reputation just as seriously. This is critical work for many organizations and should be treated with the appropriate level of concern. In fact, the most successful projects *always* incorporate multiple business units in order to gain project backing and support. The very nature of Information Security and monitoring can invoke the feeling of a "big brother" and can meet stiff resistance from employees if not approached, planned, and communicated appropriately. It is much easier to obtain the buy-in from business units prior to a major security project versus post-implementation notification that the company is "now monitoring your email" or something similar. The most successful programs I have seen build consensus from the beginning and look for opportunities to involve end users in the process rather than dictating the security program to them. We must keep in mind that if we are to be successful, we must make the end users our allies and not make them feel like they are our enemies.

The power of getting business units involved in security programs can be clearly illustrated using the following story as an example. Due to confidentiality agreements, the name of the company and specific identifying features that may be used to distinguish the company will be omitted.

We were working with a manufacturing company that had, as a portion of their business, a particular product that was subject to International Traffic in Arms Regulations (ITAR). When we met with the Information Security and Compliance teams, who were the teams that commissioned us to build the program originally, we were given a laundry list of predictable things that should be addressed by the program. First on the list was compliance with the various regulations they were subject to. This included ITAR compliance, compliance with the Payment Card Industry (PCI) Data Security Standard, and also some protections for Personally Identifiable Information for employees. The Information Security teams conceded that all design was completed in the United States and the European locations, but all manufacturing was done in China and India; but they considered accepting that risk part of the requirements of doing business in countries with a lower manufacturing cost in order to take advantage of the global economy.

Many people would be satisfied that the outcome of those interviews represented a comprehensive list of business requirements. After all, they clearly had command of the business, the regulatory environment, and had clear rationale for why Risk Acceptance was the best possible strategy. They did not, however, have the authority or responsibility to make those decisions.

The first business unit we spoke to was the business unit directly responsible for the design and manufacture of the products that were covered by the ITAR regulations, and they promptly identified additional regulations that they were responsible for complying with such as the Export Administration Regulations (EAR). While we knew these two regulations often go hand-in-hand, someone who was not familiar with the regulations may have been misled to believe that the only burden for this business unit from a regulation perspective was ITAR, and may have exposed the organization to risk up to and including termination of a military contract due to failure to comply with regulations. The other revelation from that business unit was that while the profit margins on their Line of Business were high, they only accounted for roughly 3.5% of company revenue in any given calendar year. Compliance with these regulations was important, but the risk presented to the business associated with a compliance failure was relatively low. Even an egregious lack of compliance that resulted in the cancellation of all of the organization's government contracts would not represent a catastrophic risk to the business.

After speaking to all of the business units, it was determined that due to the company's size, revenue, and market share in specific segments of the marketplace, and statistics provided about the global counterfeit goods marketplace, the risk to them from counterfeit goods represented a $50–$75 million USD annual loss in revenue. It was commonly accepted that preventing the loss and theft of design data would not eliminate the counterfeit goods market, but reducing access to designs and plans could reduce the prevalence of counterfeit goods and increase the cost and effort necessary to manufacture them. Therefore, it was estimated that an effective program to protect design data would result in a risk reduction by a percentage of annual revenue of more than the entire ITAR-regulated Line of Business. This level of insight and prioritization could not have been provided inside the Information Security team, because they simply did not have access to the information necessary to complete the exercise properly. At this point, the prioritization of what was to be protected had changed significantly. Further, determining how to accomplish this goal also required business unit expertise. The expertise that defines the specific ways information is used in an authorized and necessary fashion is what is referred to as Business Intelligence and is referred to in the next layer.

Intelligence Layer

As previously mentioned, the Intelligence layer refers to how the business or organization actually runs. The Business layer is divergent for profit-driven and not-for-profit organizations, but the remainder of the layers operate in much the same way, regardless of the presence of a profit motive. Defining the necessary portions of the Business layer is primarily concerned with what is important and how important each Information Asset is, relative to each other. The Intelligence layer is primarily concerned with how these assets are leveraged in an authorized manner in order to further the enterprise of the organization. One of the most important concepts to understand with respect to the Intelligence layer is that most of the Critical Information Assets that must be protected from a security perspective are also critical operationally in order for the organization to function properly. This fact underscores the importance of this layer, and it is the reason why it must be addressed prior to creating a strategy.

I like to say that Information Security is similar to the medical profession in that our first responsibility to the business is to do no harm. Therefore, anything we do to protect an asset must not interfere in any material way with its authorized use. This is not to say that insecure business practices must stand, but it is to say that a business process should not be blocked from occurring until an alternative process, approved by the business, is implemented that is more secure without inhibiting productivity, to the extent that both are possible. To the extent they are not, the cost-benefit analysis for accepting the risk must be weighed against the same for mitigating the risk and modifying the practice. This point once again underlines the need for support throughout the business for security measures, as changes that upset employees will not only be undermined and circumvented, but will also lead to much more difficulty when gaining support for future projects.

The Intelligence layer consists primarily of business process mapping. What we are really trying to determine and document is essentially the specific acceptable use of each Critical Information Asset from a Content, Community, and Channel perspective. It is not designed to identify all of the variations of what might be happening to the Critical Asset in the organization, but instead to map out what should happen under a normal circumstance. At this point in the process it is imperative to interview the employees who handle the Critical Assets on a daily basis, drilling down to those who actually handle and see the data. These resources are the only ones who know not only how data is supposed to be handled, but how it is actually stored and transmitted, including the workarounds that are used when business processes fail. At this point, we must remind you of the first chapter anecdote where employees wrote credit card numbers onto Post-It notes.

Remember, this step is a process designed to learn about how Critical Assets are handled and managed. Interviews with employees directly responsible for this data are extremely important and must be approached carefully; otherwise employees will become wary and fearful of the purpose of the interview. One must explain the importance of discovering how these assets are handled, including workarounds (that the employees often know are not approved), so that processes can be improved, simplified, and addressed while obtaining the input and assistance of the everyday employees.

Oftentimes an organization will discover during these interviews that Critical Assets are managed in egregious and incredibly insecure ways that are completely missed by security measures and process controls. Instead of treating these issues as problems, one should be grateful to learn about these measures as it shows that the interviewees trust and buy into the effort for improvement. It is a best practice to never block any behavior until a monitoring period has been completed and improvement steps have been identified, as there is often a disconnect between what business leaders think should happen and what necessary workarounds have been developed at the line level without sharing that information with management. The first time content and context monitoring tools and programs are deployed is often an eye-opening experience for business leaders, and it is rare to discover that processes are followed and executed as expected. Blocking without monitoring, in many cases, would result in significant harm to business practices, a lesson that many early adopters of content-aware programs learned through painful experiences, not to mention the immediate recoil that is received from employees.

Once the authorized practices are documented, the Strategy layer can then define how unauthorized behavior is going to be detected, and how the organization will respond in a given scenario. Before exploring the Strategy layer, let's return to our manufacturing company example to explore how the information gleaned through the Intelligence layer helped to significantly reduce risks to the organization that were widely accepted as risk that could not be mitigated.

You may recall that the concern about the Information Assets in this example was that the organization was losing significant revenue to the counterfeit goods marketplace. You may also recall that the company was designing products in the United States and in Europe, but their manufacturing was being done in China and India. When discussing exactly how the information necessary for manufacturing was transferred to the countries in which the manufacturing was being completed, it was quickly determined that there was no universal and secure process for completing the transfer of the data. Among the methods of transferring the information was File Transfer Protocol (FTP), which is an unencrypted and insecure protocol by nature; e-mail attachments, also insecure and unencrypted; and even transferring data to a USB storage device and sending the package via FedEx or DHL between offices.

Information Security professionals may find these methods of transmitting data appalling, but it is an important reminder that most employees in an organization have little Information Security training and awareness. It is important when building effective programs to understand the frame of reference for the average employee performing a given function.

Upon examining the cost-benefit analysis of mitigating and accepting the risks posed by the processes in place, it was determined that it was beneficial to modify the process. It is important to remember that without involving the business unit leadership in the Program Definition process, this decision couldn't have been made because the Information Security team had assumed that Risk Acceptance was the only Risk Treatment Strategy that could be employed in this situation. Once again, it is important to emphasize the inclusion of key end-user employees that will aid the improvement of processes and champion these goals with their coworkers to gain ongoing support for the project.

The end result of this example was a modification of the business process along with protections in place to ensure the old processes were no longer in use. This included education campaigns, process notifications, as well as technology controls. In subsequent layers, we will explore different examples from different industries, but it is important to compare the end state of data transfer with the old methods in order to highlight the value of the exercises in these layers. The end process was that there was a VPN tunnel created that would protect the information in transit. The specific type of technology utilized several different links sending packets out of sequence to be reassembled at the destination. In order to intercept the data in transit, an attacker would have to perform several man-in-the-middle attacks simultaneously. Compared to the simple nature of intercepting an unencrypted e-mail or FTP transfer, this measure alone exponentially increased the protection profile. Essentially, by using new technologies and a refined process, the process was made more secure by significantly increasing the level of effort needed to successfully attack the information.

The next step was to address the legitimate concerns about the possibility of theft of the sensitive assets when they reached the country of production. As a result, the customer implemented several security controls that greatly improved control over the Critical Assets. First, files were encrypted at the U.S. and European locations with a key that could only be accessed on a secure network segment by an authenticated user. Second, spear phishing or keylogging threats were addressed by implementing multifactor authentication.

■ **Note**   Multifactor authentication refers to types of authentication that use more than one of the factors for authenticating users, something you know, something you have, and something you are. A password is an example of something you know, hardware and software tokens are examples of something you have, and fingerprint readers are an example of something you are. Using multiple factors makes authentication far more secure and reliable.

Finally, separation-of-duty controls were implemented so no single employee had access to the complete set of data required to manufacture a product. Instead, several employees using multiple keys with multifactor authentication were required to complete the process. Compare these multiple layers of protection with the original process and you can see the power of Business Intelligence packaged with business process improvements.

Strategy Layer

The Strategy layer refers to the protections put in place to enforce the authorized use of Critical Information Assets as well as the appropriate responses for unauthorized use of those assets. The Critical Asset Protection Program detailed earlier is an example of a proven approach to the Strategy layer. Translating Intelligence into Strategy requires transitioning roles and responsibility from a project into a program. Doing so is best accomplished by defining two groups with separate roles and responsibilities. The first group is known as the Governance Group. It generally consists of decision makers from key business units and generally meets quarterly to review the results and adjust the strategy of the program. The Governance Group must include the main executive sponsors for any security projects, as well as the individual with the final approval for budgetary decisions. The second group is known as the Working Group. This group generally is composed of delegates of the Governance Group and Information Security teams that meets weekly or more frequently and has daily responsibilities outlined in the Tactical layer. Normally, to be successful, the Working Group is comprised of Security professionals, members of the departments that are protecting Critical Assets, and IT resources for troubleshooting efforts.

The first component of the strategy is to define what capabilities are required in order to detect unauthorized behavior with respect to Critical Assets. For example, if there is no business-use case to use removable storage media, an organization can choose to simply disable the USB and CD/DVD devices of machines in the environment. However, if some data may be transferred via removable media but Critical Information Assets are not allowed to be transferred in this fashion, there is a need to implement a capability to distinguish critical information from non-critical information.

The second component of the strategy is to determine what response or responses should be taken in order to protect each organization's Critical Assets. Many people who are new to protecting information using content and context-aware solutions assume that the best way to protect assets is to block them from leaving. Sometimes blocking is an appropriate response, but it is entirely dependent on a threat modeling exercise and identifying the threat actors that are most likely to try to compromise the asset. If the primary focus of the program is to prevent inadvertent disclosure of an asset by a well-meaning insider, it is likely appropriate to implement a blocking mechanism or an "Are you sure?" pop-up, depending on the capabilities of the system. However, if the primary goal of the program is to prevent theft by malicious insiders or outsiders, a block simply notifies the attacker of what is being monitored. No solution currently available can monitor every possible egress point and method. As such, when facing a persistent threat, it is often best to monitor Critical Assets without blocking or automatic response so that the attacker is not tipped off to the Security oversight. This monitoring is followed by aggressive response Service Level Agreements and/or Objectives that are in place and prepared to trigger strong Incident Response plans.

■ **Note** Regardless of the desired end state with respect to response options, a period of monitoring, communication, and user education prior to implementing technical responses of any kind is a widely accepted and highly recommended best practice.

Perhaps the best example of the effective deployment of a strategy that takes into account multiple factors and responses comes from a not-for-profit health care provider and research facility that I have worked with in this past. This organization is technically a government organization and has three main

Lines of Business; Education, Health Care services, and Research and Development. The results of the Business and Intelligence layers yielded two distinct groups of requirements with their own Critical Information Assets. The educational and clinical sides of the business were primarily concerned with Personally Identifiable Information, Protected Health Information, and PCI information. Another specific concern for the educational side of the organization was that many of the students also serve as interns in their clinical operations, and it is important to them to ensure that students do not use sensitive information they have access to through their internships in the public classroom setting. In an effort to address these concerns, blocking information from traversing from the clinical environment to the educational environment and using interactive messaging to remind students of their ethical and contractual obligations was deemed to be an appropriate response. As such, after the monitoring and communication period, these responses were implemented.

The second distinct group of requirements was related to the research side of the business, which was primarily concerned with protecting extremely valuable Intellectual Property that was the culmination of several hundred million dollars' worth of research. The threats against the research were largely malicious insiders and malicious actors from the spies and nation states category that we discussed in chapter 1. For these types of assets, no blocking was implemented because the strategy was to ensure there was no easy way to determine what was and was not being monitored as part of the program. The organization was able to build a program that kept research information safe from sophisticated actors, quickly responding to monitored incidents and abnormalities, while building a more automated program to prevent well-meaning students from compromising sensitive patient information by bringing the protected information into the classroom. These incidents were to be monitored and responded to in a completely different fashion. The moral of the story is that organizations do not have to treat their programs holistically, choosing one strategy or response to fit all possible use cases. Treating each threat independently allows an organization to build a comprehensive monitoring and response capability that can protect a wide range of Critical Information Assets effectively. These types of solutions require engagement from a cross-section of the entire organization.

Security strategy is unlikely to be one size fits all; it must be customized to be flexible and meet the changing needs of the business. Creativity is an asset when creating these programs, which is too often undervalued, which results in a lot of rigid and similar programs that are focused on compliance rather than flexible security. It is important to remember that the vast majority of attackers target multiple organizations looking for the easiest target, so having a program that is exactly the same as another program increases the likelihood that an attacker will know how to circumvent the program. Worse still, if the program only takes into account the minimum protections required from a compliance standpoint, attackers will have a verifiable playbook for how to defeat the countermeasures.

Picture, if you will, a sports team that tells the other team exactly what they are going to do before they do it. Would that team be successful? Likely not, but that scenario is very similar to the way many organizations build security programs based on regulations. It is important to be cognizant of compliance requirements to establish the minimum protections that are required to be in place, but those requirements should never serve as the outline or framework for the entirety of an organization's security program. It must be assumed that anyone attacking a health care company is aware of the regulations affecting the company based on its location and has tactics that will quickly defeat the minimum measures in place. It is very important to remember that compliance is not security.

Tactical Layer

The Tactical layer is where "the rubber meets the road," to borrow an old Army expression, and its importance cannot be overstated. It is important to distinguish though, that appropriate tactics can only be developed after involving the business, extracting intelligence from those conversations, and developing a strategy. The majority of programs that fail do so for two reasons, and both are addressed by applying the model properly. First, far too many organizations never develop a coherent strategy that coincides with business requirements and can be directly correlated to the bottom line. These organizations deploy point solutions, or security products designed to address one very specific security problem, tactically to solve perceived problems similar to playing the children's game Whac-A-Mole. Second, many organizations operate in silos and no one person has knowledge of the overall plan, leading to lack of visibility or discernible coherent strategy. It is because too many organizations never think above the Tactical layer that "tactical solutions" have a negative connotation in the security industry.

When applied properly, Tactical processes are crucial to the overall success of a security program. They are also extremely time consuming to create in many cases, because this is the first stage of the model where the processes are individual responsibility specific. For people familiar with the common ISO model of creating a hierarchy of Policy, Procedure, and Work Instruction, Policy would be set at the Intelligence layer, Procedure at the Strategy layer, and Work Instructions at the Tactical layer. Each capability identified as necessary in the Strategy layer will need a set of processes at the Tactical layer to ensure that every individual responsible for any portion of the security program is aware of exactly what they need to do to accomplish their strategic, and ultimately, business objectives. Creating these processes can be tedious, but it can have a tremendous positive impact in employee retention, since success criteria are clearly defined, as well as efficiency and effectiveness, since everyone knows what to do and when. A good set of tactical processes will also reduce ramp-up time for new employees and increase morale throughout the organization.

The Tactical layer is also the layer where the gap is bridged between people and process, which have been the focus of the preceding layers, and is bridged with technology, which is the focus of the subsequent layer. It stands to reason, then, that each technology that will be evaluated and eventually deployed in support of the program will need to have tactical processes assigned to it. The pioneers of the Critical Asset Protection Program, BEW Global (now InteliSecure, Inc.), identified five tactical areas that should be addressed for each technology that is deployed: Application Management, Scope and Policy Governance, Event Triage, Incident Management, and Reporting and Analytics.

Application Management refers to the processes required to keep the technology system up and running. This generally consists of some type of health checks, upgrades, change management processes, and architecture design and diagrams. These processes are generally operated by Information Security engineers and/or Network Architects.

Scope and Policy Governance refers to the translation of business requirements into rules or policies inside a technical system. This work is extremely important as the types of systems that support the protection of Critical Information Assets are generally "smart" systems. These processes consist of tuning the "brains" of those systems. These processes are generally a team effort between engineers, analysts, and business personnel who must verify the system is accomplishing the goals of the business through ongoing testing, refinement, and improvement.

Event Triage is the act of determining what events coming in are False Positives, and determining the appropriate response for events that are not. This process goes hand-in-hand with Incident Management, but is different because many events that do not fit the definition of an Incident still require some type of response. These processes are often solely run by analysts and not engineers, due to the different skillset required.

Incident Response defines roles, responsibilities, and processes that must be undertaken when an event is identified that has a significant business impact. Appropriate response is defined in an Incident Response Plan, and is generally executed by both analysts and representatives from any affected business units.

Reporting and Analytics defines the Key Performance Indicators that will help the Governance Group at the strategic layer determine the effectiveness of the program against the strategic goals outlined. This step is often overlooked, which is one of the major reasons why it is common to find disconnects between the Information Security Program and the business in many security programs. This function is generally performed by a Business Analyst or someone else who has both knowledge of the program as well as knowledge of the business as a whole. Additionally, reporting should evolve over time to not only highlight progress against initial goals but to also track issues uncovered during the project and Incident Response results.

Goals and metrics for programs can be approached in a similar way to goals for individuals. One way to design goals is using the SMART methodology, which says goals must be specific, measurable, achievable, relevant, and time bound. These same characteristics can be applied to setting appropriate goals for a security program.

Each of the above sections should not only define what needs to be done, but who is responsible for performing each task, and what frequency the task is to be performed. The processes also should be customized to the business and specifically support the strategy. Many organizations fail because they subscribe to a templated approach to how to run a program. Many times, the big four consulting firms essentially build the same program for all of their clients. The result is similar to the results of deploying a compliance program masquerading as a security program. If the processes are all the same, attackers only need one set of successful tactics techniques and protocols to exploit several organizations. It is common, especially among organized crime threat actors that a single successful attack will be repeated across as wide of an audience as possible in an effort to compromise the same vulnerability in multiple organizations. This methodology acts as a multiplier for the benefit side of the equation for attackers while only moderately increasing the cost of deploying the attack. If they are successful across multiple organizations, the criminals will often "package" their attack and resell it to other, less sophisticated criminal organizations as another revenue stream. Think of it as a kind of franchised model for cyber-crime.

Tactics can often be quite diverse even inside a single organization. I think the best example for how meticulous definition of the Tactical layer can yield exemplary results is the case of a multinational organization I have worked with that is based in London, with operations all over Europe, the Middle East, and Asia. It is important to note that the United States was not on the list of operating countries. Many security companies, consultants, and advisors are very United States-centric, but there are many global organizations that have very different concerns. When dealing with multiple locations, phases should be taken into account. The nuances involved in deploying programs across multiple locations can easily overwhelm the people and the process in place. It is important to ensure the phases are built in such a way that the resources are able to focus on implementing the program effectively while not trying to "boil the ocean" by taking on too much too fast to be effective and successful. Controlling scope throughout the project is very important when building a program.

The example organization at the beginning of the chapter had two particular operational concerns that trumped their security concerns. First, they must be compliant with all the data protection acts and works council regulations that were in place in each of the countries they do business in. Second, they stipulated that there was no possibility that any of their information ever be housed in a United States data center. Many people in the United States have concerns about housing information in China due to concerns about government monitoring programs, but fail to realize many organizations in other countries have similar concerns about housing data in the United States due to various national security acts and the public knowledge of the U.A. National Security Agency's record collection program.

This particular company was an early adopter of content-aware technology. The majority of their peers in country had decided that these types of programs could not be implemented effectively in Europe due to the privacy regulations protecting workers from being monitored in this fashion. Due to the way this particular company chose to apply the model, however, they were able to meticulously document each tactical process and technology they intended to deploy and work with their legal counsel to ensure all of their tactical processes complied with local regulations. They then submitted their very detailed plans to the appropriate works council, and after a few amendments, were granted approval for their program. Data collected in different locations was different, and staffing models had to take protections into account, but since the strategy was designed first, and all of the tactical processes were designed to support the strategy, the end result was an effective monitoring program across most countries in Europe that had been previously thought to be impossible.

Technology Layer

The Technology layer is where far too many programs begin. There are many psychological reasons for this, but regardless of the motivation, it is not the most effective way to build a program. That said, technology plays a critical role in any Information Security Program, especially when selected in accordance with comprehensive business and functional requirements. In the case of organizations using the model effectively, the Strategy layer provides business requirements and the Tactical layer provides functional requirements.

The technologies themselves are relatively fluid. What is not fluid are the key requirements the technologies fulfill. For example, since the advent of Data Loss Prevention technologies, it is difficult to imagine a time where content-aware security technologies will not play a crucial role in Information Security programs. The three technologies that form the core of content and context-aware programs are content-aware technologies, context-aware technologies, and comprehensive monitoring tools. The products we know today in each of these categories may give way to newer technologies, but these core capabilities will remain for the foreseeable future.

Content-aware technologies such as Data Loss Prevention technologies are very important parts of Information Security programs. If one agrees that there is some information that is more important than other information, there must be a way to separate the important information from the background noise, or information that is traversing the network that is trivial in nature. Data Loss Prevention technologies have been given a bad reputation in many circles as being expensive products that are destined to become shelfware. Much of the negative reputation is due, in part, to a fundamental misunderstanding of the product itself. It is truly a business product facilitated by technology instead of a technical product similar to firewalls or Intrusion Prevention and Detection Systems. When deployed as part of a comprehensive program involving business leaders, Data Loss Prevention technologies have been extraordinarily effective in certain environments.

Context-aware technologies include Security Incident and Event Monitoring (SIEM) systems as well as next-generation anti-malware products. Essentially, context-aware solutions seek to establish a baseline of normal system or user behavior in an effort to detect anomalous behavior as an indicator of compromise. These technologies are far more effective than signature-based technologies as they have the capability of being effective against zero-day threats, and are not as dependent on vendor signature updates as the signature-based technologies are. Context-aware technologies from a systematic perspective are already prevalent and technologies that have the capability of performing behavioral analysis for individuals are on the horizon. Behavior analytics has potential applications not only for cyber-security, but also for national security applications for countries around the world.

Comprehensive monitoring tools, or analytics tools, are becoming more prevalent in Information Security programs, largely because there is so much data generated by these systems, it is increasingly difficult to gather meaningful intelligence from manual review. There are many examples of these tools that are provided by product vendors like Symantec's IT Analytics or Intel Security's ePolicy Orchestrator. Additionally, independent monitoring tools like Splunk have gained popularity for their ability to perform elastic searches on large quantities of information. It is becoming increasingly common for technology vendors to include comprehensive monitoring capabilities as part of their products. Historically, it has often been the case that the context-aware tools and comprehensive monitoring and analytics tools were on a single platform, but complex security analytic capabilities are becoming an industry unto themselves.

Event Layer

The Event layer exists whether there is a program or not. This layer consists of everything happening from a digital perspective in a customer environment. Every piece of information or electronic signal between any two or more points on infrastructure that an organization controls could be monitored in some form or fashion. It is important to understand that these events are far too numerous for it to be practical to comprehensively monitor them all in any meaningful way within a realistic budget. However, appropriate programs can distinguish important from inconsequential events through the lens of the layers we have previously addressed with the requirements emanating from the business.

Program Results

Perhaps the most important part of a program is the results that come from the program. More specifically, it is common that successful programs are perceived to be failing programs due to a lack of effective and targeted results reporting being delivered to the proper people at the proper time. Analytics, Key Performance Indicators, and Metrics are of paramount importance in building and maintaining an effective program since it is highly unlikely that a business will fund an initiative in perpetuity without reliable metrics demonstrating efficacy and return on investment. It is often lamented by security professionals that business leaders do not "get it" with respect to why Information Security is important. If that is, in fact the case, it represents a failure of the security program itself to align the program to business outcomes, and to deliver Program Results and evidence of the accomplishment of those objectives. Business leaders are not responsible to become experts in security; it is the responsibility of security experts to communicate effectively with the business. Inside IT departments in general, and security departments in specific, there is often an echo chamber that convinces its members that the things they hold to be true are simple concepts and anyone who does not inherently understand those concepts is an idiot.

How many people inside an Information Security department could create a comprehensive budget or submit a Profit and Loss Statement to executive leadership? This is a relatively simple task for the finance department? How many in the IT department knows how to diagnose the degree of a torn ligament? This may be a relatively elementary task for a physician. It is important for Information Security professionals to not treat their business customers with disdain or approach them from a position of arrogance. Too often, there is an adversarial relationship between these support organizations and the business due to the fact that the business perceives their support organizations do not listen to their needs and treats them in a disrespectful manner and the IT and Security departments are of the opinion the business does not understand or care to understand their expertise. I have even heard long-time IT professionals share an old IT axiom with me that says "There is no IT problem that cannot be solved by killing the end user." This dynamic is present in the majority of organizations in my experience and is extremely harmful to not only the overall efficacy of technology and security inside the business, but also the morale of the IT and Security teams.

I often tell my Security friends that if they are doing security for security's sake, they are simply overhead from a business perspective. It is imperative that they gather business requirements and demonstrably meet those requirements in order to be relevant to the business as a whole. Similarly, I often tell my business friends that if they choose the "ostrich approach" and think they can stick their head in the proverbial sand with respect to security, their tenure will be short-lived, especially as they continue to advance their careers. The truth of the matter is, as Tom Ridge said at the 2015 RSA Conference "Your cyber-security strategy must be built into your business strategy." This means the Information Security professionals of the future will be required to be business savvy, and the business leaders of the future must take an interest in building programs to address cyber-security threats. Organizations will gravitate towards these types of leaders in order to promote the synergy between business and cyber-security that will soon become a prerequisite to doing business in a global economy and a connected world. It is also important that proper expectations are set with respect to the results the program is likely to yield. The vast majority of security issues that are highlighted by an effective program are not newsworthy events. Healthy programs identify far more broken business processes than earth-shattering breaches of large amounts of information.

To this point, the layers have been viewed from a Program Definition perspective, but the layers are also designed to filter information to the proper audiences on the Program Results side as well. The idea is that the higher up the layers we go, the more focused the information becomes. Each layer is also monitored by the layer above it on the Program Results side of the model as well. As such, the Technology layer monitors the Event layer, the Tactical layer monitors the Technology layer, etc.

As discussed previously, the event layer is where all things happen on a network. The event layer generally produces information about what is happening. Results on this layer are generally expressed in the raw number of events a system is processing over time. These types of results are generally relevant only to the Technology layer and the people directly involved in the technical uptime and availability of the system, as none of the results have yet been validated and therefore, do not necessarily have business value. That is not to say there are not important events in this layer, there most certainly are; they just have not yet been validated and therefore the results are meaningless to the layers above the Technology layer. The technology though, can use this information in order to determine if things are functioning as they should.

The Technology layer is monitoring the Event layer, and therefore captures the events that are relative to what the technology is tuned to capture and store. The results at this layer are relevant to the Tactical layer as they must review these events in order to produce their results. Far too many organizations and Managed Services providers provide executive leadership with "canned reports" from technology systems. This approach is at best ill-informed, and at worst outright lazy. The consumers of these reports will either be misled by the information, or quickly understand that the reports are not relative to their business objectives. Either scenario presents major problems for an Information Security Program.

The Tactical layer is where Key Performance Indicators begin to be generated. The Tactical layer is where day-to-day system administrators execute the tactical processes laid out on the Program Definition side at the same level in order to validate the results presented by the Technology layer. The KPIs generated at this layer will generally consist of relatively large amounts of information that will be relevant and put in context only for personnel who are intimately familiar with the program. It is important to remember that these are tactical results that have not yet been put into strategic context, which is necessary to escalate the information to the next tier. From a reporting perspective, the intended audience for tactical reports are generally the working group level and below.

Tactical Business results that are then compared to strategic objectives in order to present only strategically important information form the results of the Strategy layer. For example, if I told you there were 6,000 pieces of sensitive information that were e-mailed out of the organization in the past 30 days, would you know what that really means to the business? If you were intimately familiar with the program you might, but if you were not, it is unlikely you would. However, if I told you that according to our Critical Asset Protection Program that our primary concern was compliance with the United States Health Insurance Portability and Accountability Act (HIPAA), and we had 30 e-mails sent out containing Protected Health Information (PHI) in an unencrypted format, directly in violation of regulations we have a duty to comply with, would that information have business value to you? Certainly it would. That is strategic result information. At this level, information that did not have business impact would be dismissed, but there would still be information that does not require action or a decision. The target for this level of reporting is generally the Governance Group or business unit leader level.

At the Intelligence layer, the strategic information is further distilled to highlight risks to core business processes and changes to business processes that are necessary in order to appropriately secure the organization. These strategic initiatives use specific information to support the recommendations, but the key is to ensure that Intelligence layer reports are designed to present decisions and choices to business unit leaders and owners. For this reason, these reports are generally targeted to the vice president and senior vice president levels.

Finally, reports that go to the business are intended to only report information that is of material impact, whether positive or negative, to the business. For example, if the program has successfully integrated a system and process that significantly reduces the Annual Loss Expectancy due to regulatory violations and fines, the business would need to know that information. Conversely, if the program has identified a broken or insecure business process that is exposing the organization to a new or previously unknown significant business risk, that information should be reported to the business as well. This information is generally targeted to the executive level and above, and is generally presented in a very brief format.

Structuring Program Results reporting in this fashion will ensure the right information will get to the right person at the right time, and will be sufficient for those people to make swift and appropriate decisions that are within their sphere of influence. Enabling this capability is a critical component of an effective Information Security Program, and should be a stated goal for every organization looking to design or improve a program.

Case Study: Mastering the Model

■ **Note**   It is very rare that people with an intimate knowledge of a breach or attempted breach are permitted to speak publicly about what specifically happened. During my time as the director of Managed Services for InteliSecure, however, there is one major example in which the customer considered what happened such a success story that they have not only permitted us to speak about it, but have also spoken with us in joint speaking engagements examining the case from both sides. Express permission has been granted to InteliSecure to discuss what happened in this case with the general public. Please refrain from discussing intimate details of any breach or attempted breach you may be involved in without express permission to do so from the victim organization.

Becton Dickinson is the subject of this case study, and I will share details about their story through the reference of how they used the model successfully in order to stop a very large-scale attempted theft of Intellectual Property. Ultimately, this case was investigated by the U.S. Federal Bureau of Investigation (FBI) and the charges brought against the perpetrator were not brought by Becton Dickinson, but by the U.S. Department of Justice (DOJ). Should you desire to validate the public details of this case, simply perform a Google search for "Becton Dickinson theft," and you will find results that discuss what happened. I will, however, share details of this particular case, specific to how Becton Dickinson defined and gathered results from their program in order to protect their information.

First, who is Becton Dickinson? Becton Dickinson is a biomedical manufacturer based in Franklin Lakes, New Jersey. Many people around the world may be familiar with the "BD" logo on all types of medical devices at pharmacies and in doctors' offices around the world. Becton Dickinson manufactures a variety of products and conducts trials of their products, and distributes those products around the world. As such, their business is regulated by HIPAA regulations as well as the Payment Card Industry Data Security Standard (PCI-DSS).

When Becton Dickinson first engaged with InteliSecure to provide a program inclusive of a Data Loss Prevention system to increase compliance with both HIPAA and PCI-DSS regulations, the effort was led, as it often is, by compliance and Information Security teams inside the organization. When these teams were asked what the most important assets and concerns were for Becton Dickinson were, the answers primarily revolved around compliance concerns. Familiar refrains like "We need to protect customer credit card data!" or "we need to ensure we are compliant with respect to Protected Health Information!" were common in the initial meetings. However, Becton Dickinson's Chief Information Security Officer (CISO) was also involved in the effort and agreed to allow InteliSecure to leverage their methodology in accordance with the model in order to define the program appropriately. Throughout the model, several key decisions were made that led to the successful mitigation of a major threat to the organization.

The first step was the meetings with the business. At the beginning of these meetings, as is often the case, there were different levels of engagement from different business units. The compliance and legal business units were very vocal in their support for monitoring regulated data and ensuring compliance with those regulations. It is not the intent of the Business layer to eliminate or prioritize assets, which is accomplished at the Strategy layer. We were skeptical those assets were the only important assets; nevertheless those concerns were noted as an output of the layer as other business units were encouraged to share their concerns. The vice president of Research and Development eventually stood up and shared a concern around a new epi-pen injector that was under development. Her specific concern was that the injector was almost complete from a Research and Development perspective, was largely developed by contractors who were nearing the end of their contracts, and represented significant portions of global projected revenue for Becton Dickinson over the next five years. There were other assets of concern, but for the purpose of this case study, we will focus on this specific concern, as it is the one that eventually yielded the results publicized in the media.

The Intelligence layer is designed to yield authorized processes with the intent of creating the capability to detect and react to unauthorized processes. With respect to the assets that were necessary to manufacture the epi-pen injector in question, the rules were relatively straightforward. There was a project team internal to Becton Dickinson that was authorized to access, modify, and save information related to the project on Becton Dickinson-owned IT assets. There was no authorized process in which these assets could be saved to removable media, posted via the Web, transferred via FTP, or e-mailed outside of the company. There was no business need to print the data or to transfer it to an IT asset not owned and controlled by Becton Dickinson.

The Strategy layer played a key role in the success of this particular program in this particular case. The key portion of the Strategy layer is defining exactly how to react to unauthorized use of a Critical Information Asset. Since this use case and threat modeling exercise was most concerned with intentional theft instead of well-meaning insiders and accidental exposure, the decision was made to not utilize the technology to prevent any transfers of information. Many people may find this decision counterintuitive, but it is common for sophisticated attackers to test defenses by sending out small pieces of information to see if the transactions will be blocked in order to find a gap in the technology. By focusing on closely monitoring user behavior instead of blocking, you deny potential malicious actors key reconnaissance and intelligence they may gain by probing the defenses you have put in place.

It was an important component of the Tactical layer to build mechanisms to respond to threats quickly and appropriately and involve the right points of escalation due to the strategic decision that was made not to block activity related to the asset using technology controls. As a result, the monitoring program had to be extremely vigilant in order to appropriately protect the critical information. It was determined that users displaying risky behavior were going to be reported to Human Resources and monitored closely in an effort to build a quick reaction capability in the event that a breach took place.

The Technology layer for this use case primarily leveraged Symantec's Data Loss Prevention solution, which is a leading enterprise-class Data Loss Prevention solution featuring comprehensive protection for data being stored by the organization, data as it traverses the network, and data as it is being used on a laptop or desktop by an end user. Data Loss Prevention solutions are a type of content-aware solution.

Program Definition yielded a few keys to success for Becton Dickinson. First, due to the decisions made at the Tactical layer, it was deemed to be very important that there was a capability to review and react to incidents and events very quickly, and at a level that internal staff at Becton Dickinson could not meet. The solution to this problem was for Becton Dickinson to engage InteliSecure Managed Services to manage their program and Data Loss Prevention system. Second, it was determined that the deployment of the program and the technology specifically to the engineering use case was time sensitive, due to the impending end of the contract and the development project. Finally, due to the risk identified related to contractors that have access to internal Becton Dickinson communications and the lack of any blocking activities, it was decided to deploy the system in a covert fashion and not announce to users they were being monitored.

▪ **Note**   It is important to remember before deploying any of these advanced security solutions to end-user populations to clear your intended actions with your organization's legal counsel. The reason I specifically mention that is because it is illegal in many countries to deploy Data Loss Prevention technology comprehensively and covertly. Becton Dickinson is headquartered in the United States, which has no prohibitions against doing so.

Rather than reviewing the Program Results on a per-layer basis, we will explore exactly what happened from the InteliSecure Managed Services team perspective as well as the perspective of the U.S. FBI as published in the media in reference to the story.

(Source: http://www.northjersey.com/news/business/becton-engineer-sentenced-in-theft-1.1111183)

In May of 2013, an engineer on contract with Becton Dickinson, by the name of Ketankumar Maniar, began to show up on the list of users who were exhibiting risky behavior. The beginning of the suspicious behavior involved Maniar transferring small amounts of sensitive information related to Becton Dickinson's self-administered injector known as Vystra. An InteliSecure Information Security Analyst by the name of Molly Stolpman was able to identify the anomalous behavior as he transferred data to a removable storage device and then sent some information to his personal e-mail address. The activity was reported to Molly's Becton Dickinson contacts immediately, and she continued to monitor the user for additional behavior in accordance with the program that was built to protect the Information Assets.

The behavior stopped for a few days, but Maniar remained on the user watch list. Suddenly, Maniar called in sick and started to transfer massive amounts of information to removable storage devices and began forwarding large amounts of information to his personal e-mail account. Becton Dickinson was immediately notified and they, in turn, notified the FBI, who obtained and executed a search warrant and seized Maniar's storage and computing devices.

It is critical to remember that the people involved with the program are an extremely important element. Molly was one of the most intelligent and vigilant people I have ever had the privilege of meeting, and it was her skill, expertise, and knowledge of both the processes put in place through the model and the technology she was charged with using that facilitated this success.

The devices contained roughly 8,000 files with alleged plans to relocate to India and sell the stolen trade secret information. According to authorities, "The materials Maniar allegedly downloaded essentially comprise a tool kit for mass producing the pen injector."[1]

Becton Dickinson did file a civil case that they eventually dropped, but they did not have to file criminal charges against Maniar. The U.S. Attorney's Office instead charged Maniar themselves with the attempted theft of trade secrets. The ultimate result of the case was 18 months in federal prison and restitution of a little over $32,000. It was also discovered in the federal court case that Maniar had stolen trade secrets from his former employer as well.

The Becton Dickinson case is an example of an overwhelming success utilizing the model effectively. The case is a great example not only because the perpetrator was caught, but more importantly because the perpetrator was caught before the information was used to harm Becton Dickinson. Perhaps the best piece of evidence that it was, in fact, the model and its proper operation by dedicated and trained professionals at every layer and not coincidence that Maniar was caught is the fact that he had used the same behavior to steal information at a previous company and was not detected. The primary difference between the two breaches, one successful and the other unsuccessful at the two companies, was the model and its operation.

For everyone of these types of success stories, there are thousands of stories of breaches that costs companies and governments large sums of money, or sadder, still, cases where breaches led to the ultimate demise of a previously profitable organization.

There is no one strategy or methodology that can provide guarantees that an organization will not be breached, or will be able to comprehensively protect themselves from harm should a breach or attempted breach occur. However, involvement of the business in the Information Security Program has been proven both empirically and anecdotally to reduce the cost of breaches that do occur, and successfully prevent breaches from occurring.

Conclusion

Creating a Comprehensive Information Security Program is difficult. There are many moving parts and pieces that are necessary for the program to be relevant and effective. Threats and the Information Technology landscape are also rapidly evolving further complicating the effort. Therefore, it is imperative for organizations to follow a model and methodology rooted in best practices in order to build a program

---

[1]http://www.northjersey.com/news/former-engineer-at-bergen-county-based-becton-dickinson-charged-with-stealing-trade-secrets-1.626124

that can be effective in the moment and also stand the test of time. The model presented in this chapter has been applied effectively hundreds of times and forms the basis of many effective security programs that have stood the test of time. The strength of the model is in its flexibility. Rigid programs do not work as they fail to adapt to changes in the threat landscape and the business. There is no prescription for success. Effective security is a journey, not a destination, and it certainly cannot be purchased in the form of technology.

CHAPTER 5

■ ■ ■

Incident Response Planning

People can either deal with cyber threats through leadership, or they will be forced to deal with them through crisis.

—Leon Panetta

We should start our discussion of Incident Response Planning by defining exactly what an Incident is in Information Security parlance. However, in order to truly understand an Incident, you must first understand an event. An event is something that happens inside an organization that is possibly of concern. An Incident is a confirmed event that has a significant impact on an organization from a financial or an operational perspective.

Incident Response Planning is an exercise designed to ensure organizations are prepared for the inevitable event of an Incident. There are variations of quotes on the subject that have been attributable to a variety of sources, but essentially the consensus wisdom is that there are two types of organizations: organizations that have been attacked by an external threat, and organizations that do not know they have been attacked by such a threat yet. Many experts warn that the companies that do not know they have been attacked yet fail to make the proper changes to their security program through the Incident Response Process to help prevent similar attacks. This failure to address inadequate processes or system vulnerabilities makes such organizations far more likely to be attacked again, potentially by a much less sophisticated attacker using a commoditized form of the attack that was successful the first time. Incident Response Planning, then, can be seen as preparing for the inevitable, as well as building a mechanism to learn from past mistakes in order to provide for a stronger security posture in the future.

Chicago Mayor Rahm Emmanuel has said, "You never let a serious crisis go to waste. And what I mean by that it's an opportunity to do things you think you could not do before." The idea is as applicable to Information Security as it is to politics. There are countless examples of organizations that did not allocate resources to security adequately until they were the victim of a major cyber-attack and afterwards spent money freely on initiatives. The key to capitalizing on this type of event though, is that the event is discovered and properly treated as an Incident in accordance with a proper Incident Response Plan.

Ensuring that money is spent appropriately is very important, as too often the impulse to freely purchase applications and throw bodies at a problem results in overspending that fails to follow a strategic program as discussed in chapter 4. The Incident Response Planning process, specifically as it relates to post-incident activities, provides a framework and a justification with respect to lessons learned and opportunities for improvement specific to the attack itself.

Benjamin Franklin famously said, "By failing to plan you are planning to fail." I often like to tell people that the worst time to teach someone how to fight a fire is in the midst of an inferno. Regardless how we choose to phrase it, it is prudent to ensure everyone knows exactly what to do in case of emergency. This is why schools and workplaces have fire drills and there is a safety briefing every time we board an airplane before it takes off. If something happens, we all must understand the basics of what is expected of us, and where we can find the resources that must be deployed immediately in order to contain the impact of the Incident. It is for the same reason that every organization should have a tested and effective Incident Response Plan.

© Jeremy Wittkop 2016
J. Wittkop, *Building a Comprehensive IT Security Program*, DOI 10.1007/978-1-4842-2053-5_5

I have been involved in several active breach situations and I have sat in boardrooms post breach trying to help organizations put the pieces back together. These have been some of the saddest moments of my life. I have seen chaos inside of organizations with people running through hallways in a literal panic, communicating with each other in written form because they did not trust the security of any of their electronic communications. During my time in the Army, I have experienced actual war zones that are less chaotic. At least in the war zones, people knew what needed to be done, had a plan for several contingencies, and knew exactly what their role was in the effort. This did not happen by accident. The simple truth is that when human beings are under extreme stress, they cease cognitive function and rely on what psychologists call the "reptilian brain," which only focuses on behaviors that are second nature. The commonly understood "fight or flight" response is an example of this phenomenon, which is a relic from a time in human history in which when people were stressed, their lives were literally in danger. You can be sure that in periods of extreme stress, people will not be able to choose the best course of action from possibilities that they are first thinking through in the situation. They will instead fall back on behaviors that are familiar to them.

The difference between success and failure in these chaotic scenarios is a good, well-formed, thoroughly tested, and optimized plan. If the plan happens to be well-tested and the key personnel have been trained with respect to their role in the plan and have practiced its execution, the likelihood that the plan will be effective in its goals increases exponentially. The key to a well-tested plan is not only that the plan itself is tested, but also that the people involved in executing the plan have practiced their responsibilities enough times that it has become second nature.

The military is a good example in this scenario because branches of service have perfected the art of training individuals to function predictably in high-stress situations. If you have ever seen a movie that depicts basic training, you will see that the Drill Sergeants, or Drill Instructors, depending on the service depicted, spend a lot of time yelling at recruits. These people do not yell because they are mentally unstable; instead the objective is to trigger the fight or flight response in their recruits and confront them in a way that will not allow them to think clearly. By doing so, they can train those recruits to take certain actions in those situations. From personal experience, I can tell you that type of training is invaluable in a combat situation as trained individuals know exactly what they need to do in situations of extreme stress without rational thought.

I am not suggesting that Incident Response training and practice drills should include leaders screaming in the face of their employees. These tactics are far less socially accepted in the private sector than they are in the military. However, creating surprise scenarios in which key participants in the Incident Response process are asked to perform their duties without warning repetitively can accomplish similar goals.

Similarly, conducting surprise simulated attacks through penetration testing for the purpose of evaluating not only vulnerabilities, but also whether the response was appropriate, while amending the plan as necessary can be very useful in the process. It is important that these types of plans are exercised. If they are written and put on the shelf, it is unlikely that the response will be effective when it is needed.

Elements of an Incident Response Plan

Too often people get hung up on creating a perfect plan. There are a variety of military sayings regarding planning that I believe have strong applications in Information Security. The two that are prevalent on my mind are "A plan is simply a basis for change" and "No plan survives first enemy contact." The idea behind both sayings is that the plan will change, but having a basis for that change and a guideline to direct people's efforts is of paramount importance to the overall capabilities and probabilities of success. Any plan is better than no plan. Even a basic plan that simply identifies who should be involved in the response and naming their roles and responsibilities greatly reduces the per capita cost of a breach, according to the 2014 Ponemon Cost of a Breach study,[1] and greatly increases the chances of a successful response and recovery.

---

[1]"News & Updates," Ponemon Institute Releases 2014 Cost of Data Breach: Global Analysis. Accessed May 21, 2016. https://www.ponemon.org/blog/ponemon-institute-releases-2014-cost-of-data-breach-global-analysis.

It is also important that there be a mechanism for improving the plan after the plan is executed and an after action review is conducted. There are many methodologies for building Incident Response programs, but most have a few common elements. The Incident Response Planning Model we will explore in this chapter is a basic model that is applicable to any industry. Figure 5-1 shows a simple illustration of the model.

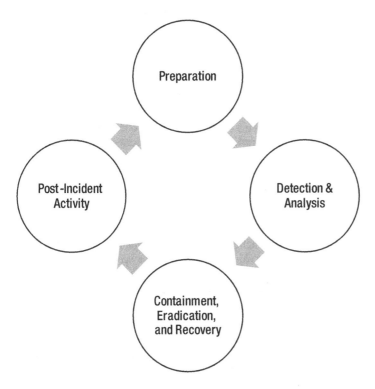

Figure 5-1. *Incident Response Planning Model*

Preparation

In the book *The Art of the Start*, Guy Kawasaki made a simple but profound statement: "The hardest part of doing anything is getting started." This quote is beautiful in both its simplicity as well as its universal truth. Especially in large organizations, it is difficult to escape the tyranny of the "analysis to paralysis" paradigm, which prevails when people, groups, or organizations are so consumed with building a perfect solution, that they never implement a solution or vastly exceed original timelines and budgets. In terms of Information Security, we are talking about an incredibly complex and ever-evolving problem to which a perfect solution will never be found. Since there are human beings on both the attacker's and defender's side, perfection is impossible, and even the best approach is constantly changing. The key to building programs is to understand that improvements to Information Security programs and posture are made and measured incrementally rather than on predetermined and absolute original goals.

Any effective Information Security Program must contain a mechanism for Continuous Process Improvement (CPI) in which processes can be improved at any time as lessons are learned or as circumstances change. Incident Response is a particular example of the power of such an approach as this model is designed to be continuously operated and improved during and after each process iteration. As such, getting started is time critical because every time there is an event or an incident inside an organization where there is no Incident Response Plan in place, not only does the organization suffer the negative consequences of an unprepared, inappropriate, or inefficient response, but a vital opportunity to improve the plan is wasted. In that sense "analysis to paralysis" is particularly damaging and counterproductive. Creating any plan and using it as a basis for change represents an incremental improvement. It can be as simple in the preparation phase as setting a framework for documenting the results of any exercise, the people who should be involved if an incident occurs, and who is responsible for what. This simple exercise that would take minutes or hours to complete in most organizations can impact the efficiency and effectiveness response in an impactful way by reducing confusion and duplication of effort.

Kitty Genovese

There is a popular study of psychology involving the case of Kitty Genovese, in which Catherine Susan "Kitty" Genovese was brutally murdered in plain view of several people in Queens, New York, in 1964. By many reports, at least thirty-seven people heard the attack taking place. All of those people had at least the ability to call the police if not intervene directly, but no one did, all thinking someone else would do the right thing. The end result was that many people witnessed the horrible crime and this poor young woman died in a horrible way unnecessarily.[2] This is a horrible example of the natural tendency of people to refuse to volunteer responsibility during a crisis situation. This phenomenon requires assigning personal accountability and responsibility as part of any plan. It must be clear to an individual that they are responsible for a certain action, and they must acknowledge responsibility for the same. If you were to simply yell "Help" in a crowd, people would be paralyzed by confusion in many cases. However, if you were to say "John, I need you to get the fire extinguisher in case of a fire," if John was standing there and you yelled "John, get the fire extinguisher!," it is far more likely that John would behave in the way you would like him to.

While we aren't generally dealing with life and death threats from a human perspective when we are examining cyber-threats, we are often dealing with threats to individual and organizational livelihood, which are severe threats indeed.

■ **Note**   Our brains are hardwired to identify threats to our livelihood similarly to threats to life and limb. This is why a person may sweat profusely or exhibit signs of an elevated heart rate and muscle tension before an important meeting or interview. These reactions that may help evade a predator or physically confront an adversary may be useless in the business world, but it demonstrates the fact that the human mind can subconsciously make the connection between financial livelihood and actual survival. It is especially interesting in a society that makes that connection between financial livelihood and actual survival with diminishing frequency rationally, can retain that connection subconsciously.

If no one knows their responsibilities in the case of a breach generally one of two scenarios will play out. First, everyone may do the same things since no one knows what their role is supposed to be, which causes chaos, confusion, duplication of efforts, and people working against each other based on opposing viewpoints of what must be done. Alternatively, the situation may result in no one doing anything, assuming someone else is going to take a leadership role. Either situation is destructive to the overall goal of containing and remediating the Incident.

---

[2]Martin Gansberg, "37 Who Saw Murder Didn't Call the Police," *New York Times*, 1964. Accessed May 21, 2016. http://www.nytimes.com/1964/03/27/37-who-saw-murder-didnt-call-the-police.html?_r=0.

Building the Plan

The output of the planning phase is the development of the actual Incident Response Plan. As discussed, this plan does not have to be perfect, but it needs to document the basics of the response at a minimum, which is inclusive of roles and responsibilities as well as what specific actions need to happen in order to respond to a situation. Many Incident Response Plans get complicated as they try to anticipate every possible scenario. There is an alternate approach that I recommend to my customers, which is to be able to fit the entire plan on a single page, while having a separate plan for each threat actor we described in chapter 1. This will result in a seven-page plan as a place to start. Certainly, the plan may grow over time, but when organizations approach me with questions about how long a plan should be, I generally recommend making the plan as short as possible while being comprehensive and effective for a given situation. It is important to remember that the overall quality of the plan is inconsequential. The only thing that matters is the quality of the portions of the plan that each person involved in the response *remembers* in case of emergency.

■ **Tip** My experience in combat tells me that no more than seven steps will be retained for a given situation for each person. If a person is expected to perform more than seven responsibilities as part of the plan, my recommendation would be to involve an additional person and share that responsibility between multiple people.

Detection and Analysis

The next step in the planning process is to address Detection and Analysis. In the 2015 Verizon Data Breach Investigations Report, it was reported that the average amount of time it took an organization to detect a breach was eighteen months after an attacker first compromised a network.[3]

Dedicated attackers can do immeasurable damage to a network given eighteen months of unfettered access, including the ability to implement security measures and to fix vulnerabilities so they are not detected by outsiders or those within the network. The majority of the time, when dealing with detection times that long, it is not the organization itself that is responsible for the detection, but they are alerted to the breach by a law enforcement or government agency that has seen information that belongs to them for sale on the Dark Web, which is the side of the Internet not accessed by the majority of users that acts as a black market for stolen information and illicit activity. Any organization's Detection and Analysis program's goal should be to reduce that Mean time to Detection (MTTD) and Mean Time to Response (MTTR) from months and years to hours and minutes. Ideally, the best programs will either be able to respond so quickly, or will have protections in place, where information does not actually leave the organization and result in financial harm. The Becton Dickinson example that was explored in the Mastering the Model chapter (chapter 4) is a good example of a very rapid response that resulted in neutralization of the threat prior to harm coming to the business as a result of the breach.

Another important part of the Detection and Analysis section of the planning effort is to identify all of the sources that may contain information that is material to a breach, and how that information will be gathered and analyzed in the event that it is necessary. Every time a new detection capability is deployed, a new potential for identifying a breach is added, if not more than one. Therefore, every time a capability is added or changed, the Detection and Analysis portion of the plan should be updated.

---

[3]"Verizon 2015 Data Breach Investigations Report," *About Verizon Enterprise Solutions*, 2015. Accessed May 21, 2016. http://news.verizonenterprise.com/2015/04/2015-data-breach-report-info/.

■ **Tip** When adding capabilities with respect to Detection and Analysis, it is important to consider factors such as the type of information that may be detected, the present maturity of the capability, the long-term desired state for the capability, and the difficulty and the timeline associated with maturing from present state to desired state.

Many organizations perform their threat modeling exercises by attempting to imagine all of the different things that can happen to their assets and modeling the responses to those imagined attacks. This approach is serviceable, but often leads to the tendency to purchase new applications as a first step, or "boil the ocean" by attempting to tackle too many problems at once. It is critical to avoid situations where new applications and processes are not improved and optimized, which leads to frustration and the lack of ROI that was discussed in previous chapters. Instead, there is another approach that could help stimulate more ideas for the organization, by taking a capability-centric approach.

That approach looks at the tools and programs deployed and imagining the different scenarios that they could detect, rather than trying to think of every possible scenario without boundary. This keeps the exercise grounded in the capabilities present, and also identifies gaps in detection that may exist. If someone says, "What about if the attacker does x?" and the response is that "We don't have capabilities to detect that," the next logical question may be "Why not?" While we don't want to allow those types of questions to paralyze our Incident Response Planning process, we do want to park those conversations so we can address them at a later time, and apply a Risk Treatment Strategy to what has been identified. For the purpose of the Incident Response Plan, the most important consideration is the fact that if we do not possess the capability to detect a certain action, the response to such an action is inconsequential because we would never know it happened even if it were to occur. As the program matures, we may be able to answer "Why not?" with something like "We have identified that risk, evaluated the Risk Treatment Strategies, and have determined that we will accept that risk until we can find a mitigation technique that has a favorable cost-benefit analysis to address that threat." That would be a very good answer!

Each Detection and Analysis capability should have a subject matter expert identified as part of the Incident Response team who has the expertise to assist in an Incident Response Plan to utilize what is available through that individual capability. The information that should be immediately gathered and shared with the Incident Response team should also be documented and shared with each of the capability representatives, so the basic and universally necessary information can be provided quickly as soon as an Incident Response begins.

Containment, Eradication, and Recovery

Before undertaking an in-depth discussion of Containment, Eradication, and Recovery, it is very important to remember that there are three parts. I have personal experience with many organizations that do a very good job of containing and eradicating a threat, but a very poor job of recovering. By doing so, they have inadvertently contained and eradicated their future earnings and customers as well – often with disastrous results that can open the door for competitive vultures to strike. In fact, there have been breaches that I have seen where more than half of the harm to the business was self-inflicted as a result of their containment and eradication efforts. When building a plan for Containment, Eradication, and Recovery the goal should be to contain and eradicate the threat and get back to normal operations as quickly as possible. For that reason, I often recommend having Business Continuity Planning experts participate in this portion of Incident Response Planning to help set up a comprehensive plan to return to normal operation. Depending on what is necessary for containment and eradication, this may be as simple as backing out the changes that were necessary for containment, or it may be as complex as activating part or all of a hot site, warm site, or cold site in accordance with the larger Disaster Recovery plan. Additionally, don't underestimate the value of a predetermined strong public response plan to minimize the loss of trust and future revenues. All of these scenarios should be taken into account.

To give an example of how severe this can be, there have been Incident Response situations that have rendered entire data centers unusable by a force outside of their control that they could not predict. However, almost all organizations have plans for such events as part of their Business Continuity and Disaster Planning efforts. Leveraging the work already done in order to reduce impact to the business in the case of an act of nature to improve Incident Response planning is a practice that makes a lot of sense.

Containment

The first step in the process is Containment, which is defined as ensuring the threat cannot continue to propagate itself or traverse to other areas of the business. The definition of containment, then, can mean many different things given the type of the threat and the nature of the threat, but it often involves isolating machines or network segments for the duration of the Eradication activity. If the threat affects a single machine, for example, containment may be as simple as removing that machine from the corporate network. Often, breaches and compromises affect more than a single machine, so it is important to have a plan to quickly identify the scope of the problem, and act quickly to isolate it by isolating the affected network segments from other network segments. Part of this exercise should be the communication plan to let any users who may be affected know that emergency measures are being undertaken to neutralize an active threat and enumerate the services and machines that will not be available for the duration of the exercise. Creating notification templates as part of the plan is a best practice in this area.

There are certainly different scenarios that dictate different specific actions as part of the containment effort. For example, there may be times where the most prudent response is to monitor a threat and not allow it to propagate throughout the environment, but also not to alert the attacker to your knowledge of their attack in order to gain evidence against them or to try to determine their motive. In order to make that determination, one of the first steps of containment should be to engage an internal or external forensics expert. Depending on the desired outcome on the part of the victim organization, there may be specific actions the organization must take, such as preserving a forensic copy of the affected machines and maintaining a proper chain of custody in order for evidence to be admissible in court.

■ **Note** While each situation may be different, including the criteria that will be used to determine whether the response will include gathering forensics and preserving a chain of custody or if it should be focused on Containing, Eradicating, and Recovering from the Incident as quickly as possible, without forensic consideration, should be clearly outlined in the Incident Response Plan along with the person or people who are responsible for making that decision.

An increasing number of organizations are signing retainer agreements with organizations to provide Incident Response experts very quickly in the caser of a confirmed Incident. These retainers are a good option for organizations that do not have full time Incident Response or forensic experts on staff. Retainers can offer peace of mind at a relatively low price point. Many of the Service Level Agreements provide for experts to be on site within forty-eight hours of being called in order to assist in the response and can begin advising their clients immediately over the phone. This type of agreement is similar to an insurance policy; you hope you never need it, but if you do, you must be confident that you have the right organization on your side.

Eradication

Think of a cyber-attack in progress as a rapidly spreading cancerous tumor. Identifying it quickly will limit the damage. Once the scope of the cancer is identified, the tumor is removed while affecting as little healthy tissue as possible. Take too much, and you are causing unnecessary damage to the host. Take too little, and the cancer comes back stronger than before, often with dire consequences.

Eradication refers to the process of removing the threat from an environment. This can be a single action in the case of a simple malware infection affecting a single machine, or may require tearing down and rebuilding an entire network or a section of a network. There is a balance that must be struck since it is important to eradicate the threat completely, but if the eradication is too far reaching, it will unnecessarily add time, effort, and expense to the recovery process. In the case of a significant Incident affecting more than a small subset of users, the effort to identify the entire scope of the problem and formulate an eradication plan will require security experts working in concert with desktop and networking resources. The effort should be coordinated with the senior person in the organization with "Security" in their title, often the Chief Information Security Officer, with oversight from the Chief Information Officer.

In the case of a simple infection of a machine, for example, the eradication step should contain procedures for how identified threats are to be removed. Sometimes it may include erasing the storage on the affected machine completely and rebuilding them to perform their original function. For some threats, it may be as simple as changing all passwords, or running a utility to remove the threat. For more advanced threats that are starting to be identified, the entire machine may need to be replaced in order to fully eradicate the threat, at least until more effective eradication methods are available.

The Sony attack represents the other end of the spectrum. The attack against Sony was a vicious attack that appears to have been conducted as a terrorist attack against Sony, likely with some form of state sponsorship. The reason I classify it as a terrorist attack is because the intent of the attack appears to be to cause harm or embarrassment rather than to steal a piece of information. Essentially, the attackers used a type of malware that overwrites all data, including the master boot record, which renders the systems useless as they are unable to start properly. This type of malware does not appear to have any ability to exfiltrate information, but serves to destroy information in a way that makes it very difficult to recover from.

Sony was certainly the first high-profile attack of this type against an American corporation in recent times, but many experts do not think it will be the last. Tom Kellermann, chief cybersecurity officer with security software manufacturer Trend Micro said it best when he said, "I believe the coordinated cyber-attack with destructive payloads against a corporation in the U.S. represents a watershed event, Geopolitics now serve as harbingers for destructive cyberattacks."[4]

Recovery

Recovery has been the subject of a good amount of discussion to this point, but it is important to address it through the lens of the planned containment and eradication steps. Any functionality or connectivity that has been deprecated as part of Containment and Eradication must have a clear Recovery plan. Taking a methodological approach to these three steps is likely to make the effort much more efficient and effective than trying to put the pieces back together after a breach response in an ad-hoc manner.

I often liken the Information Security profession to the medical profession in that the first rule of both is to do no harm. This does not mean that security professionals should hesitate to take swift and decisive actions in order to protect their organization, just like doctors make take risks to save a life, but it does mean that every action taken by security should balance the benefit of the corrective action with the potential collateral damage to productivity and the overall organization. Taking special steps to ensure the proper recovery of an environment after Containment and Eradication efforts will ensure no undue harm comes to the business and the overall cost of the breach for internal restoration is limited to whatever extent limitation of that cost is possible.

There is a cost to any business associated with the amount of time services are unavailable to their authorized users. Therefore, Recovery is time critical and the plan should define Recovery Time Objectives (RTO) and Recovery Point Objectives (RPO) similar to a Business Continuity Plan (BCP) or a Disaster Recovery (DR) Plan.

---

[4]"Exclusive: FBI Warns of 'destructive' Malware in Wake of Sony Attack," Reuters, 2014. Accessed May 21, 2016. http://www.reuters.com/article/us-sony-cybersecurity-malware-idUSKCN0JF3FE20141202.

To this point, the focus has been on recovering systems and capabilities, which is only the first step. There also are public relation considerations to the recovery step since a large part of recovery from a public breach is recovering an organization's reputation. It is important to clearly define roles and responsibilities in terms of communication in the Incident Response Plan. The organization should have a group of people who are controlling the narrative. It should be clear to the entire organization who is authorized to publicly release information and who is not. Generally, it is the role of the Chief Information Officer or Chief Executive Officer to designate the people who should fill this role. It is often a member of the public relations team if one exists. If not, the marketing department is another logical place to find people who can fill this role well.

Many times there is also a legal component to a breach. In cases of the exposure of regulated information, there may be a burden on the organization to report the breach, and it is often prudent to engage legal counsel so they may guide the effort to minimize penalties and fines that may be assessed, as well as to anticipate what types of lawsuits and settlements may result from the breach. Any agreements with customers or suppliers should also be evaluated in order to determine if the Incident has caused harm to a partner or customer that may need to be addressed by the legal team. In other cases, even if there is not a likelihood of suits or penalties against the organization, the organization may choose to press charges against the attacker if such an action is feasible. Simply put, part of recovery should always be to engage legal counsel to quantify, and to the extent it is possible, limit the organization's exposure as a result of the breach.

Recovery Time Objective (RTO)

Recovery Time Objective refers to the maximum amount of time services will be unavailable to authorized users in case of emergency. In many ways, a documented Recovery Time Objective is a contract with business unit stakeholders. It is important to remember that a stated RTO should be a maximum amount of downtime and not a best-case estimate or a target the team will aspire to. RTOs should not be exceeded under any circumstances so the plan should account for unforeseen delays that may take place, and additional time is provided for inevitable delays and imperfections in the process that may be identified as the process is exercised.

Recovery Point Objective (RPO)

Closely related to a Recovery Time Objective, a Recovery Point Objective is the maximum amount of data that will be lost in such a case. An RPO is generally used to determine the appropriate frequency of backups and other types of activities that can allow organizations recover data in case of a disaster. A good example is the previously discussed Saudi Aramco hack where tens of thousands of computer hard drives were erased. If there were a very short RPO in place, the damage from that attack would have been significantly limited. However, if backups are only performed monthly, there is a possibility that up to thirty days' worth of information could have been lost from each of those systems.

Post-Incident Activity

The process improvement portion of the cycle begins in earnest in the Post-Incident Activity. This portion of the cycle includes a review and documentation of the efficacy of all of the preceding steps. These may be known as After Action Reviews or Lessons Learned sessions, but regardless of what they are called, they should be honest assessments of what went well and what did not go well as part of the process. Immediately following an honest evaluation of the performance of the plan, should be a brainstorming session for how the plan should be improved, through the lens of the other steps.

In terms of preparation, ideas of who should've been involved that wasn't or identification of things that were required but not adequately prepared prior to the activity should be explored and resolved. In terms of Detection and Analysis, if there was a significant gap between breach and detection, ideas should be put forth for how the same type of threat could be identified more quickly in the future. This may involve creating a new program with new capabilities, or improving an existing capability or program. In the Containment, Eradication, and Recovery section, ideas for how to better contain the threat, more quickly eradicate it, or more quickly recover to a pre-breach state of operations should be explored. Finally, even the Post-Incident activities themselves may have opportunities for improvement should be explored.

Any Incident Response activity that does not generate some form of process improvement is a wasted opportunity. These plans, by their nature, can never be perfect. Therefore, simply saying "We did a great job" and moving on is not only arrogant and ignorant, but also wasteful. Further, the lack of an improvement from a poorly executed Incident Response can expose the organization to future gross negligence accusations and lawsuits should a similar incident occur in the future. Leaders of organizations should demand accountability for not only what happened and an honest assessment of how well the response was executed and how effective it was, but it should also demand a detailed list for future improvement including an owner for each process. It is a leadership responsibility to ensure processes are constantly improving throughout the business, but especially in Information Security. Apathy and complacency are the biggest threat to any organization's Information Security program. I cannot tell you how many times I have worked with organizations who sat across the table full of hubris and told me they had a perfect program and it was not possible for them to be breached, only for me to see them in the news a short time later with an entirely different team responsible for their program. Let me be clear: just because there is a breach does not mean the Information Security team should be cleaned out and replaced. These things can happen, and as we have previously discussed, a targeted attack is almost impossible to successfully turn away without some damage. However, any Information Security leader or team member who is arrogant enough to put forth to leadership that a breach is not possible is derelict in their duties and does not have a firm grasp on the industry and threats as they exist today. That person is clearly unqualified for any position on the Information Security team.

Testing the Plan

There are two reasons that every organization should do some type of testing of an Incident Response Plan. First, any plan should be tested once it is developed in order to find fatal flaws. Second, and perhaps more importantly, since the plan is built to improve any time it is exercised, performing realistic exercises allows for improvement without having to wait for a breach.

Red Team Exercises

The most common types of simulated attacks are commonly known as "Red Team Exercises." Essentially, there are two teams. There is the Blue Team, which is the internal Information Security team that has no indication a simulated attack will happen ("defense"). There is also a Red Team, which is a team of people with skills to simulate attacks who are paid to attack an environment in order to assess the Blue Team's capabilities to stop an attack. These exercises can be extremely valuable for an Information Security program.

The first time I ever conducted a Red Team exercise, I had a team in a Security Operations Center. I went out and hired some of the best Certified Ethical Hackers I could find. I set the rules of engagement, gave my Red Team an objective, and let the attack commence. As I suspected, the Red Team was able to defeat my Blue Team with relative ease. We continued running the exercises on a continuous basis, and over time, the Red Team became less successful, and the Blue Team was consistently winning. At first glance, it seemed as if my efforts were an overwhelming success! Unfortunately, the trend was far too clean to be believable. Under further investigation, I was able to determine that the Red Team and the Blue Team had become friends, and the Red Team did not want to make the Blue Team look bad. Therefore, the Red Team was increasingly tipping the Blue Team off about timing and tactics, and only making half-hearted efforts to attack systems. This is not what I was trying to accomplish at all! But what went wrong?

In the real world, the attackers don't know the defenders, and they couldn't care less about how the malicious activities could affect them. How was I to re-create that dynamic? I didn't want to mandate or manipulate my teams to dislike each other or have a general disregard for the well-being of their coworkers. The real world also had another difference. There was a profit motive for the attackers. I could re-create that! Moving forward I offered a $1000 bonus to each of the Red Team members if they successfully stole the data, and that money went to the Blue Team if they were able to prevent the attack. You would be amazed how the results of the exercise changed! The exercises were also far more valuable to the organization.

Some organizations choose not to re-create the profit motive as part of their exercises. If it is preferred, re-creating the dynamic of the attackers not knowing the defenders can also inject realism into the process. This objective can be accomplished by utilizing a third-party Red Team rather than hiring the Red Team into the organization. This also offers the added benefit of providing the capability to change teams, and therefore tactics, periodically.

Regardless of how the exercises are conducted, the emphasis and the reason for conducting the exercises is to improve the security program. These types of exercises can and should be fun ways to provide Information Security professionals an opportunity to compete and learn at the same time, but the primary reason for spending the time and the money on the exercise is to offer opportunities for improvement.

When conducting Red Team exercises, effective leadership and messaging after the exercise is important. In order to build a highly performing Information Security team, the team must understand that it is acceptable to have an attack be successful one time; what is unacceptable is the failure to improve the program as a result of the exercise.

Purple Team Exercises

There is an evolving concept that is known as purple teaming that is gaining popularity. Purple Team exercises differ from Red Team exercises in that Purple Team exercises have the Red Team and the Blue Team working together throughout the exercise. This approach has some advantages and some disadvantages when compared to traditional Red Team exercises. The benefit is that the Blue Team is able to step through the attack piece by piece to see all of the elements of the attack through the lens of the Detection and Analysis systems at their disposal. This approach also helps to highlight particular portions of the attack that may be undetectable with the current systems and programs in place.

The downside of Purple Teaming is that it does not allow evaluation of the Incident Response Plan and the associated opportunity for improvements that Red Team exercises offer because it is not a realistic attack simulation. I do not see Purple Team exercises as a replacement for Red Team exercises. Instead, I see Purple Team exercises as training camp and practice, whereas Red Team exercises are more like a scrimmage or a game, to borrow a sports analogy.

Both Red Team exercises and Purple Team exercises are most effective when they are used as part of a CPI model designed to constantly be evaluating and improving the security program. Red Team exercises and Penetration Tests are too often deployed only for compliance reasons, and their value to the overall security program is therefore not realized. Also, many organizations use the results of the test as a report card, rather than a specific set of lessons learned that could be used to improve the program.

Tabletop Exercises

Another form of testing the plan deals far less with the capabilities of the security team to detect and respond to a plan, and far more with testing the ability of the organization at the leadership level to mount a comprehensive response. I have recently conducted some of these exercises, and they have been extraordinarily effective in both educating executive leadership about threats that exist and likely scenarios that may occur, while simultaneously identifying gaps in communication that may exist as part of the plan.

There are many parts of an Incident Response Plan, specifically in the recovery phase, that transcend technology and security teams and rely heavily upon public relations and legal. These groups are unlikely to benefit from a Red Team or Purple Team exercise, but can benefit greatly from a tabletop exercise.

Tabletop exercises can vary greatly in scope between a simulated exercise lasting a few hours, and an exercise that asks each participant to actually perform their portion of the response while role-playing with a facilitator, which may last a week or so.

A tabletop exercise begins with a realistic scenario that has a significant business impact. As the information is provided to the participants, they are asked to explain or act out their portion of the response. What is interesting is the majority of the value of a tabletop exercise is realized after technical Containment, Eradication and Recovery. Who is going to answer the media's questions? Who is responsible for communicating with internal employees that may be affected? Who is responsible for fielding calls from concerned customers or partners? What is the strategy related to settling lawsuits or preempting them by negotiating compensation? All of these things are very important and are tested during the exercise.

Security Assessments

Red Team exercises could be considered a specific example of a type of Security Assessment, but the term Security Assessments refers to a much broader set of activities that are designed to assess the current state of an organization's security posture and look for critical weaknesses and vulnerabilities. A thorough Security Assessment will highlight vulnerabilities regardless of how secure an organization is. It is not always appropriate to attempt to mitigate all of the vulnerabilities identified. The proper response to an identified vulnerability, in my opinion, is to do a cost-benefit analysis in an effort to determine the proper Risk Treatment strategy in a given situation. There are three levels of depth and rigor when it comes to Security Assessments: scanning, assessment, and penetration. These terms are not universal, and are often incorrectly applied, so it is important for an organization to ensure they explicitly spell out the scope of an assessment to ensure everyone is on the same page with respect to what is being done.

Vulnerability Scanning

Scanning is the least in-depth type of Security Assessment and consists of scanning the perimeter of a network (firewalls), inside of the network (between trusted systems), or application scanning (such as application code that requires a periodic request for update) with a tool that is looking for well-known vulnerabilities. This level of scanning is very cheap to perform and seldom requires verification that the targets belong to the organization performing the scan. These factors make scanning an inexpensive option for an organization to identify vulnerabilities in their network, but the same factors make these types of scans an inexpensive and unsophisticated method for attackers to do the same. If you aren't familiar with basic Vulnerability Scanning, imagine a situation where a home intruder is surveying a house. He might wait in the neighborhood to record patterns of when residents are home and away, and might occasionally check to see if doors or windows are unlocked.

I often tell people that if they are not scanning their public-facing IP addresses to identify known vulnerabilities, they are at a major disadvantage because someone else is. We've already mentioned that external scanning is cheap and easy to perform because it based on already-known vulnerabilities that have not been fixed in a timely manner. This process refers back to the "outrun the bear" analogies where all one has to do is be faster than another person to avoid the bear's attack. At a minimum, organizations should perform these scans on a recurring basis (monthly or quarterly) as basic due diligence. Often the vulnerabilities identified are easy for attackers to exploit, and easy and inexpensive for an organization to patch.

Vulnerability Assessments

True assessments take the scan one step deeper. Instead of simply looking for known vulnerabilities, an assessment will evaluate how easily a vulnerability could be exploited. This often stops short of taking control of a system or stealing certain types of data, but does endeavor to validate that the vulnerability could be exploited and sometimes may also assess the level of skill and resources that would be required to take advantage of the vulnerability. In this example, the home intruder might be confident enough to attempt to slide a window open or push hard on a door to test for structural weakness.

Penetration Testing

True Penetration Tests are exercises in which all bets are off and the assessor does everything they can to compromise a system in a full-blown simulated attack. These assessments are difficult to perform because the overall quality of the assessment is wholly dependent on the individual skill of the assessor. Often, the term Penetration Test is used when the exercise in question is really more of a scan or assessment. Many people claim to have Penetration Testing capabilities, when in truth, a small percentage have the skills and experience necessary to provide a realistic simulation of a sophisticated attack. There are organizations that are now beginning to certify individuals and companies to perform this type of work as there has been an identified need in the marketplace to be able to universally identify which companies and individuals possess the proper skills and experience to perform a thorough Penetration Test. If you were having a Penetration Test done on your house, the assessor would attempt to break into your house and load your belongings into a moving trailer without triggering any alarms.

A well-recognized certification for Penetration Testing is the Certified Ethical Hacker (CEH) Certification. This certification tests the skills of the applicant and also requires that he or she adheres to a code of ethical conduct. While this certification is well-known, it does little to distinguish the testers with world-class skills from those who are pretty good. The need to further delineate individuals and organizations has given rise to organizations like CREST, which offers a Registered Penetration Tester certification that is, by all accounts, far more difficult to achieve than a CEH certification. Certification bodies can play a crucial role in the development of an industry or service so long as they maintain integrity of the testing and they are well represented by their certification holders.

The Erosion of the Perimeter

Since the turn of the new millennium, Information Technology has undergone a dramatic shift in the way that organizations structure their infrastructure. At one time, it was realistic to believe that every information asset owned by an organization was contained inside a perimeter protected by firewalls and Intrusion Prevention and/or Detection systems. In those days, it was a logical strategy for a company to focus on keeping everything that wasn't authorized outside the perimeter, and the data would be secure. Another benefit to security professionals in those days was that transfer speeds were relatively slow, so even if they were to be compromised, it would take significant time and resources for the attackers to move the data from inside the perimeter to outside the perimeter. Throughout the vast majority of the world, those days are gone. As often happens, advances in capabilities that make it easier to share, work on the go, collaborate, and lower infrastructure costs, has also made it much easier to attack, infiltrate, and steal from organizations. The modern world is full of vague terms and buzzwords such as "The Cloud," mobile devices, tablets, smartphones, and e-readers. The entirety of the wealth of human knowledge sits in the palm of a user's hand. With that great power comes great responsibility, and great opportunities for peril for organizations trying to protect the digital property they hold most dear. To make matters worse, there are many buzzwords that are thrown around that truly mislead people into thinking the new capabilities are magical creations. I will use two examples of brilliant terminology for ideas that may not be so attractive to people when the layers are peeled back: Next-Generation Firewall and the Cloud.

Next-Generation Firewalls

Many years ago, the world was introduced to a type of product that was intended to be a single-box solution to a variety of security challenges. It was commonly known as a Unified Threat Module (UTM). A UTM was a device that contained inside it, among other things, a firewall, an Intrusion Detection System, a Web Gateway, and an antivirus solution. The device worked very well when only a few functions were used simultaneously, but it did not work very well when all of the functions were competing for the same resources. As a result, there was relatively low adoption of the technology that quickly waned as the industry decided that having dedicated hardware and software to perform each function was the best approach. Not only from a resource perspective, but also so each of the vendors would focus on what they were best at rather than trying to be a jack of all trades. Enter Palo Alto and its Next-Generation Firewall. What is a Next-Generation Firewall? Simply a repackaged and rebranded Unified Threat Module. There really is no difference between a Next-Generation Firewall and a UTM other than the fact that the hardware and software have improved. All of the drawbacks of a UTM still exist. Yet, Palo Alto has proven what a good rebranding campaign on top of a recycled and largely failed idea can do. The purpose of this example is not to downplay the efficacy of the Palo Alto product; each organization should evaluate every potential solution under consideration on its own merits. The purpose is, instead, to provide a warning to the industry to be sure they truly understand what is being presented and that they look deeper than the advertising and marketing campaign and into the problem they are trying to solve and their individual requirements for doing so. Any time a buzzword is used by a sales person, the buyers in an organization should immediately grasp their wallets or purses tightly and challenge the salesperson to explain in simple terms exactly what they mean.

The Cloud

The second example is the idea of the cloud. It is as if the whole world has become convinced that they can house their data in the sky and access it whenever they wish. Unfortunately, there is no cloud: it is simply someone else's computer in someone else's data center that houses data and applications as a service to customers. If you ask an organization that has adopted cloud technology where, specifically their data is, they will tell you "it's in the cloud."

The cloud is not a location. The truth is, many of these people have no idea where their data is actually being housed, and where else it may be replicated. The terminology and advertising behind the cloud has made it a very attractive model, but let's examine how attractive it is once we explain it simply for what it really is.

If I told you that I wanted to store all of your data in my data centers, wherever I choose to put it, and you would have no input or visibility into how I secured your data, would that seem like a good idea? What if I told you that you would have access to your data twenty-four hours per day, seven days per week, which meant by consequence, so would anyone who wanted to steal it, with no restrictions or monitoring with respect to access patterns, would that inspire confidence? That is essentially what the cloud model is, but when people tell us to put our data in the cloud and not worry about it, we tend not to ask many clarifying questions. The point of this example is not to say that the cloud does not have a role in collaboration and storage, but simply to say that prior to investing in a technology, it is important to remember what it truly is and how it works. Otherwise, we expose ourselves and our organizations to undue risk.

Evolving Infrastructure

How many modern organizations have all of their data contained within a traditional perimeter? I have not encountered any in several years, and a large part of my time is spent speaking with organizations about their security posture, so I am exposed to a reasonable volume of organizational infrastructure. By the same token, very few organizations have all of their information stored in the cloud. There is often a balance between what is stored in the cloud versus what is stored on premise. The problem is, those decisions are rarely made with security in mind. In general, the data that the organization wants to be most accessible to those who need it is stored in the cloud. Consequently, that important information is also often sensitive and should be protected. Part of the cloud puzzle is solving that very problem. Many organizations are not policing what goes up to the cloud, but rather trying to control how the data is put there. For example, if I encrypt my data prior to storing the data in the cloud, and I secure the keys on my premise, anyone who breaches the cloud environment would not also breach my data unless they also breached my keys. Solutions such as this are helping organizations store data in the cloud with confidence.

Digital Protectionists

There is another developing trend around the world that is similar to a protectionist sentiment. Essentially, world governments have realized that information is power, and have decided that it is important to them to ensure information generated in their country by their citizens remain in their country. There have been numerous laws around the globe that enforce these rules, and there are likely more to come. This trend of deglobalization is gaining momentum that is likely to continue for the foreseeable future.

All of these factors have resulted in heterogeneous networks that complicate the problem facing Information Security teams around the globe. These changes do not make it impossible for organizations to secure their most critical data, but they do make it imperative for organizations to take a data-centric approach and map the life cycle of their Critical Information Assets. It also means that Incident Response Plans must take the changes into account and be prepared to respond to an Incident regardless of where the data resides and who has access to it.

Conclusion

The modern digital world is dangerous. Reading a newspaper or watching the nightly news often will highlight the growing prevalence of cyber-crime. There are many reasons for the increase in these types of activities, but the results are clear. More than ever, organizations need to prepare themselves for the inevitable possibility of an Information Security Incident. An incident does not necessarily mean a breach either. An incident may be something that requires investigation that does not result in harm to the business, or it may be an emergency where seconds in the response translate to enormous sums of money in terms of damages. Regardless, a clear plan that details how an organization would respond to such an incident is necessary.

A plan does not need to be perfect in order to be valuable, because a good plan will include a mechanism for testing and continuous improvement. There are various methods of testing the plan including Red Team exercises, Purple Team exercises, Security Assessments, and Tabletop exercises.

The most important part of building an effective Incident Response is to get started. If your organization does not have a plan today, build one! If a plan does exist, test and improve it. Having an effective plan with clearly defined roles and responsibilities is one of the easiest and least expensive methods of reducing the cost of an Information Security breach.

CHAPTER 6

■ ■ ■

The People Problem

Amateurs hack systems, professionals hack people.

—Bruce Schneier

It is widely accepted that people are the weakest link in the security triumvirate of people, process, and technology. There is a general lack of awareness among the user community that leads to disturbing trends continuing, and even worsening in some cases. Examples of these trends include creating weak passwords, a lack of awareness of the value of their identity, clicking on links on e-mails, opening attachments from unknown senders, holding doors for people into secure areas, and a propensity to share information over the phone without verifying the identity of the caller, among others. Worse still, there is a growing trend of people intentionally taking data from their employers with the intent to use it for purposes that may be detrimental to their organization. The people problem is growing.

Conversely, people can also be the greatest asset in an Information Security program. Well-meaning are often the first line of defense an organization has with the capacity for rational thought. When these people are armed with the information and tools necessary to protect sensitive data, they can make it significantly more difficult for an attacker to compromise a network, as the majority of attacks begin with a social engineering campaign of some kind, which is designed to trick a user into giving the attacker information he or she should not have. Social engineering takes many forms, including following authorized personnel into a secured area, sending an infected attachment to a user, e-mails that fool a user into clicking on an illegitimate link, or convincing a user to give the attacker their password over the phone, to name a few.

Attackers are also increasingly relying on smart and adaptable people rather than solely utilizing technical exploits. This is not to say that technical exploits do not still play a role, but sophisticated attackers are taking advantage of the fact that human beings can adapt to changing circumstances in order to defeat technology countermeasures. It is imperative for the success of any program that people are part of the solution rather than part of the problem.

In short, the actors, whether malicious or defenders of their own cyber realm, that are winning the cyber-security battle are learning to leverage people for all of their strengths and support their weaknesses with processes and/or technologies that are designed to enable people to be at their best, while enabling these resources through ongoing training and feedback loops. Those that continue to lose are the people or organizations that continue to lament the "stupidity" or "ignorance" of the end user without offering solutions to the problems at hand. In this chapter, we will explore how to use people as an effective tool in building an effective cyber-security program as well as how to minimize the likelihood that a user will be the cause of the downfall of your carefully constructed program.

© Jeremy Wittkop 2016
J. Wittkop, *Building a Comprehensive IT Security Program*, DOI 10.1007/978-1-4842-2053-5_6

What Would You Do for a Klondike Bar?

According to an article from BBC in 2004, "More than 70% of people would reveal their computer password in exchange for a bar of chocolate," and "34% of respondents volunteered their password when asked without needing to be bribed."[1]

A lot has changed since 2004, and I certainly hope these statistics would be much lower today. However, I would hazard to guess the number could still be greater than 40%, because a lot of users have no idea how valuable their password actually is. Most users go about their daily business utilizing assets that are extraordinarily valuable, blissfully unaware of just how valuable the assets are. This lack of understanding is demonstrated daily by how many people within everyday situations share common usernames and passwords with coworkers, not understanding the perilous situation that one can be subjected to if another user violates predetermined rules for use of that machine.

Educating end users is certainly part of the solution but can lead to other problems as well. Many of the same users that are causing security issues today because they are unaware of the value of the assets they are using may become insider threats once they are made aware of the value of the assets they use. In today's marketplace, it is more important than ever to do comprehensive background checks on every employee. There was a time when only certain individuals had access to information that may be of commercial value. Currently, there are very few members of an organization that do not have access to some assets of value. In addition, attackers have become very adept at utilizing one set of compromised credentials to compromise an entire environment and successfully elevate their permissions from the original point of compromise.

Finally, few organizations have implemented Concept of Least Privilege or Separation of Duties necessary to ensure access is limited to only those who need it, and a single set of compromised credentials could not cause widespread damage or data loss.

Concept of Least Privilege is a best practice that states that a user should have access to the minimum amount of systems or information that they *require* to perform their job function. It is important to emphasize that access is granted based on requirements and not desires. Many users want access to everything, but that does not mean that they require it. This can become especially problematic when dealing with high-ranking members of an organization.

Separation of Duties is a best practice that states that no single user should have the ability and the responsibility to perform all parts of a process. This best practice is generally thought of as a prevention technique for internal fraud, but also helps to secure systems from external attacks by ensuring a single set of compromised credentials cannot result in external fraudulent activity.

Few breaches highlight the failure to implement these best practices quite like the eBay breach of 2014. The eBay compromise began when a small number of user credentials from trusted employees were compromised, resulting in the exposure of 145 million users' information. The information compromised was inclusive of Personally Identifiable Information and user passwords, but exclusive of credit card information. Essentially this means the attackers could potentially use their accounts to purchase items but did not have access to their actual methods of payment. They could also sell the users' identity information on the Dark Web. What possible reason could there be for such a small subset of corporate users to have access to all of that information? Often, administrative users who need access to make changes to the system are given unrestricted access to data, which may not be necessary in order for them to do their job effectively. On a positive note, eBay did a good job of separating their user information from their Card Data Environment (CDE) where credit card information is stored. This segmentation limited the scope and the impact of the breach by protecting the credit card information for those users.

Given the fact that the average user does not understand the value of their password, three essential best practices should be implemented by every organization that seeks methods to strengthen their security posture. First, the Concept of Least Privilege should be universally adopted. Second, requiring users to change their passwords frequently can limit the effect of a single loss of credentials. Third, two-factor and multifactor authentication should be implemented whenever possible to limit the ability of an attacker to leverage stolen credentials.

---

[1]BBC News, 2004. Accessed February 4, 2016. http://news.bbc.co.uk/2/hi/technology/3639679.stm.

Multifactor authentication refers to the use of multiples of the three possible ways users can identify themselves to systems. The three possible factors of authentication are something you know, something you have, or something you are. Something you know is the most commonly implemented factor of authentication and includes things like passwords or answers to secret questions selected to secure an account. Something you have is most commonly implemented in the form of a hardware or software token that has a code that must be entered in conjunction with password authentication. Something you are is also known as biometrics and consists of things like iris scans and fingerprint readers. Two-factor authentication means using a factor of authentication from two of the three categories; multifactor authentication has been expanded to include two-factor authentication as well as authentication that uses all three factors of authentication.

■ **Note**   asking for a password and a birthdate is not two-factor authentication because both methods of authentication are from the something you know category. In order to implement two-factor authentication, the factors must be from different categories.

There was a time when biometrics was difficult to implement, and a second factor based on something a user had was expensive and time consuming to implement and maintain. Those days have largely passed as most users have a smartphone with fingerprint technology to allow the user's device to become the device necessary to implement biometrics. The same device can be used to implement a software token solution where the device receives the token from the server, eliminating the need to distribute hardware tokens to employees. Organizations can go one step further and require any mobile device that has access to corporate information to have a password. Implementing this type of solution allows an organization to implement true three-factor authentication with little impact to the end user. Essentially the user would log into their phone and request a code that would challenge them for their fingerprint. Upon successful fingerprint authentication, a code is generated that can be entered into the system they are trying to access. This scenario is very secure. If the organization chose to remove the password requirement, then two-factor authentication and neither of the factors is a password. It is much more difficult for an attacker to convince a user to give them their phone and their fingerprint through social engineering than it is to convince a user to give up their password. Also, since the fingerprint is validated at the device level, it is never transmitted, limiting the efficacy of phishing attacks. Bring Your Own Device (BYOD) has been bemoaned as a security nightmare by many security professionals, but it is not going away in the foreseeable future. Therefore, the most successful security organizations seek opportunities to make BYOD part of their solution rather than part of their problem.

It is a worthwhile pursuit to educate users with respect to keeping their passwords secure; but regardless of awareness training, human error and ignorance will continue to put passwords at risk. It is prudent to implement measures to limit the impact on the organization of a lost password. Some organizations have implemented their measures so elegantly that it is actually easier for users to perform multifactor authentication than it was for them to access systems with a password only. This is especially true when users have access to several systems or networks with different password requirements for each. If something you know is a desired method of authentication, passphrases have become increasingly common. In short, regardless of the overall authentication strategy, passwords are becoming far less popular and effective as technology continues to advance.

Why Don't They Get It?

Information Security and Information Technology professionals often lament their collective plight in dealing with the end user. There is even an axiom common in many Information Technology circles that states "There are very few problems that cannot be solved by killing the end-user." The axiom is intended to be a macabre joke, but it highlights the thinking that must be changed in order for technology and business to work seamlessly together.

First, security professionals must address a fundamental flaw in their thinking. Inside the echo chamber that is the Information Security community, security professionals often allow themselves to be convinced that anyone who does not understand basic Information Security tenets must be stupid or naive. If everyone across the many disciplines required to make up a successful enterprise thought the same way, would security teams not be ignorant if they don't know how to build a financial forecast model? That is a relatively basic finance function. They must be idiots if we don't know how to effectively manage the performance cycle, correct? That is a relatively basic Human Resources function. They may be so simple-minded as to not know how to effectively forecast revenue and make commitments to sales projections, for isn't that a relatively simple sales function? Too often people fall prey to the tyranny of our limited frame of reference. The first thing security professionals must do is learn to communicate more effectively with business users and approach them with an attitude of mutual respect, rather than one of arrogance.

Second, it is very important that organizations shift the paradigm from blaming the end user to helping to empower the end user. The end user is not the enemy: he or she is often the victim. This is the reason that next-generation Information Security programs focus on people, and the authorized manner in which they handle Critical Information Assets, rather than on the bits, bytes, and signatures that may indicate a system is compromised. Instead, we build content- and context-aware programs that will give us indications that people or their accounts have been compromised, willingly or unwillingly. Victim blaming is strongly frowned upon in the real world across most developed nations; why would it be acceptable with respect to Information Security?

The ultimate goal should be for us to shift the paradigm from a culture of "us against them" with respect to how Information Technology and Information Security teams interact with the end-user community, to a culture of mutual respect and empowerment. In order for us all to be successful, we must work together. Information Security professionals must endeavor to make it easier for end users to meet and exceed corporate security standards. End users must make an effort to understand the role they play in keeping information secure. Business users will start to "get it" with respect to Information Security only when Information Security professionals do a better job of communicating with the business and helping to explain how security problems are business problems.

The Insider Threat

According to research performed by the Systems Administration, Networking, and Security (SANS) Institute, 96% of data leaks are accidental.[2] Regardless of the origin of the leaks of the data, however, the consequences are the same for the organization who has lost it. In addition, the other 4% of data leaks often represent very large and very costly breaches. Further, many organizations' security programs are designed to keep outsiders out, but what happens when the threat is already inside the organization? There are three categories of Insider Threats that essentially every breach I have ever studied, involving a trusted insider falls into: the Malicious Insider, the Misguided Insider, and the Well-Meaning Insider.

Malicious Insider

An inconvenient and inescapable truth of security programs is that not all data loss involving trusted insiders is accidental. It is human nature to assume that all of the individuals inside of an organization want the best for their organization and the people they work with. They don't. Any organization of any size invariably has unscrupulous, unhappy, or disenfranchised individuals inside the organization. These individuals would intentionally cause harm to the organization if it would be of benefit to them personally or help them gain revenge for a real or perceived slight or instance of disrespect.

Malicious Insiders will often probe defenses for weaknesses and opportunities to exfiltrate data. Moreover, due to the fact they have malicious intent, they will intentionally target the information that is most

---

[2]Peter Gordon, "Data Leakage - Threats and Mitigation." *Data Leakage - Threats and Mitigation.* Accessed May 23, 2016. https://www.sans.org/reading-room/whitepapers/awareness/data-leakage-threats-mitigation-1931.

beneficial to them, usually information that is the most valuable on the open market, which tends to be the information that is most damaging to the organization. Malicious Insiders represent the vast minority of users in an organization, but also present the greatest risk of the three groups since they intend to cause harm, and when given the opportunity, will cause as much harm as possible to maximize their personal benefit.

There are two types of Malicious Insiders. The first type is an insider that is not malicious when they join the organization. Many times employees are alienated or become disgruntled for a variety of reasons during the term of their employment. Of the two, these are the easier to detect because at some point, there is a change in these employees' behavior. A monitoring program that includes behavioral analytics can be designed to detect deviations from baseline behavior that may indicate a user's behavior is changing. These changes may be due to a change in role or business process, or they may indicate a change of intentions.

The second type is an insider that is malicious before joining the organization, and joins the organization with the intent of stealing information. These types of insiders are much more difficult to detect, but are also far less common. Organizations that have data that is likely to be specifically targeted by sophisticated and well-funded adversaries are encouraged to perform extensive background checks for potential employees, including using every method available to attempt to gain an understanding of the candidate's associations such as social media, in an effort to identify any potential conflicts of interest that may exist.

Misguided Insiders

There is another group of people who believe they can take information with them that may be of benefit to them at another company, but would not cause harm to the organization they are stealing from. These people are rationalizing their behavior similarly to a car thief who believes he or she is morally superior to other car thieves because he or she steals only from large dealerships who are insured against their losses. These people live in a fantasy world in which their crimes are victimless. The truth is, anything that has value to a competitive organization would cause damage to the originating organization, simply because it helps a competitor. This is inescapable.

There is a second group of Misguided Insiders that has misconceptions with respect to the ownership of the data they use or even create. Most employees in Western countries sign an employment agreement that states any Intellectual Property they create as a course of their employment belongs to their employer. However, if you ask many people who create Intellectual Property if it is wrong for them to keep copies for themselves to reuse after they leave the organization, many would say it is not. This attitude presents major problems to organizations that develop Intellectual Property like code because large parts of code development activities in many cases are performed by contractors. If those contractors then resell the code they created to a competitor, they have immediately commoditized their own work. The organization that has paid for the work, then, has immediately lost the exclusivity they are entitled to by commissioning the creation of the Intellectual Property in question. It is difficult for many people to understand, but the concept is quite simple if you think about it. Essentially, if you create something on your own time, you own it. If you are paid to create it, it almost certainly belongs to the individual or company who paying you. It really isn't any more complicated than that.

Different cultures have different ideas with respect to ownership. Many countries, like the United States and Great Britain, have concepts regarding individual property rights, where a person or an organization that creates something has the right to ownership and exclusive use of the creation for a period of time in order to allow them to profit from it and to encourage continued innovation. There are many countries around the world, however, that believe that any creation that would be beneficial to society as a whole belongs to all people in society. The Chinese culture, and other cultures based on socialism or communism largely agrees with this philosophy. The intent is not to opine on which system is better or worse, but to highlight the fact that cultural attitudes toward Intellectual Property ownership play a major role in the security programs of multinational corporations, especially as it relates to the insider threat. The person that is an insider threat to a U.S.-based company with operations in China, may be acting in accordance with their own values and, in their minds, doing nothing wrong. It is important to distinguish that not all malicious actors actually have malicious intent. In the global economy, leaders must be cognizant of the fact that a globally shared value system does not currently exist. Risk factors associated with culture and location must be taken into account when doing business internationally.

Regardless of the intent, or the ways in which the perpetrator rationalizes his or her actions, insider theft hurts organizations. Insider theft of information is also far more common than most people would like to believe. There are countless statistics detailing insider threats from a variety of sources, and the statistics do change from year to year. What does not change is the fact that the vast majority of data leakage initiates from inside an organization rather than outside. It is also true that the majority of security technologies deployed inside an organization are designed to prevent intrusions from external threats. Why would we pay more attention to external threats than internal threats?

Well-Meaning Insiders

The vast majority of users that present an insider threat to an organization are Well-Meaning Insiders. These people have pure intentions and end up representing a threat due to their own ignorance of proper security practices, an insecure business process that exposes information through no fault of the user, or an honest mistake. Each of these issues can be identified and mitigated with a comprehensive and effective IT security program, but the aggregate of these three problems accounts for 96% of data loss incidents, according to the Symantec research that was previously cited. Many organizations have quarterly or annual Information Security awareness training. This training by itself has been proven ineffective. Basic human psychology mandates these types of education programs be supported by continuous and on-the-spot corrections of improper behavior. There are a variety of technologies that can be deployed and configured to provide these corrections in a way that reinforce Information Security awareness training in an effective manner.

Internal and External Threats

There are a variety of reasons why addressing external threats is more popular and politically expedient than addressing internal threats. First, it is simply easier and less intrusive to keep an outsider out than it is to monitor authorized user behavior for improper use of company assets.

Second, it is easy for an organization to say "there are bad people out there we must protect ourselves from" than it is to say "there are bad people in here, amongst your friends and co-workers who would cause you harm." Most people simply do not want to believe the second statement is true, regardless of the statistics.

Finally, external threats can be addressed to some extent with technology solutions and insider threats are largely process and people problems. We are conditioned to prefer the multiple choice problems technology solves over the critical thinking and creative process required to solve complex process and people problems. As a result, far too many organizations choose the right solution to the wrong problem and remain blissfully ignorant of the most prevalent threats they are facing, which are the users they have entrusted their Critical Information Assets to.

User-Generated and System-Generated Events

Many forward-thinking technology solutions, when combined with expert people and well-defined processes, enable programs that can address both internal and external threat actor groups.

Data Loss Prevention systems (technologies that can examine the content of messages) and SIEM systems (technologies that can identify contextual anomalies in systems or networks), which are rapidly evolving toward Security Intelligence platforms, enable these types of programs to be built by leveraging the capabilities necessary to correlate large volumes of disparate data, and the flexibility to take context into account. Some companies have gone so far as to build their entire corporate strategy around educating and empowering the end user to be more secure rather than relying on a technology to enforce rules and regulations. Sometimes both can be done in conjunction with each other.

It is important to note that Data Loss Prevention technologies are really content-aware technologies and SIEM systems are essentially context-aware solutions. The reason it is important to make that distinction is that the individual product names will likely change over time, so the need to analyze content and context will be a requirement for security programs for the foreseeable future.

Content-aware solutions refer to any solution that can inspect the content of a transfer of information to discern important information from trivial information. Many times these types of systems also allow for some programming to take place with respect to what is authorized and unauthorized based on the source of the information, the destination, and the amount of sensitive information that is contained in the transfer. The first content-aware solutions were the first Data Loss Prevention solutions. These solutions have been difficult for many organizations to implement successfully due to the fact that they are not technical tools; they are business tools facilitated by technology. In order to be able to successfully operate these systems, both technical and analytical resources are necessary. In my career, I have been personally involved in more than two hundred successful implementations of these technologies and they have been extremely valuable when implemented properly. The events generated by these technologies are often referred to as user-driven events because they generally monitor actions taken by a user. The addition of behavioral analytics in order to make predictions on the user's intentions or predict future actions are the emerging capabilities being developed to make these technologies even more effective. Data Loss Prevention is currently experiencing a resurgence in popularity, but even if DLP tools eventually disappear from the Information Security landscape, organizations will always need the capability to make qualitative determinations with respect to the value of the contents of a transfer of data.

Context-aware systems define normal behavior of a system or application in an effort to alert security professionals to changes in an environment. SIEM systems are the most common example of these types of technologies. The events generated by these devices are often referred to as system-generated events because they examine the environment from a systematic perspective, in most cases without concern for end-user behavior. Baselines and deviations from baselines are examples of programmatic elements that require monitoring of system-generated events.

Combining both user-generated and system-generated events into security analytics is critical for the success of a Comprehensive IT Security Program. When both are leveraged effectively, organizations can identify a wide range of threats including insider threats, advanced persistent threats, undue risk caused by insecure or ineffective business process, and well-meaning insiders that are subjecting information to risk through ignorance or willfully circumventing authorized processes. Building such programs is difficult, but the increased risk exposure for organizations that choose not to is often more expensive than building the program itself. Simply put, the cost-benefit analysis of building a Comprehensive IT Security Program is often favorable.

The Evolution of Attacks

There have been several evolutions of cyber-attacks over the years since the Internet was invented. The first attacks could be classified largely as cyber-mischief. Many of the original hackers were not professionals, but people who had an interest in and a talent for technology, and who were largely attacking systems to gain notoriety for themselves. These attackers were very similar to graffiti artists. They would attempt to gain access to a secure system, and leave an artifact to prove to everyone they were successful. These types of attackers were often a nuisance, but generally did not cause much harm.

The next iteration of cyber-mischief turned significantly more serious as the same types of actors that were involved in defacing web sites, moved toward denial of service attacks, in which they would up the ante by causing outages to web servers or services. This type of mischief caused damage to organizations due to lost productivity, and products were developed in order to prevent these types of attacks. The attackers were generally not sophisticated, and the threats themselves were not generally adaptable.

Then came the first pieces of malicious software, and with them, the advent of cyber-terrorism. The first types of malware were generally viruses and worms that were designed to cause damage to infected systems. They generally did not yield much benefit to the attacker, but they did cause significant harm to victims. These types of software gave rise to traditional signature-based anti-malware and antivirus solutions.

A major evolution subsequently hit the Information Security world when attackers began to adapt these types of malicious software designed to exfiltrate information from their victims. Many infamous types of malware, like Zeus and many others, were a product of this time period and ushered in the Information Security industry for the types of businesses that were often targeted. The most common targets were financial services as these types of malicious packages became the bank robberies of the Information Age.

Speeds of network transfer and processing power have continued to increase, and with more powerful systems came more sophisticated attacks. At some point, large-scale data transfers over the wire became increasingly feasible from any source to any destination. This change gave rise to Advanced Persistent threats as we know them today, which are well funded, and they originate from very sophisticated individuals that dedicate their lives to stealing information or causing harm to systems. Whether they are cyber-spies, cyber-criminals, cyber-terrorists, or hacktavists, the overwhelming majority of the people carrying out these attacks are very well-trained professionals. Understanding this fact is key to combating modern threats because organizations must employ and deploy their own groups of highly motivated, highly skilled professionals in order to have a chance at protecting themselves. People play a major role in this cat and mouse game, and organizations that do not have the right people on their side are like lambs to the slaughter. They will be completely unaware of the threats they face until it is too late. Very large organizations suffer massive damage from breaches, but smaller organizations that don't generate headlines often never recover and disappear forever.

One prominent example is a Dutch certificate issuer called DigiNotar. DigiNotar was a SSL certificate issuing authority that is essentially in the business of verifying that a web site a user visits is actually who they claim to be. DigiNotar was targeted by a terrorist group who targeted the Dutch company because the group felt the Dutch government was complicit in a specific event involving the massacre of Muslim civilians during the 1995 Bosnian war. While DigiNotar was not affiliated with the Dutch government, they were the certificate issuer for the government. The attackers used their illegitimate access to generate several hundred fake certificates signed by DigiNotar. The public release of this information resulted in an immediate loss of trust from the marketplace.

Based on post-breach forensic analysis, the breach likely began in June 2011, and was uncovered in July 2011. By September 2011, DigiNotar had filed for bankruptcy and was no longer in business. This is an extreme example because a company like DigiNotar is far more dependent on public trust based on their business model than most organizations, but there are countless other examples of organizations closing their doors forever in the wake of a cyber-attack. The simple truth is that if a business loses the trust of their target market, they will suffer significant loss of revenue. In most cases, publicly disclosed breaches result in a loss of public trust, regardless of the circumstances. Many of the victims will never recover.

Security Humanistics

Throughout this chapter we have examined the people who cause organizations to lose data and categorized them in an effort to define their behavior profiles so the risks they present can be more easily identified and mitigated when a security program is being built. With respect to external attackers, regardless of the threat actor group and the resources at their disposal, it is generally true that the people behind the attacks are smart and adaptable. We, as human beings, have many shortcomings when compared to technologies. For instance, I cannot process several billion calculations per second like many computer processors can. I do, however, possess the capability for rational thought and the innate ability to adapt to the situation and circumstances around me that those same processors do not. The most successful attackers from any group harness the inherent strengths that people have while using processes and technologies to support their weaknesses.

Successful Information Security programs must harness the power of people as well. The study of how we effectively leverage human beings as an integral part of a comprehensive Information Security program has been called "Security Humanistics" by InteliSecure founder Robert Eggebrecht. The central premise is that the only way to respond appropriately to an enemy employing smart and adaptable human beings is to ensure our security programs are designed to leverage the strength of the human mind as well.

People, Process, and Technology

One of the most universally understood, yet poorly implemented ideas inside of the Information Security community is the concept of people, process, and technology. Many organizations understand that they need all three. What seems to be lacking is the understanding of the strengths and weaknesses of each and how to build a program that utilizes all three to support each other, capitalizing on the strengths of each while supporting each of their weaknesses.

Before exploring people, process, and technology in detail, I would like to share a story that drives to the heart of why companies, specifically American ones, seem to fail at implementing this concept effectively inside their programs. After speaking to the Pittsburgh ISACA chapter at the Rivers Casino one afternoon, I was approached by a Polish American woman who had some insight to share with me. I had just presented about Information Security programs, lamenting the fact that far too many programs I have interacted with took a technology-centric approach. She told me that there was a good reason for why American executives prefer to select technology solutions over solving people and process problems, and it is ingrained in Americans from the day they first start school. Her juxtaposition between her education in Poland and her daughter's education in the United States would prove to be insightful.

She started by explaining that in Poland, there is no such thing as a multiple choice test. All testing in Poland gave a student a question to which they must write out a response. Her daughter's education in America was predicated on multiple choice tests in which her daughter was asked to select the best answer from the choices presented.

In America, there are plenty of good reasons for multiple choice testing. First, there is a desire to ensure all students are treated fairly. If all students are presented with the same options, one of which is correct for each question, there is less room for bias to affect student scoring than if the questions are scored subjectively. Essay answers, on the other hand provide large amounts of subjectivity for the teacher and introduce more opportunities for bias to exist in the classroom, which is something the American education system is committed to avoiding. Second, there is a desire to compare large numbers of students across wide-ranging geographies through standardized testing. It is nearly impossible to provide standardized testing without allowing for multiple choice testing. Finally, the school system in America does not allow for families to choose which school their children attend inside the public school system. In order to ensure every school provides a similar level of education, then, it is necessary to have teachers teach to a multiple choice standard rather than one that would require the teachers to comprehend the material at a higher level, like the system in Poland would require. My intent in listing the above reasons for why American schools need multiple choice testing is to ensure it is clear that the following paragraph is not an indictment of the American school system, but simply an observation that offers an explanation as to why American graduates think in ways that are different from their peers on a global stage, and are sometimes detrimental to them when attempting to counteract global and evolving threats.

Solving people and process problems require critical thinking. In fact, if you were to put a people or a process problem to a child in the Polish school system, it would resonate immediately with them because they would be presented a problem, and asked to create a solution in a very similar fashion to how they were tested during their formative years. In contrast, the problems Americans are accustomed to solving are much more similar to technology problems. When we endeavor to solve a technology problem, we are generally presented with options, in the form of technology vendors, and asked to select the vendor that best suits our needs, very similar to a multiple choice test. In fact, many American students are presented with very few problems they need to solve outside of multiple choice until they reach college, which many Americans never attend. There are certainly exceptions to the rule; some American high school teachers rely heavily on essay tests, and some American universities rely on multiple choice tests, but in general, Americans are far more comfortable selecting from a menu of available solutions than creating solutions for problems with no options to choose from. In my opinion, this dynamic is a major contributing factor to the situation that exists, especially in America, where companies have purchased copious amounts of technologies without building the programs to support them. Although this example is only a theory and one possible solution to the puzzle, it is interesting to consider differences like this one when attempting to understand why certain issues exist and why people operate as they do throughout their lives.

People – What Would You Do for a Klondike Bar?

People, in the context of an Information Security program, are generally the weakest link. Information Security Awareness Training is not futile and has been demonstrated to have a tangible impact on the relative security posture of an organization. However, the undeniable truth is that the majority of users who have access to Critical Information Assets have no idea what the assets or their credentials are worth. They perceive the data they interact with on a daily basis as a commodity, since interacting with it is a normal part of their business functions. If you use something every day, how rare or special would it seem to you? If this frustrates you from a management perspective, remember that not everyone has a reason or impetus to see the forest for the trees. Proper valuation is often a matter of perspective. As previously discussed, these problems exist not because people are stupid or negligent, but simply because their area of expertise lies outside the Information Security realm. It is incumbent upon the security program to support these people with processes and technologies that can protect them from making mistakes due to their lack of awareness of the threats they face or the value of the information they interact with.

For example, I used to visit my wife while she was working at a hospital doing scheduling. To her, scheduling patients for their next appointment was a pretty normal activity. When I visited, her door was generally open and there was no privacy filter on her computer screen. As she went about her day, people could overhear her using names or see her screen as she was working to schedule patients to see their doctors. In her mind, she was not exposing Protected Health Information because she never said on the phone or put on the screen what they had been diagnosed with. However, she worked in the part of the hospital that was a blood cancer clinic, so simply saying a patient's name and scheduling them with a doctor in that particular clinic was a pretty reliable indicator that they had some form of blood cancer. My wife is a very intelligent woman, but the processes and technologies deployed in the clinic did not help her keep this type of information secure, and privacy training was clearly needed. Further, the program did not support her in order to make her aware that what she was doing represented a violation of her patients' privacy rights.

The other side of people as they relate to Information Security, particularly with respect to Security Humanistics, is the people that are responsible for building and maintaining the Information Security program. As previously discussed, attackers have smart and adaptable human beings on their side, so Information Security teams need the same if they wish to be successful. People working directly on a security program need to be knowledgeable of the processes and technologies that are deployed in order to be successful. Those technologies and processes also need to be selected and designed to support people as they work to secure the environment. Remember, implementing a security program that makes end users miserable is the easiest way to make sure that the security program is circumvented and results in failure. People are often simultaneously the security program's weakest link and greatest asset. The importance of good people in security programs cannot be overstated.

The other side of the people equation is the end user who interacts with sensitive data daily and likely does not have a security background. They must also be thoroughly trained on their processes and the parts of their everyday processes that are designed to keep sensitive data secure.

Culture Wars

Many of the organizations that I have worked with that have been the most successful pay special attention to their culture. Creating a "culture of compliance" or a "culture of security" is often a difficult undertaking, but one that yields extraordinarily results when effectively applied. Integrity at the individual level is doing the right thing even when no one is watching. Your corporate culture dictates what the right thing to do is for a person in the eyes of their peers. Additionally, a company's workers must know, understand, and truly believe that reporting gaps in security will result in praise, reward, and never punishment. Integrity is very important in every organization because it is social norms that influence values in individuals, and adults often spend more time with their coworkers than their own families. This is not to say that people's core values change at work, but even individuals who have never done a certain thing before might begin to do so if it is cultural acceptable in an environment.

Changing culture is not easy. Most employees resist change and have worked for previous employers where mistakes were punished through disciplinary action or termination. Positive culture change requires a commitment from the top down, constant communication, consistent corrective action (when needed), and a demand for excellence. In short, it requires strong and effective leadership, and it is a slow process. Many books have been written on the topic of building a positive corporate culture, and there are many approaches that have proven effective over time. I do not have a preference on how it is accomplished in order to support a comprehensive security program, but creating a culture that is aware of the dangers that exist and the value of the assets an organization possesses is a key element for an effective program.

The Talent Gap

Based on my experience, there is a severe shortage of experienced and effective security personnel that an organization can hire, for many reasons. The focus on Information Security is new due to the advancement of the Internet and the availability of mass data in a digital form. Training and education for both corporations, universities, and the general public is improving but is still behind the curve. Also, consider all of the factors that we've previously discussed; when a breach occurs Information Security employees become unemployed, non-security employees resist security improvements and process changes, return on investment is difficult to quantify for general business process improvements (as massive breaches are uncommon), and targeted attacks are almost impossible to prevent. These factors do not facilitate vocational interest when there are many less-risky career options.

Additionally, many of the knowledgeable security professionals exploit the talent shortage and move from job to job, commanding a higher salary with each move. These types of "security mercenaries" make it very difficult to maintain continuity in a comprehensive Information Security program, and only further exasperate the problem. Further, in some locations, it is difficult to attract top security talent at all. The talent tends to congregate in heavily populated metropolises or desirable locations since their salaries are normally high enough to afford them a decent quality of life even in areas where the cost of living is exorbitant.

The talent gap in Information Security is real and growing.

Interestingly, all of the reasons above have led many organizations to seek an outsourced security solution. This solution is a remarkable change from ten years ago, where the mention of outsourcing these critical duties was not even within consideration, which makes perfect sense. If this information is this critical to my business, how can I trust another company to hire the correct people to understand my business and protect my data, when I can hardly do so myself? There has been a fundamental change in thinking recently, however, which explains a shift toward outsourcing as much as possible, including critical data and applications in the form of cloud technologies. Outsourcing these critical pieces of infrastructure would have been unthinkable not long ago.

When building a program in accordance with the ideas outlined in this book, however, a traditional tiered managed services model is often insufficient. These types of programs require intimate knowledge of the business and a model that is more similar to an extension of the business, rather than the traditional reactive, ticket-driven service that has been the hallmark of Managed Security Service Providers (MSSPs) traditionally focused on signature-based technologies such as Intrusion Detection and Prevention Systems (IDS/IPS), traditional Antivirus, and Firewalls. Next-Generation MSSPs are starting to emerge that can address the people problem presented in a more collaborative way than traditional providers. These newer service offerings provide a good option to organizations seeking to solve the talent gap while still building, operating, and maintaining a world-class Information Security program.

Process

Effective processes drive technology decisions in effective security programs, not the other way around. The technology should be selected to fit the business rather than business processes being amended to fit the capabilities of a selected technology. Far too often, technology drives decision making inside an organization, which makes sense considering the historical emphasis to stop external threats by implementing technologies such as firewalls. However, in today's age, this technology-based decision is the wrong way to approach Information Security. The state of Information Security technology currently is such that if you have a business requirement that is not being filled by a certain technology, it is highly likely that making a different technology choice and applying a proper process with skilled people will solve that problem. This is the reason why the Information Security Model presented in chapter 4 is important to implement appropriately. In the model, you will define strategy and tactics prior to selecting a technology. I firmly believe this is the proper approach, but far too often I see organizations purchase a technology first and then engage with someone like myself to help them fit the technology into their process. This is similar to purchasing a hammer only to find out you really needed a screwdriver. Purchasing a tool before you have defined what you are trying to accomplish is ineffective in any context. It seems that that mistake is made disproportionally inside Information Security circles, but my proximity to the problem and my frame of reference may color my thinking on the topic.

Process also needs to be designed to support people. People are fallible by definition. People also need to be trained on the process to execute it effectively, and need to buy in to the program in order for the program to succeed. Organizations that are effective at modifying human behavior often deploy processes that are designed to have minimal impact on the end user, or ideally, actually provide a productivity benefit while simultaneously increasing security posture. People, like electricity, can generally be relied upon to take the path of least resistance, so providing a process that is simultaneously more secure and more efficient is a true "win-win."

Secure Process Design

In the early days of software development, until the recent past, software was designed to perform a certain function. Only after the software was finished and released to the marketplace, was it examined for security flaws. The flaws that were found were then patched after the development cycle. As security became more of a concern, a concept called secure software design was developed to ensure the software was being developed with security in mind. It started to become widely accepted that functionality was not the only concern.

I posit that business process design is ripe to make the same transition. When building business process, productivity should not be the only concern. Rather, security should have a seat at the table in order to ensure that the process is built not only to accomplish a stated goal, but also to do so in the most secure manner possible.

For example, the most expedient way for a hospital to transfer patient information to a billing facility may be through an unencrypted File Transfer Protocol (FTP). The transmissions in this example are likely to contain multiple records in a batch. Depending on the size of the organization, these transfers could become very large. Unencrypted transmissions are not secured and, in many cases, are violations of regulations designed to protect the consumer. Rather than deploying the FTP technology and later attempting to secure the transfer, understanding security as a requirement while designing the process may have yielded a transfer method that was just as expedient but also did not expose the information to undue risk. This is an obvious example, but the idea is that all business processes be designed with two objectives: accomplish the objective as quickly as possible, while protecting the Critical Information Assets throughout the process. I am confident this approach would yield much better results.

Building secure processes also supports culture shifts within the psyche of the people inside of an organization. The phrase "we've always done it this way" is often dangerous in business, especially in the context of security. However, if processes are designed to be secure from their inception, the way users have always performed a task becomes the proper method from a security perspective.

For example, I worked with a manufacturing client that was making an effort to bolster their security posture with respect to Intellectual Property, in general, but specifically their trade secrets. Many people don't know this, but trade secrets are the only form of Intellectual Property that does not have any legal protection. A trade secret is only protected by the extent to which the organization who owns it is able to keep a secret. Why would an organization choose to use a trade secret then, rather than a copyright, a trademark, or a patent? The answer lies in the concept of public domain. Any piece of Intellectual Property that has legal protection also has an expiration date. There have been changes to Intellectual Property law for some high-profile companies to be able to extend internationally recognized trademarks that demonstrate the problem. The most recognized example is Disney. Mickey Mouse has been on the verge of going into the public domain several times, which would be disastrous for Disney. This is the reason that many things, including recipes for popular products such as Coca Cola, Pepsi, Kentucky Fried Chicken, and many others are trade secrets and not protected in other ways.

My client was beginning the process of making changes to their manufacturing process in order to take advantage of cheap labor in China. But in order to do so, it would be necessary for their trade secrets to be transferred to China. Instead of transferring that data to China in a traditional way, they designed their process in a secure manner. They would use encryption that could only be decrypted when a user was connected back to the corporate network through a VPN using two-factor authentication. The file could not be opened without retrieving the key, which resided at corporate headquarters in the United States. Had the process been in place using a more traditional method, it would have been much more difficult to change to this process later, as is evidenced by other manufacturing clients I have worked with who have attempted to do so, with mixed results.

The idea of behavioral inertia is very real. Essentially, just like physical objects, human beings will continue to do things the way they always have unless great effort is exerted to modify the behavior. Secure Process Design is a methodology designed to use behavioral inertia to the benefit of the security program rather than to its detriment.

Technology

Technology plays a critical role in all of our lives. It has enhanced and streamlined countless daily activities and has improved the quality of life of countless people around the globe. Overdependence on technology has also caused harm to basic human skill sets as well. One does not have to look further than Facebook posts to see how technology can have a negative effect on how people communicate with each other. Surely, there are benefits to social media platforms, but basic knowledge of effective communication has eroded as technology has become a crutch for many individuals. The same could be said for countless business applications as well.

In general, technology has a net positive impact on productivity, but relying solely on technology rather than as a triumvirate of people, process, and technology is a recipe for failure that has manifested itself in countless breaches around the globe. Technology certainly has its proper placer in a program, but choosing to implement a technology as an easy solution that allows an organization to ignore the often more difficult challenges of designing processes and educating people is ineffective and misguided. Regardless, the vast majority of organizations possess plenty of technology to secure their environment, but it is rare that the technology is deployed, integrated, and operated properly.

What is the proper role of technology in an organization? Technology is good at many things, and just like people or process, it has some inherent strengths and weaknesses. Technology is very good at completing complex calculations in real or near real time. It is also very effective at scanning and matching large volumes of information. It is not good at prioritizing which functions it should or should not perform, identifying and solving business problems, or determining the intent of human behavior. Therefore, it is often best to build the process and engage the right people prior to making a technology decision. Far too often, organizations choose to approach a technology purchase in the opposite order.

Look at All My Features!

A core problem leading to the prevalence of shelfware technologies, meaning technologies that are never deployed and utilized to their full potential, is the way they are often bought and sold. It is important to understand whenever there is a failure in the way things are sold, that failure is shared by the buyers, as they influence the sellers. Similarly, sellers often lament the fact that every organization seems to buy at the end of a quarter or of a year, but it was the sellers who conditioned them to do so by offering the best incentives during that time period. The following is not purely an indictment of technology vendors, since these tactics would quickly cease should they become ineffective.

Technology vendors often sell their products, in conjunction with their counterparts in marketing, by first inventing or recycling buzzwords. They will use whatever resonates the best in the marketplace at the time. At the time of this writing, some of the most popular buzzwords are "cloud," "big data," "analytics," and "next-generation." Then the vendor will build a list of features and some talking points related to why customers should want the features they are presenting. Essentially, the vendors are introducing the business problems they can solve without really finding out if they are relevant to the customer.

On the buying side, customers and prospects hear the buzzwords and they hype around the offering and get interested in the product for all of the wrong reasons. They take the list of features the vendors told them they should want and seek out parts of the organization that may have some of the business problems the technology can solve.

A Different Approach

The approach is broken. We explored the Security Intelligence model in much more depth in chapter 4, but it is important to understand for the purpose of this conversation that in my opinion, no organization should ever evaluate technologies without first working with the proper resources inside the organization to establish business and functional requirements for the system. Doing so not only ensures a better fit with respect to technology, but also forces the organization to think about what they are trying to accomplish in a more holistic fashion. This approach leads to better outcomes for both the customer and the vendor.

Business Requirements

Business requirements should be gathered from as wide of an array of business unit leadership as possible. In the context of security, these requirements should be gathered on a continual basis whether or not there is a technology purchase being considered. With a comprehensive list of current business requirements, the security team can array different types of technologies to the requirements and prioritize the needs of the business without falling victim to the "shiny object syndrome" or simply chasing after the "next big thing." Once the purchase is deemed necessary from a business perspective and a preliminary budget is determined, functional requirements may be developed.

Functional Requirements

Functional requirements should relate to one or more business requirements. Essentially, the more technical team members should be allowed to develop the functional requirements of a technology, but there should be rules that dictate that the functional requirements be related to a current or future business requirement. If there are functional elements the Information Security team would like in a product that is not related to a business requirement, this is not, in fact, a requirement, but a "nice to have."

Many successful organizations build a spreadsheet or other template to track all business and functional requirements and their relationships to each other. Once those requirements have been documented and ratified by the team members, technology selection may begin.

Technology Selection

Selecting technologies once business and functional requirements have been established becomes a far less subjective and a more structured process than selecting technology for technology's sake. When vendors are invited to present their technologies in this scenario, they will know exactly what problems the organization intends to solve and will have the opportunity to tailor their presentations to the requirements. Generally, the result is a much more thorough evaluation, a better fit for the customer, and a shorter sales cycle for the vendor. It truly is a situation where all parties benefit from a more comprehensive and methodical approach.

Back to Basics

Solving the people problem requires a return to tried and true best practices. Throughout the years, many organizations have been turning to increasingly complex solutions where simple best practices would have been much more effective. Table 6-1 shows a table of famous breaches where the damage could have been mitigated significantly by the proper application of a best practice.

Table 6-1. *Breaches and Best Practices That Could Have Been Beneficial*

Name of Company	Beneficial Best Practice
eBay	Concept of Least Privilege
Sony Pictures	Records and Information Management
Target	Third-Party Access Control
Saudi Aramco	Separation of Duties

eBay and Concept of Least Privilege

The example of Concept of Least Privilege and the eBay breach has been explained in detail earlier in this chapter. The eBay example is a great example of why the Concept of Least Privilege is important. It is a concept that is easy in theory, and much more difficult to implement. That said, Concept of Least Privilege is a great practice to minimize the potential harm that could come to an organization based on the compromise of a single set of credentials or a single identity.

Sony Pictures and Records and Information Management

The attack on Sony Pictures is well known and has been referenced both in this book and many other places. The part of the Sony breach that is often overlooked is the Records and Information Management implications.

Records and Information Management (RIM) is a best practice related to retention periods for information. Many organizations look at RIM as a mandate to maintain records, but from a security perspective, it is also important to understand what information should not be retained, and to destroy that information. Most organizations keep the information they are mandated to keep, but few aggressively target and destroy obsolete or expired information. As a result, the amount of data the average organization is storing is often ever expanding. The Sony case showed just how much damage over-retention can cause.

Throughout the details becoming known in the Sony case, many people were focused on who did it and why they did it. Many speculated based on the type of information, with seemingly little business value, that the attack was perpetrated only to harm Sony as an organization. It is my personal opinion that is likely the right answer to the wrong question. The real question is this: why was Sony storing that information in the first place? This is the question some organizations are starting to ask for the first time due to the harm caused to Sony by over-retention.

Target and Third-Party Access Control

The Target case is an example to support the need for both Third-Party Access Control and Separation of Duties. Reports say that the initial intrusion into Target's network was accomplished by an organization that compromised credentials from an air conditioning and heating provider. Any time a third party is granted access to systems, that third party's security policies should be vetted as part of that due diligence, which would comply with the best practice of effective Third-Party Vendor Management.

Third-Party Access Management is important, but the Concept of Least Privilege question revolves around why would that company need access to Target systems? Especially a level of access that would allow attackers to install software on Target systems that could then be used to push malicious software to payment systems. Organizations should grant the Least Privilege necessary for trusted third parties as part of their Access Control program.

A more effective Third-Party Access Control program combined with a Least Privilege review of the access granted would have likely prevented, or at least significantly mitigated, one of the most famous breaches in history.

Saudi Aramco and Separation of Duties

The best practice known as Separation of Duties is defined earlier in this chapter, but as a reminder, it refers to the practice of ensuring no single person, or in the case or Aramco - system - has access to everything that the person or system needs to perform a task. It is often used to prevent fraud, but in a security context, the idea is to prevent a single set of compromised credentials or a single compromised system from causing an inordinate amount of damage.

The Oil and Gas industry has embraced Separation of Duties, especially as it relates to systems, much better than many other industries. Most oil companies separate networks containing things like drilling rigs, research equipment, and other connected devices related to the operation of finding and extracting oil, known as Operational Technology (OT), from networks containing more traditional systems that are referred to as Information Technology (IT). This separation has been widely embraced in Oil and Gas for a number of years, until Enterprise Resource Planning (ERP) systems became widely deployed technology.

ERP systems are designed to manage business processes and automate certain functions. For example, if there is a business process related to the sale of a barrel of oil, it may automate the billing for that oil as well as the shipping of that barrel the moment that order is placed in the system. In order to perform this level of business process automation, the ERP system was granted access to all systems in the Aramco case. This effectively allowed a point for a terrorist attacker to pivot from the IT network to the OT network and cause financial harm to Aramco by disabling computers responsible for things such as processing payment and dispensing products to customers.

Had the Separation of Duties between the OT network and the IT network been upheld, it would've resulted in degraded functionality for the ERP system, but likely a less impactful attack on the company. This is a great example of Separation of Duties in a security context.

There are far more examples, but the general premise is that the vast majority of breaches start with people and are actively perpetrated by people. While people can be the weakest link, they can also be the greatest asset for an organization when they are properly supported by processes rooted in best practices. Those processes are most effective when monitored and enforced by technologies that have the capability to stop harm from coming to the organization in real time when proper process is not observed. People perform their best when they understand the processes and technologies that are put in place to support them and they truly believe in the mission of the organization. There is no single solution that will secure an organization. Nor is there a magical process that will solve all of the challenges an organization will face. There is certainly not a perfect person that I am aware of walking the earth today. However, when people, process, and technology are deployed effectively to support each other, organizations can achieve unparalleled levels of risk reduction. Figure 6-1 shows a Venn diagram of the strengths and weaknesses of each of people, process, and technology, and how they all fit together to form effective protection.

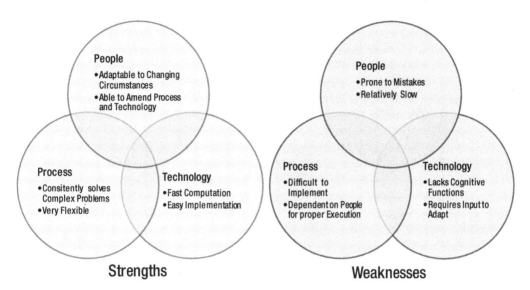

Figure 6-1. *People, Process, and Technology Venn Diagram (Left Diagram lists strengths, right lists weaknesses)*

Conclusion

People, process, and technology have to be deployed effectively and work together in concert to create an effective IT security program. In general, people are the weakest link, but only because the process and technology are not adequately supporting the people in the majority of implementations I have seen. In reality, since all three are codependent, one area cannot be lacking without also having failures in the other areas. In order to solve the people problem, process and technology must play a major role.

CHAPTER 7

■ ■ ■

Assigning Accountability

When it comes to privacy and accountability, people always demand the former for themselves and the latter for everyone else.

—David Brin

I have spent a significant portion of my time since 2012 working with customers and speaking to audiences about the fact that Information Security is a business problem. Many executives were resistant to the idea because they did not want to be responsible for something they did not understand. Further, as long as senior executives could turn a blind eye to the problems presented by Information Security and simply fire their Chief Information Security Officer if something happened, they did not see it as something they needed to concern themselves with. Target changed everything.

Who Is Responsible for Security?

In the wake of the massive Target data breach, Target CEO Gregg Steinhafel, who spent thirty-five years at Target and six of those years acting as their CEO, abruptly resigned. His resignation made a lot of waves inside of the business community as the timing of his departure was quite suspect. Still, the argument could be made that his departure had to do with other concerns inside the business and not the breach directly, at least until the rest of the aftermath began to play out. The next domino to fall was Target's CIO. If his ouster alone was not a clear indicator that senior leadership, investors, and board members were expecting a stronger security direction from their Chief Information Officer, the fact he was replaced by Bob DeRodes, who has a strong security background as well as several executive leadership roles on his résumé, made it abundantly clear that security was to be an executive responsibility inside of Target moving forward. In perhaps the most shocking personnel decision made after the massive breach, significant pressure from investors led to the ouster of seven board members. Anything that can cause seven board members, a CEO, and a CIO to lose their job is clearly a business problem. When people ask me when security became a business problem, I would argue that it always has been; but when asked when the world took notice of security as a business problem, in my opinion it was sometime in May of 2014, when the long-tenured CEO of Target lost his job because of a security breach.

The Target case featured a multitude of mistakes that were made by many people throughout the organization that led the attack to be far more damaging than its level of sophistication would warrant. Still, the notion that business leaders would be held accountable for something related to Information Security was relatively foreign in the enterprise business community. There have been subsequent cases of breaches and the precedent set by Target has proven to be more of a trend than an isolated incident. It does not mean that CEOs are fired any time there is a data breach, and I am not advocating that they should be. There are many times where breaches could not have reasonably been prevented regardless of the level of care given to the Information Security program, or breaches concern less financially impactful information that may not have warranted the attention of senior executives. It does, however, mean that the failure at the highest

© Jeremy Wittkop 2016
J. Wittkop, *Building a Comprehensive IT Security Program*, DOI 10.1007/978-1-4842-2053-5_7

levels of leadership to define and protect information that could cause financial harm or reputational loss to the organization is a dereliction of duty and an offense that could result in immediate dismissal. This is a palpable shift in accountability for this problem, and one that requires business leaders to delegate responsibility throughout the business instead of trying to depend solely on the Information Technology or Information Security departments to protect them with tiny budgets and understaffed teams.

In many government and military circles, there is a phrase that says "Communications Security (COMSEC) is everyone's responsibility." That mantra is beginning to be adopted by private enterprise as well. The idea that a small subset of employees that have very little day-to-day interactions with business units could comprehensively protect all Critical Information Assets in an organization without business unit engagement is laughable. The role of the security department should be to build a framework for business units to operate within and provide subject matter expertise and guidance to enable business units to secure their most important data. A healthy program features mandatory protections for assets that are subject to regulations and assets that the executive leadership team has deemed critical as well as capabilities for business units to designate levels of sensitivity for assets outside of the scope of corporate security governance and have that information be protected appropriately. The latter has given rise to Data Classification products as a security tool.

The Rise of Data Classification

Data Classification tools like those developed by Titus Inc. were originally developed in order to mark documents for secrecy and clearance levels inside of government organizations. In private enterprise, Data Classification was often a dead-end project that seldom yielded valuable results. It was for this reason that I was originally a Data Classification skeptic. In order to explain the rise of Data Classification as a security tool, I will share my Data Classification journey as many other security professionals have taken similar journeys from skeptic to proponent, and many more are likely to do the same in the coming months and years.

The Genesis of My Skepticism

At the time I was first introduced to the idea of Data Classification as a project, I was myopically focused on the benefits of DLP solutions when deployed as part of a comprehensive content- and context-aware Information Security Program. Many organizations that were evaluating Data Loss Prevention as a solution, which was far less common at the time, were simultaneously looking at the value of Data Classification. There was much debate of the seeming chicken or egg scenario involving Data Loss Prevention and Data Classification. Some people were of the opinion DLP should be implemented first, followed by a Data Classification Program. This approach worked fine for me because it did not interfere with my objective. The second group posited that deploying Data Classification first was the best approach. This vexed me terribly.

I looked at Data Classification as a utopian idea. Essentially, it was a great idea that no one really knew how to implement effectively, and I was beginning to believe it to be impossible to implement in the real world. I had never seen an environment where all of the data was classified in neat little labels and protected based on those labels, and disposed of based on an expiration date like expired food at a supermarket. It is not that I did not agree with the premise; it's that the execution was invariably flawed.

Effective Deployment of Data Classification Tools

There are two parts to building an effective Data Classification Program. First you must have a user-friendly mechanism to classify data as it is created. Second, you must have a methodology to classify all the data that already exists. The former is generally the first step and it could be done by some organizations effectively. The latter was the portion that no one could seem to figure out.

My primary problem with Data Classification was the fact that people were terrible at it. Essentially, there were very few organizations that actually got their programs off the ground. To me, Data Classification was synonymous with the bridge-to-nowhere project. It was essentially a time and money pit where nothing was ever accomplished and it only served to delay what I was trying to get accomplished. I shouted from every mountaintop I could find that Data Classification was a great idea with little practical application. In many cases I was right.

The *idea* of Data Classification, though, was a good one. It is difficult to identify the sensitivity of data just by looking at a file, especially if you are not an expert in the content. The people who created the asset, or who interact with it the most, are in the best position to determine how sensitive the asset is, and therefore, drive the methods in which the asset is treated by the organization. Data Classification had the potential to involve users in a security and data retention program in a meaningful way, which was unprecedented and impractical previously. There had to be a better way to accomplish this goal.

Data Classification Technology

Data Classification products were just beginning to emerge at that time, and while they provided a system for labeling data, I had not yet come across a methodology that worked. Looking back on the situation, I was making the same argument against Data Classification that people were making against Data Loss Prevention. InteliSecure, Inc. (then BEW Global) had successfully built a methodology to effectively deploy and manage Data Loss Prevention to get business value out of the tool in a way that was previously not realistic for many organizations. I had completely ignored emerging technologies such as Titus, Bolden James, and Secure Islands that were not only developing software solutions but effective methodologies for the effective deployment and use of their solutions.

The people I first encountered from the Data Classification product development space were employees of Titus and are some of the most intelligent and practical people I have ever met, especially within the software development space. Many developers do not have enough experience in the real world to develop their products in a way that makes them easy to deploy and maintain. The Titus team was different, and their approach to business problems helped to change my negative disposition toward Data Classification. Their technology solution was rooted in their consultancy practice, which predated the software company. The founders of Titus clearly understood the challenges their customers were facing and set out to create a solution to a business problem rather than to compile an impressive list of features that may or may not have impactful practical applications.

■ **Note** This example is not intended to discount the other technology vendors in the Data Classification space. The products operate in a relatively similar fashion, and it is likely there are similar anecdotes related to those solutions. However, the specific experience that shifted my perspective was my experience with the team at Titus.

It was my own self-interest that led Data Classification products and myself to cross paths for the first time. I needed a solution for the challenges being presented by International Data Protection regulations that were emerging in Europe and the Asia Pacific regions. The Titus product specifically, and Data Classification products in general, had the ability to use X-headers to classify messages, which I could use to force my DLP solutions to ignore messages that were marked personal by employees, and which put me on the right side of many of the Works Councils that were beginning to hold more sway in support of these emerging Data Protection regulations. Suddenly, the effective deployment of Data Loss Prevention solutions in certain regions required integration with a Data Classification solution, since certain governments had mandated that users be given a mechanism with which they could mark their communications private and have that privacy respected by their organization.

Data Classification and DLP: Better Together

Around the same time, I started to reevaluate my perception of Data Classification. Rob Eggebrecht and Chuck Bloomquist strongly encouraged me to read pretty much everything Jim Collins ever wrote, as his works helped to shape their careers and visions for their own personal growth. Jim Collins has written many best-selling business books such as *Good to Great, Built to Last, Great by Choice*, and *Why the Mighty Fall*. The books each have their own focus but they all revolve around the central theme of examining current and past companies looking for the specific decisions and habits that separate companies that are good in a specific time period from companies that are great and stand the test of time, often through several generations and through many iterations of leadership. While rereading Collins's work, I had a thought related to his concept of "the genius of the AND" versus "the tyranny of the OR." Essentially, the concept is there is genius in looking at doing both things, in situations where a choice is generally presented. Instead of doing Data Classification or DLP, why don't we do Data Classification and DLP! They could be better together! Further, if we could combine the efforts of creating the programs for both, perhaps we could find the economies of scale necessary to make the entire engagement cost effective and high value to a variety of organizations!

Throughout my time deploying Data Classification and Data Loss Prevention systems together, I began to realize the unforeseen result that blending these two products had on the topic at hand: assigning accountability within the organization. Data Loss Prevention tools are generally a "top-down" approach to Information Security. There is a central console where all of the rules are housed and information is reviewed. This type of arrangement is appropriate for assets that are deemed critical across the organization and are well understood by the security teams. However, there was also a need for a "bottom-up" approach that enabled individual business units to assign levels of sensitivity to data as it was created.

The essential premise is relatively simple. The organization dictates three or four generic sensitivity labels such as "Internal Use Only," "Restricted," or "Confidential." Each classification level then has rules with respect to how information in that classification level can be stored, used, or transmitted. Security tools are then programmed to read these sensitivity labels and enforce the rules related to the classifications. Each of the solutions works slightly differently, but the majority require users to classify new or modified information starting at a specific point in time. The solutions are more divergent with respect to how they handle legacy data that exists inside an organization that will not be modified, but must be retained. The approach to those pieces of data range from accepting the risk associated with it to performing scans of historical data with the intention of achieving 100% classification of stored data. Classification labels allow business units to protect their sensitive information without having to build these data elements into the larger corporate governance infrastructure. Effective programs also build in responses based on these sensitivity levels. Historically, many organizations have expected employees to protect sensitive information without empowering their employees with the tools to do so or giving them a mechanism to communicate effectively data sensitivity across the enterprise. This process is a good first step toward arming employees with the tools they need to remain compliant with corporate policy and demonstrate that compliance.

Shifting Accountability

The global marketplace has begun to shift accountability for Information Security failures from technologies and security professionals to business leaders as evidenced by the board response to the Target breach as well as similar responses in subsequent breaches. Security has truly become a business problem.

Simply stating that security is a business problem may be accurate, but it is not enough to actually solve the problem. Businesses solve problems by first mandating they be solved from the highest echelons of leadership. The board is generally the highest level of leadership inside of an organization, especially a publicly traded one.

Establishing Mandates Using Earnings Reports

In most global markets, publicly traded companies must report their earnings to the marketplace. In the United States, one report that is relatively well known is the Form 10-K report, which is usually filed annually and is a way for the board and executive leadership teams to communicate their intent and their performance to shareholders. The Form 10-K report is regulated in format, so they all have the same sections, regardless of the company or the industry. Section 1A requires the organization to list their risk factors. Increasingly, I have been able to find listed risk factors in those reports that relate to Information Security. By doing so, you have a written mandate from the board that is being presented to shareholders to secure the company's information. That is a large burden, but a great opportunity for Information Security professionals to demonstrate to their counterparts, who may not have a deep understanding of Information Security, that the problem is real and understood by the highest levels of the business. InteliSecure founder and former CEO Rob Eggebrecht liked to define his role as CEO as "providing guidance, budget, and air cover." I think that is a great way to define executive leadership in terms of Information Security as well. A truly supportive executive team will provide all three in order to enable their organization to be more secure.

Many times after I speak, I hear from frustrated Information Security professionals who are in organizations that don't seem to care about Information Security, at least one level above them. I tell them to look at their Form 10-K report and see if they find a mandate for Information Security. If they do, make sure their leadership is aware of the mandate. They may have a divergent opinion of how to execute the intent from you, but if they ignore it completely, simply wait until they are replaced. If the organization does not take Information Security seriously all the way to the top levels, I generally suggest they look for another job, because efforts to educate will fall on too many deaf ears to make organizational change a realistic possibility. I strongly believe that organizations that do not take Information Security concerns seriously are unlikely to survive in the long term due to the growing emphasis on this topic. The first secretary of the U.S. Department of Homeland Security Tom Ridge said, "Your Information Security strategy must be part of your business strategy" when asked what advice he had for America's CEOs. Those who choose not to heed that advice generally do not last in the globally connected marketplace. I expect this trend to not only continue, but to grow in the coming years as cyber-attacks become more prevalent, and the patience for executives who fail to take Information Security on the part of board members continues to wane.

It's MY Problem, Now What?

The first step to solving any problem is to admit you have one. Once someone inside the organization takes ownership, it is important that they know exactly what to do. The first six chapters of this book can be used as a guideline for building the program. There are many roles and responsibilities, however, that must be defined in order for the program to be successful. It is important to remind participants throughout the process that this is a business problem and requires business involvement throughout in order to be successful.

Information Security programs are different from other business initiatives in content, but they do not need to be wildly dissimilar in terms of execution. The steps to creating an Information Security program from a macro perspective are quite similar to anything else. First there must be a charter that establishes what is to be established and why. Second, a budget must be identified. Third, a plan must be built with milestones that identify the steps and time frames required to get from the current state to the desired end state. Since programs do not end by their nature, the desired end state could be the desired state at the end of any given month, quarter, or year in the form of a "road map" or a series of milestones with set evaluation dates.

Flexibility within a Framework

I was recently reminded by a visit to an organization of a common mantra used in many organizations that I've always loved: "Flexibility within a Framework." Many organizations mistakenly think that they must choose between a completely flexible environment that doesn't allow for discipline or a rigid framework that does not allow for flexibility. You can do both and allow people freedom and flexibility inside of a framework that provides boundaries.

Many frameworks exist to provide guidance to organizations for building a comprehensive Information Security program. Many are location and industry specific, but one that seems to be the basis of many others and is internationally recognized is International Standards Organization (ISO) 27001. ISO establishes the guidelines for how to build a Quality Management System (QMS) and what types of controls should be implemented, at a minimum, but leaves a vast amount of room for flexibility and building secure business processes into the program. It is very important for modern organizations to be flexible to meet the demands of a rapidly changing world. It is also important for business outcomes to be predictable and consistent. Flexibility within a framework offers opportunities to simultaneously do both.

Using a RACI Matrix

RACI matrices are commonly used in the Project Management arena to determine who is responsible, accountable, consulted, and informed in a project. An effective Information Security program is essentially a project that is designed not to end with every lesson learned becoming a new improvement project inside of the program. An effective RACI matrix does not consist only of broad categories, but also breaks down the individual tasks that must be performed in order to make the broader initiatives successful.

■ **Note**   The goal of the matrix is to ensure everyone involved in the program understands *exactly* what is expected of him or her, so the more specific the RACI matrix is, the more effective it will be.

In order to understand how to effectively build a RACI matrix for Information Security, we must first understand how a RACI matrix is built. First, tasks may be allocated to either individuals or roles. For example, many people in a role may be responsible for performing a task while an individual is likely to be accountable for the task being completed appropriately. Each of the assignments Responsible, Accountable, Consulted, and Informed have slightly different guidelines for how they should be applied. We will explore each in detail in the following sections.

Responsible

The responsible party is the person or group of people who will actually be performing the task in question. Responsibility is often assigned to teams of multiple individuals or multiple roles.

For example, when I was building out the RACI matrix for the Security Operation Center inside of InteliSecure's Managed Services Department, one of the daily tasks was to complete health checks on all of the servers under our management. Each team had several Information Security Engineers supporting customer systems. Instead of assigning specific engineers to that task in specific customer environments, I found it much more effective to assign all of the like tasks to the role of Information Security Engineer instead of to specific employees. Doing so ensured that people with the proper skill sets were performing the work, but also gave the team managers the flexibility to deploy their resources as the situation dictated on any given day. This is an example of building flexibility into a framework by assigning responsibility for a certain task to a role instead of an individual.

The Responsible designation can also be given to several roles or individuals as some tasks require multiple skill sets to work collaboratively in order to complete the task with excellence. Anyone who is completing work on a task should be given the Responsible designation for that task. However, if multiple people or roles are assigned to a single task, it is prudent to examine whether that is truly a single task or can be broken into subtasks to track what each party is responsible for. It is important to remember that the intent of the matrix is to provide clarity to all participants in the program with respect to what their role is. The most effective matrix is the one that accomplishes this goal with the least amount of complexity possible.

Accountable

Groups may be responsible for tasks, but individuals should be held accountable. The accountable party should be the ultimate authority on the proper completion of the task. This should be the person who will be most negatively impacted by a failure of the task to be completed appropriately. The person who is deemed accountable should have the authority to delegate tasks to responsible parties and should review all work before it is considered complete.

Many organizations struggle to assign accountability for tasks until there is a problem. Once something goes wrong, the higher levels scramble to hold someone accountable to deflect accountability from themselves. This is not only unfair, but it is also ineffective at achieving better results and eliminating the need to find someone to apply negative consequences to in the first place. If someone knows they are going to be held accountable before something goes wrong, they are more likely to ensure the task is completed correctly. Further, accountability for security Critical Information Assets should not always be assigned to Information Security leadership. These individuals may be responsible for tasks within the program, but accountability for security in business should ultimately roll up to line of business owners, and eventually senior business leadership. Recent events have demonstrated they will be held accountable ultimately by the board in the case of a large-scale failure, so it is appropriate to ensure the RACI matrix for the program demonstrates this reality.

■ **Note** Assigning accountability in advance and assigning it fairly are keys to success in any endeavor, but especially in building effective Information Security programs.

Fair Assignment of Accountability

People should always be put in a position to succeed. Setting a person up for failure is not only morally wrong, but also jeopardizes key business initiatives in many cases. Security initiatives often fall into this category. Far too often, security programs are given nearly impossible goals with very small budgets and very few personnel who have only partial responsibility for security. It is key to ensure that accountability is assigned, but it is equally crucial to ensure that accountability is assigned fairly. There are several elements to assigning accountability fairly.

First, accountable parties should always hold some level of authority over responsible parties. This approach makes sense as the accountable party is held accountable for the responsible party's work, but this best practice is not always observed. One of the best ways to phrase this best practice is everything someone is to be held accountable for should be within their "sphere of influence," meaning if they are incapable of having complete influence over the outcome of a task, they should not be accountable for the task. One of the easiest ways to conform with the best practice is to assign accountability for a task or subtask to the lowest ranking management individual who has all of the responsible parties within his or her sphere of influence. Doing so ensures the accountable party is close enough to the responsible parties to monitor their work, but also has the proper level of authority to shoulder the accountability.

Second, accountable parties should have some level of understanding of the actual work being performed. For example, making an Information Security Engineering team lead accountable for a financial forecast is not fair to the individual and is unlikely to produce the desired results. Similarly, making the CFO accountable for tuning a firewall rule set in accordance with the latest best practice is similarly unfair and unlikely to yield the desired results. These are extreme examples that seem like common sense, but far too often accountable parties lack an appropriate level of understanding of the tasks they are accountable for.

Finally, accountable parties should be given the appropriate resources to accomplish the task within the given time frame. These resources include the proper responsible parties with appropriate skill sets, sufficient budget to accomplish their tasks, and guidance from senior leadership along with an escalation path should they need assistance along the way.

Consulted

Consulted parties are parties that do not have responsibility or accountability for outcomes, but should be consulted and given an opportunity to provide feedback related to what is being done and how it is being done. Consulted parties often possess expertise that can be leveraged to improve the outcomes of a given activity. In many cases, Subject Matter Experts (SMEs) that do not hold responsibility for a task will be consulted on the completion of the task.

Consulted parties, by their definition, engage in two-way conversations with responsible and accountable parties. It is important that responsible and accountable parties take counsel from consulted parties in order to achieve optimal outcomes.

The consulted designation can, and often should, be given to many individuals or roles, as gaining insight and feedback from as many SMEs is generally advisable. It is important to find the balance though in order to ensure "analysis to paralysis" is not reached. In other words, having too many consulted parties can paralyze progress as the program stalls while awaiting feedback to an unmanageable number of parties. One way organizations can gather a wide spectrum of feedback while ensuring the breadth of the feedback requested does not paralyze the program is to request feedback from a large group of experts with a deadline, saying the program will move on without waiting for feedback that has not yet been gathered within a specific time frame.

Informed

Informed parties are parties that have a need to know about the progress or results of a program, but are not responsible or accountable, and whose feedback is not consulted or required for the program to be implemented. These parties often include peripheral interests who are not considered stakeholders in the process.

Many tasks have a wide range of informed parties whether or not all of them are documented. It is important, however, to enumerate informed parties in order to ensure that proper communication is taking place throughout the program. The other advantage of documenting informed parties relates to building the reporting requirements of the program. As discussed previously, proper reporting is critical to the overall success of a program. Documenting informed parties within a program serves to enumerate the interests that reporting must address.

Building a Matrix

Once the different options are understood, the different tasks required for a successful program must be enumerated. Once they are, the involved individuals and roles must be defined. Finally, the matrix must be completed. Figure 7-1 shows a very high-level sample matrix that demonstrates a sample program and how the RACI matrix is built.

Sample Information Security Program RACI Matrix

Role / Project Deliverable (or Activity)	Governance Group					Working Group					Business Units				IT Support Personnel					
	Executive Sponsor	Program Sponsor	Steering Committee	Advisory Committee	Program Manager	Team Lead	Team Lead	Security Engineers	Security Analysts	Consultants	Business Unit Executives	Business Unit Liason	Business Unit Analyst	Business Process SME	IT Help Desk	Network Engineering	Desktop Support	Messaging Team	Storage Team	Network Architect
Program Design Activities																				
-Project Chapter	A	R	C	C	C	I	I	I	I	I	C/I	I	I	I	I	I	I	I	I	C/I
-Input for Critical Asset Protection Program	R	R	A	R	C	I	I	I	I	R	R	C	I	C	I	I	I	I	I	C/I
-Input for Program Design Run Book	I	I	I	I	A	R	I	I	I	R	I	R	I	R	I	I	I	I	I	C/I
-Program Documentation					A	R														
Technical Implementation Activities																				
-Change Management Activities					I	I		R	R											A
-Email Integration					I	I		R	C							R		R		A
-Web Integration					I	I		R	C							R				A
-Endpoint Agent Deployment					I	I		R	C								R			A
-File Share Integration					I	I		R	C										R	A
-Database Integration					I	I		R	C										R	A
-Technical Documentation					I	I		A	R						C	C	C	C	C	C
Platform Engineering Activities																				
-Daily Health Checks						A	R	R	I	I										
-Version Upgrades	I	I	C	C	C	I	R	R	I	I										A
-Change Management Activities						A	R	R	I	I										
-Quarterly Architecture Review	I	I	C	C	C	I	R	R	I	I										A
Incident Traige Activities																				
-Daily Incident Traige						A	I	I	R	C	C	R	R	C						
-Incident Response Activities						R	I	I	R	R	C	R	R	C						
Scope and Policy Governance Activities																				
-New Policy Development	I	I	C	C	C	C	C	R	R	R	A	R	C	C						
-Continuous Policy Improvement					C	C	C	R	R	R		A	R	C						

Figure 7-1. *Sample Information Security Program RACI Matrix*

The matrix demonstrates that a single person should be accountable for every task, and different functions and teams can share responsibility and work collaboratively. Building an RACI matrix greatly increases the probability that disparate groups will have the ability to effectively collaborate toward a common goal.

The act of building a matrix by itself can be a helpful exercise in identifying and addressing misunderstandings, but it is equally important to ensure the matrix is kept current as the program changes. Since a program is designed to evolve and change over time, it is generally prudent to establish a recurring review of the entirety of the program including the RACI matrix. This review is often conducted annually, but the frequency may be adjusted in order to fit the needs of the organization and of the program.

Effective Leadership

Effective leadership plays a critical role in the overall success of most endeavors in the professional world. Leadership has an added importance in the context of security though, as organizations struggle to retain top talent and security teams struggle against overwhelming odds. It is incumbent upon Information Security leadership to work to get the best out of every employee and to strive to retain skilled workers. Studies show that high-performing team members expect their leadership to hold them and their coworkers accountable for their performance. Therefore, leadership, specifically as it relates to accountability, is critical to employee retention as well as the overall success of the program.

What are some of the elements of effective leadership as it relates to accountability? The first aspect is setting proper expectations. It is important to inform employees when they will be held accountable for something, but simply informing them is not enough. Leadership must also set the parameters by which success and failure will be measured for each task that accountability is assigned for. Another key element of leadership is effective communication. Great leaders are great communicators. Finally, delegation is critical to ensure the overall success of an Information Security program. Therefore, proper delegation is critical to the overall success of the program.

Setting Proper Expectations

Assigning accountability is important, but it is only half of the equation. In order to hold someone accountable, they must know what objectives they will be measured against. Setting expectations and goals is an important exercise at all levels of the organization, but it is especially important inside of security programs since responsibility spans across multiple organizational units and is often cross-functional. Organizations that have an exceptional security posture make everyone responsible and accountable for some aspects of security. For example, some companies I have been a part of write a paragraph into every job description detailing the individual employee's responsibility for adherence with the security program. Doing so ensures personnel are aware of their responsibility for security even before the term of their employment begins.

Proper expectations should be documented and reviewed in person by the accountable party and their leadership. The meeting should be established with the goal of gaining consensus, and the documentation should be signed by both parties acknowledging that they both understand where accountability lies for the specific expectations and how success or failure with respect to those expectations will be measured.

Communication

Communication is important in any interpersonal relationship. Fostering an environment of honest communication is an important function of leadership as leaders set the tone for what is and is not acceptable inside of their organizations and their teams. If employees are afraid to report failures or negative observations, the organization is not likely to solve the problems that exist, but rather remain blissfully unaware of them as they blissfully march toward the abyss. Leadership is particularly affected by communication as it is a key component of building trust between leaders and employees. Leaders who prioritize transparency and honesty are far more effective than leaders that do not. Many of the best leaders I have had the privilege to follow make a concerted effort to build personal relationships that transcend the workplace. This type of leadership is especially important when referencing security teams as they are often asked to accomplish much with too few resources, and the stakes are often very high. People are far more willing to sacrifice for people they like and respect than they are for a set of tasks or a job description.

It is often uncomfortable for people, especially leaders, to let their guard down and communicate openly with their teams. These challenges are often due to fear of vulnerability and deep-rooted insecurities in the leader themselves. However, leaders who are confident enough to show that vulnerability and humility to their teams are far more likely to get optimal performance from team members.

Effective Information Security programs require smart people to come up with creative solutions to complex problems. There is simply no other way to combat evolving threats in a universally connected world, especially since many of our adversaries are utilizing smart people to find new ways to circumvent security systems and compromise Critical Information Assets.

In order to foster a creative culture that has the capability to create these types of solutions, leaders must reduce the fear of failure that is deeply rooted in the psyche of most human beings. For every creative solution that is effective, there are many creative solutions that are not. Organizations that promote a fear of failure are far less likely to innovate than organizations that create a safe environment where revolutionary solutions can be developed and tested. Culture is often established by leadership, and one of the major contributing factors to creating the type of environment that fosters creative solutions is humility on the part of the leader. If a leader communicates to his or her employees that they are not perfect and they make mistakes and it is acceptable for all team members to make mistakes in the pursuit of excellence as well, it is far more likely that such a leader will have team members more willing to take risks. Far too many leaders are afraid or unwilling to admit that they are fallible human beings.

Delegation

One of the most important skills a leader or manager can master is delegation. Delegating responsibility is critical to the overall success of a manager or leader inside an organization as it is impractical for members of leadership to perform every task themselves.

■ **Note**   *Responsibility* can be delegated, but *accountability* ***cannot***. It is important to remember the person who is accountable cannot transfer that accountability. "Passing the buck" is a form of transferring accountability, usually to a subordinate.

Proper delegation not only expands the influence a leader can have, but also builds trust in a team and inspires team members to improve. Failure to delegate results in micromanagement and the eventual turnover of skilled employees. Since accountability cannot be delegated, the process of delegation requires the leader to monitor the progress of the responsible party or parties, since the leader will be held accountable for the results. Many people are uncomfortable with being held accountable for things they do not directly control. There is nothing wrong with this perspective, however, in my opinion; it is impossible to be an effective leader without developing comfort with this dynamic. There are many uncomfortable aspects of leadership, which is why leadership is a burden.

Millennials

Increasingly, an effective leader must have the ability to lead the millennial work force. A millennial is an individual born between 1980 or the early 1980s, depending on the source, and 2004. Millennials are a growing part of the workforce, and are at the time of this writing, the generation with the largest number of active workforce participants.[1] Millennials have been much maligned by older generations and have been characterized as lazy, disloyal, and unmotivated. In my career, I have found that is not the case. I have found, however, that getting the best possible performance from the millennial generation requires great leadership, whereas that level of leadership may not have been a prerequisite to get the best possible results from other generations. Millennials also have some advantages in the workplace as well, especially as it relates to high technology careers and cyber-security. In the following sections, I will address some of the negative perceptions of millennials along with my experience with the generation and the ways in which I've been able to leverage a predominantly millennial work force to build a revolutionary Information Security Operations Center that protected the most Critical Information Assets for some of the largest organizations in the world. My intent in sharing this insight is not to boast about what we were able to accomplish, but in hopes that other Information Security leaders can learn to leverage millennials effectively.

Laziness

The most common misconception I have heard as it relates to millennials is that they are lazy. The perception comes from the fact that millennials place a high importance on work-life balance. Some millennials hide behind the term "work-life balance" to cover the fact that they do not want to work. In my experience, this is not the case for the vast majority of millennials.

---

[1]Richard Fry, "Millennials Surpass Gen Xers as the Largest Generation in U.S. Labor Force," Pew Research Center RSS, 2015. Accessed May 27, 2016. http://www.pewresearch.org/fact-tank/2015/05/11/ millennials-surpass-gen-xers-as-the-largest-generation-in-u-s-labor-force/.

117

Millennials are as hard working as any other generation I have had the privilege of leading in my career, but their motivations are different. Millennials tend to be far less motivated by money than other generations, so if you are trying to motivate millennials with material things, you are unlikely to stimulate their work ethic. Instead millennials are very idealistic and are much more motivated by being a part of something special that makes a contribution to society. The issue with many leaders comes in their discomfort with transparency. Simply put, in order to provide millennials with the motivation they need to be at their best, a leader must trust them enough to share what the overall mission and vision of the organization is, and how their individual roles contribute to that mission and vision. Failure to do so will result in a disengaged workforce who will likely put forth the minimum required effort at work. Doing so effectively will result in a workforce that will gladly think outside the box and put in immense amounts of effort in order to contribute to the overall success of the organization in achieving the mission and realizing the vision you have articulated.

In order to honestly and fairly explore the reasons why it is difficult to retain top millennial talent, we need to look into the history of generations. Millennials are the children of both the baby boomer generation and generation X. Many of those generations are the children of the greatest generation, or the generation that was of age during World War II. In order to understand the attitudes of millennials toward employers, we must understand how their grandparents and parents were treated by their employers.

Members of the greatest generation were raised to value job security above all else. They were taught that the ideal work scenario is to work for the same company their entire working lives and to retire with a nice pension. Due to this preference, companies realized that they did not have to compete for talent, and they did not necessarily have to treat their employees well in order to retain them, since employees rarely left a company unless they were changing careers. As a result, organizations began to cut pensions and cap raises at a very low percentage in order to cut costs. These changes were not well received by the children of this generation, who felt these organizations were taking advantage of their parents.

The baby boomers and generation Xers who watched their parents have their options and benefits severely limited by their employers were far less loyal to a company. It was not uncommon for these generations to move from company to company in order to increase their earning potential. Organizations also further exasperated the disloyalty between employers and employees by arbitrarily laying off employees in order to make financials look better. The perception was jobs were being cut not out of necessity, but to ensure bonuses for well-compensated executives of wildly profitable companies. Most millennials had their childhood significantly impacted by a well-performing family member being laid off for reasons that did not seem to be existential to the business.

As millennials came of age, it was commonly believed that they should look to change employers every eighteen to twenty-four months in order to advance their career. This is not due to a lack of values on their part, but due to three generations of training by their parents and grandparents' employers. The problem for all organizations is that it is very expensive and disruptive to replace team members with that frequency. As an employer, in order to combat this situation, we first have to address the problem head on while acknowledging the situation that exists and also presenting a career path to our employees to demonstrate that they do not need to leave the organization in order to build their career.

The first step to solving any problem is to admit you have one and to take ownership of the problem. When I bring a new employee on board, one of our first conversations is about what their career aspirations are. This conversation presents an excellent opportunity to explain that while you have to leave many organizations in order to advance, it is part of the corporate strategy and vision in our organization to develop our talent and promote from within. Regardless of any assumptions you may make about what employees should intuitively assume, this needs to be said.

Second, the organization must commit to actually developing talent. InteliSecure CEO and cofounder Rob Eggebrecht pioneered a quarterly exercise for my team members called career mapping. Essentially, every quarter, we reviewed short- and long-term goals with each employee along with performance and education goals that must be met in order for the progression to be made. Committing to such a process allowed us to communicate effectively with our teams and retain much of our top talent. The added benefit was clearly understanding where people's passions and interests were concentrated so we did not promote people into positions they did not like. This last point is personally important to me because I have seen many times where organizations promoted an individual as a perceived reward, only to have the individual leave the organization shortly afterward. This often perplexed the organization, as they believed they were offering the employee a superior position. More than any other generation, millennials are particular about what they want to do as a career, and some of them have no desire to be in management. In order to retain top millennial talent, it is important for organizations to be sure they know what employees want from their career. There must be possibilities for advancement financially and through avenues of training and expertise that exist outside of upwards mobility through management. Listening is key.

Gossip

Another criticism of millennial workers that I often hear is that they are prone to gossip and destructive "water-cooler talk." In my experience, it is true that millennials will fill voids in information with rumors and conjecture Those rumors can be quite destructive but are relatively easy to counteract with frequent and honest communication. In my career, there was one specific time where I found misconceptions were rampant in my department and the misconceptions were causing a toxic environment and I was losing great talent due to the things people were saying that were at best stretching the truth and at worst, outright lies. The solution to this problem and the subsequent end to my turnover issues was ridiculously simple.

I created an all hands team meeting every Friday afternoon at 2:00 p.m. Generally, the team would leave each day around 5:00 p.m. The first part of the meeting would cover all of the topics that were covered with any and all meetings with senior leadership throughout the week. Certainly, there were things that could not be shared from those meetings, but in those cases, I simply told the team that we had a conversation that was confidential and I could not share the details. After I was finished sharing information, I opened the floor for any questions the team would like to address with the group. Nothing was off limits and if the answer to the question was confidential, I would explain why I could not answer in a public setting. After the group session was complete, any employee who wanted to speak with me in private could do so in my office. Anyone who did not choose to was free to go home early and enjoy the afternoon. After implementing this system, the gossip greatly decreased because there were no longer gaps to be filled with rumors or conjecture.

Finally, I wrote a "Personal Leadership Philosophy," which was a concept I was introduced to by Don Jenkins in a leadership training opportunity that I was given at InteliSecure. This Personal Leadership Philosophy was designed to explain the way my mind worked, after reviewing the results of a personality test, explain my values and expectations, and also challenged any of my team members to confront me in person if they believed I was not living up to this philosophy. This accomplished two key objectives with respect to leading millennials. First, it provided a unique level of transparency to the team members. Second, it gave my team the permission and responsibility to hold me accountable for my actions just as I would hold them accountable for theirs. Third, it established shared values we would all strive to demonstrate on a daily basis. All of these things sent the message to the team that while we had different responsibilities, I did not elevate myself above them, and we all should hold ourselves and each other to a very high standard.

Comfort with Technology

It is widely accepted that the average millennial is far more technologically savvy than the average member of any other generation. This fact is largely due to the fact that the majority of millennials spent their formative years surrounded by technology, and are the first generation to do so on such a large scale. This particular fact is a double-edged sword as millennials have a much steeper learning curve for technology, but also have far fewer inhibitions about sharing information in a public forum.

It is incumbent upon leaders to leverage and nurture millennials' natural love of and comfort with technology, while also educating them on the types of information that should not be shared in public forums such as social media posts. There are countless examples of accidental disclosure by millennials since they have become so comfortable with sharing every detail about themselves online. There are very few secrets for this generation, so it is important for organizations to understand that they must stress the importance of company secrets to millennial employees and to connect cyber-security to the overall mission and vision of the organization.

Privacy in the New Millennium

Privacy is the subject of much debate around the world. Technology is rapidly advancing in the area of monitoring electronic communications. Concurrently, an ever-increasing percentage of interpersonal communications are taking place in the digital world. The combination of these factors is leading to very real concerns about what, if anything, remains private in the Information Age. The issue is further exasperated by the fact that the millennial generation is increasingly voluntarily surrendering their privacy and living a good portion of their lives in the public eye through social media. Privacy concerns are driving many new regulations throughout the world designed to create mechanisms in which individuals can choose to maintain privacy, but those regulations are still forming, and the issue of privacy is far from settled.

Many things in life require balance to be effective. With respect to Information Security, we as organizations and governments grappling with striking the proper balance of security and privacy must weigh both sides of the argument in such a way that allows us to build programs which can simultaneously provide individuals with a reasonable expectation of privacy while allowing organizations to protect the Critical Information Assets they own and their employees' use in performance of their duties. Building Information Security programs that are focused on specific content rather than monitoring the entirety of communications on a network are not only more feasibly implemented within the confines of a realistic budget, but are also more likely to appropriately balance between privacy and security since the capture of data is targeted and not indiscriminate.

Conclusion

IT is very important to assign accountability in anything that is done. If people are not clear that they will be held accountable for a task or outcome, they are less likely to be personally invested in that outcome. Communication is key for assigning accountability fairly as well as for accountable parties to delegate responsibility for the tasks at hand. Leadership also plays a key role, since simply holding someone accountable for an outcome is unlikely to guarantee a positive experience. Assigning accountability to strong leaders, however, will often greatly increase the probability of good results.

Accountability is also shifting in many organizations up the management hierarchy, especially with respect to Information Security. IT is no longer acceptable for senior executives to stay above the fray by pointing the finger at IT Security or IT departments. Securing an organization's Critical Information Assets has clearly become an executive-level responsibility.

CHAPTER 8

■ ■ ■

Shifting the Paradigm

Usually the first problems you solve with the new paradigm are the ones that were unsolvable with the old paradigm.

—Joel A. Barker

There are many dangerous precedents in Information Security that need to be changed in order for organizations to be more successful in securing their most Critical Information Assets. There is danger in continuing to do things a certain way simply because that is the way it has always been done. Often, these precedents are reinforced despite the fact that an examination of their efficacy would suggest a change is necessary. There are also entrenched interests representing these antiquated approaches that will vehemently oppose any changes to the old guard. The simple truth is that the threat landscape is changing, and Information Security programs must also change to meet these emerging and evolving threats. Sometimes when I speak to audiences, people tell me the ideas I am presenting are common sense solutions. I take that as a compliment. Good solutions should make sense when you hear them. Great ideas should make you wonder why everyone isn't doing what is being suggested. The problem is not that no one knows what to do, it is that people are still not doing the things that need to be done in order to secure programs properly. These ideas may seem simple at their highest level, but implementing them properly and protecting Critical Information Assets comprehensively is still a challenge, and a challenge that is highlighted every time you read yet another story of organizations failing to protect their assets.

There are many major paradigms that must shift, but they essentially fall into two categories: people and process. Traditional Information Security programs are technology-centric. They focus on buying the next shiny gadget that promises to solve all security problems with the click of a button. Unfortunately, any solution that does not require people and process in the modern world cannot possibly protect against threats that use both in order to compromise systems. Technology-centric solutions can only be successful against technology-centric attacks, which are the lowest form or threats that an organization faces. It is not to say that programs should not also address those threats, they certainly should, but due to the relative ease of defeating such threats, the majority of time, effort, and budget should be spent on countering more complex and potentially harmful threats.

Why do organizations choose to focus on technology, given that threats are evolving? First, it is much easier to combat threats with technology. Until recently, it was reasonably acceptable in most organizations to purchase technology to address a threat, and when the technology failed, to blame the vendor and replace the technology. This solution also often allowed organizations to "meet the compliance check box" to prove that they were doing something to address security in the event of an audit or regulatory review. Additionally, Information Security was seen as an IT problem and not a business problem, and therefore, wasn't allocated enough of the budget to properly fund a comprehensive security program. Even in programs that did not count lack of funding among their issues, generally there was difficulty getting the proper level of attention from business leaders in order to integrate their security systems into their business processes. It is much easier to meet minimum requirements, but this book is entirely about building programs and making effective decisions. The old business paradigm toward security is shifting or has shifted in the majority of organizations. I often tell people Information Security became a business problem when board members of Target were asked to leave following their breach. In truth, the trend started well before the Target breach, but it is hard to say Information Security is someone else's problem if it can cost you your job.

Businesses are increasingly concerned with Information Security at the board level. Most countries around the world require public companies to submit corporate summaries and results on a specific frequency to potential investors. Some countries require certain details to be released to the public regardless of whether the company is private. The details in these reports vary, but the majority contain either specific risk factors that threaten their business or their standing in the marketplace. Even if it is not explicitly stated, reviewing regulations that may be applicable to an organization or the products and services they provide can clearly communicate what is important to the organization from a regulatory perspective. One simply must know where to find the information and how to analyze it. Chapter 7 contains a specific example from the Form 10-K reports filed by companies who publicly trade equity in the United States.

Budgets for Information Security are expanding, and with the rising budgets come rising expectations. Meeting those expectations will require Information Security professionals and teams to reevaluate how they are doing business, and also require them to put security initiatives and results in business terms, while proving return on investment as previously discussed. There is a fundamental rift between business users and Information Security teams in many organizations that will need to be healed in order for security programs to achieve their true and highest purpose, which is to serve the business interests of their organization, namely, in protecting assets whose loss or inappropriate exposure could cause the business irreparable harm.

The current state of the Information Security landscape shows an increasing number of security technology companies that are trying to capture the capital that is flooding into the marketplace as businesses understand they need to spend money on security, and continue to try to spend money on the technology because that is the most comfortable way to solve the problem. Unfortunately, simply spending more money on technology will not make an organization inherently more secure, and will often make the problem worse as the people responsible for managing the systems are spread thin with very little guidance for their efforts. Simply put, you cannot buy your way to security and no technology will comprehensively protect your organization with technology alone. There is no product that is the panacea, and I am relatively confident that there is not a security technology that is completely infallible on the horizon. You must focus on the people and process as well if you want to be successful. Regardless of what you think of his political ideology, U.S. President Barack Obama is widely accepted, even by his harshest critics, as a master orator. A major element of his original campaign message was the theme of change and his ability to speak eloquently about how change is a major contributing factor to him becoming president. One of his quotes about change that is specifically relevant to the current position many Information Security professionals find themselves in is this: "Change will not come if we wait for some other person or some other time. We are the ones we've been waiting for. We are the change that we seek." Many Information Security and even business professionals are moving from shiny new object to shiny new object waiting to find a technology that will solve their hard people and process problems. Artificial Intelligence is being developed, but as of the time of this writing, there is no technology commercially available that eliminates the need to involve people and process in a comprehensive security program.

Education Reforms

In chapter 6, we explored an anecdote about the differences between an education predicated on multiple choice questions and an education that relies more on problem solving and explanations of solutions. The reason for the comparison is not to say that one is unequivocally better than the other and therefore should be used universally. Like many other scenarios in life, the best solution lies in striking the right balance between the two.

Students should have elements of their education delivered in a format that allows them to select the best options from a defined list of options. There are many scenarios we face personally and professionally that would require us to make similar choices between options that exist, even though our perfect solution may not be an available option. Also, there are questions that have absolute and specific answers. However, there are also situations where professionals must solve complex problems utilizing creative solutions that they are not presented with. This develops skills in critical thinking that are important skills that should be developed.

There are many opinions related to education, and I am not claiming to have all of the answers, but it is my opinion that the more we try to ensure educational experiences are the same for all students inside societies around the world, the more quality education and phenomenal teachers are marginalized. We must not accept the premise that we must sacrifice quality in the name of standardization.

I have friends and family members that are current and former teachers, including my sister, who have a passion for teaching children the skills they need to be competitive in the global marketplace. However, many of them are frustrated by the fact that they are actively prevented from providing higher quality education than is mandated by the school district. Essentially, they are required to deliver educational services that are on par with expectations: no better, no worse. My frame of reference in terms of education is limited to the United States, but I am confident that similar conditions exist in other societies. We must stop the insanity!

As human beings, we must demand the best for our children, not only for their benefit, but for the benefit of all of humanity. There are many ideas that I have heard that may or may not improve the situation, but the forces of the status quo are strong enough to overwhelm the ideas for change. In my personal opinion, instituting a profit motive for schools by allocating funding by allowing parents to choose the school they believe is providing the best educational opportunities to children, or taking feedback from parents into account when allocating funding to schools and districts, would create a situation where competition could drive improvement in the quality of education. Another positive output from this type of change would be that there would suddenly be competition between schools for the best and brightest teachers who deliver the highest quality education because those teachers would be elevated from a commodity in the eyes of the administration to a critical contributor to the revenue coming into the school. This competition would likely lead to higher wages for the best teachers, and a merit-based system for valuing teachers rather than the current seniority-based system. This is simply my opinion on a single possible solution; each person may agree or disagree with it. However, I believe most people would agree that there is an opportunity to improve education in terms of how prepared students are for the workforce when they complete their education, and we should do what we can to achieve that outcome.

I have previously stated my theory that the current education system being disproportionately reliant on multiple choice questions drives the tendency of organizations to prefer selecting technology to solving process problem. Some may say that the correlation is oversimplified, but I am convinced that the two are related, although there are likely other contributing factors. Regardless of the reason, though, the tendency of organizations to attempt to leverage technology, especially in Information Security programs, without instituting the proper policy and procedure changes or addressing the people problem is something I have observed throughout my career.

It is critical that organizations break the habit over overreliance as technology as a simple solution to complex problems by any means necessary. The need to have creative solutions to complex problems with respect to Information Security cannot be overstated. Many adversaries in the Information Security realm are smart, creative, and adaptable. Our teams must be the same in order to be effective. Marshall Goodman wrote a book called *What Got You Here Won't Get You There: How Successful People Become Even More Successful*. That is a good quote to explain the current state of many Information Security programs. We cannot stem the tide of increasing cyber-attacks by doing the same things that made our organizations vulnerable to attacks in the first place. We must be passionate about what we do, and we must be the change we seek in order to improve our security posture and secure our most Critical Information Assets.

Traditional Information Security Professionals and Effective Information Security Teams

I was approached by another individual after giving a speech in Seattle, Washington, who was very interested in my point of view. He was telling me that there is still a prevailing attitude in the industry that everyone in Information Security needed to know how to do malware analysis, scripting, or other similarly technical tasks. This individual was extremely intelligent, very articulate, and had a background in investigations. He had a passion for Information Security, but he found it very difficult to find a job. The truth is many people have Information Security Engineers in mind when they think of Information Security professionals. These traditional technical skill sets are still relevant to the industry, and these individuals are necessary to an effective program, but there are far more roles that need to be present in effective Information Security teams.

Shifting the paradigm and becoming more successful at protecting our most Critical Information Assets will require creative thinking and challenging the status quo with respect to how we build our programs. This is inclusive both of the methods we use to run our programs as well as the people we choose to employ in support of our programs. Building more effective Information Security teams will require programs to employ a more diverse skill set than has historically been part of these types of programs to include people who understand human behavior and social dynamics, instead of myopically focusing on technologies.

Traditional Information Security Professionals

Information Security professionals are often seen as essentially Network Engineers with a focus on protecting systems. While these types of professionals certainly have a place inside an effective Information Security program, they do not represent a comprehensive set of skills that will help to solve the problems of today and tomorrow.

A major contributing factor to the over-reliance of Information Security programs on technical skill sets is the fact that cyber-security education programs in major universities throughout the world are focused on the technical elements of Information Security. Students learn about things like cryptography and access control lists, firewalls and how to open and close specific ports, and best practices with respect to complying with government regulations. All of these skills are important, but represent only part of the skills that are necessary to be successful on the digital battlefield.

The first major shortcoming of these traditional education programs is that security is truly a business problem. Although an increasing number of Information Security professionals recognize security as a business problem, very few Information Security programs include curriculum related to teaching students core business concepts. The result is that the students get into the workforce without the skills necessary to relate to their business stakeholders and cannot effectively build a cost-benefit analysis for the security proposals they are making. Business education programs also rarely teach elements of Information Security, so the result is a chasm in communication between the business and security teams. This chasm leads to disengagement from both sides, which often has disastrous consequences for the business itself.

Another major shortcoming is the fact that security is a people problem, which is not reflected in the curriculum. Behavior analysis and basic human psychology are important elements for students to learn if they are to become effective in determining intent and predicting future behavior patterns, which are key elements of a successful security program.

Education will not change overnight, but ultimately higher education is a competitive business. If students demand a wider range of education that is more relevant to the emerging threats and problems faced by the wider Information Security industry, more comprehensive education options are likely to emerge.

Until education programs change in order to educate Information Security professionals with a more comprehensive skill set, organizations will have to search for talent in less traditional places and with less traditional credentials. I have had success building teams that contained traditional Information Security and Network Security majors along with business majors, finance majors, people with degrees in Criminal Justice, former police officers and federal agents, and also people who would consider themselves data scientists. Teams built with an aggregate of these skill sets have proven to be far more effective for me than teams full of more traditional Information Security skills.

Effective Information Security Teams

In order to discuss the evolution from traditional Information Security teams to the more effective and more skill-diverse teams that I advocate today, I will tell the story of my personal journey as the first Managed Services Director at BEW Global, where my primary responsibility was to build and manage the teams charged with protecting Critical Information Assets for our customers. Before telling the story, I want to take a moment to make it clear that I am not claiming credit for the advancements made during my time as Managed Services Director. There were many people who contributed to these advancements, some of which made contributions that may be greater than my own, including Rob Eggebrecht, Chuck Bloomquist, Graham Laird, and others.

In the beginning, every member of the Managed Services teams used a generic skill set that we called Data Protection Analysts. These people were assigned to manage systems for customers in an outsourced model. In many ways, this arrangement was similar to how many organizations' Information Security teams internally operated at the time, and many still operate today. It was apparent to me and others, however, that people were different with different strengths and weaknesses inside the program, which in and of itself was not surprising. The more profound discovery was that it became apparent to us that there were different *mindsets* required for different parts of the program. It was not that the strengths and the weaknesses were unique between individuals, which would only be natural and could be easily addressed by expanding the size of teams to a size in which people's strengths and weaknesses naturally aligned. There was a pattern emerging.

We found through observation, trial, and a whole lot of error, that people who were very good at engineering had a certain mentality. They liked to look at problems as black and white where there is a tangible process that will fix the same problem the same way every time. To them, every solution should be repeatable. Also, finding a suitable solution that transitioned a system or element of a system between two defined states as quickly as possible was often the objective they were most comfortable with. An example is taking a server from a nonworking state to a working state as quickly as possible.

These people were not nearly as good at looking deeply into an incident in an effort to determine the reasons why someone took a certain action. They were often looking at exactly what happened in order to make an expedient determination, when effective Incident Triage and Response must take into account not only *what* happened but ***why*** it happened. Also, the natural curiosity into human behavior drives the most effective analysts to look for patterns of human behavior and would bore most engineers I know. Their natural curiosity lies in how systems behave and how to optimize them, not in how and why human beings behave the way they do.

Further, engineers have earned the reputation over a variety of years, of lacking in documentation and communication skills. Further, there are few engineers that take an interest in business and finance. All of these lacking skills are important in order to deliver impactful reports and analytics to business leaders. As a result, many times if you ask an engineer to create a report, the resulting report will be unlikely to contain information that would be relevant to a business executive. This is not because the engineers do not have every intention to provide value to business stakeholders; it is because they are not naturally well versed at speaking the language of business and do not see the world the same way as others.

Many of the people we found that were good at performing Incident Triage and Response and building reports were the type of people who did not possess an overwhelming amount of technical skill. These types of individuals were far more comfortable looking into human behavior than they were in troubleshooting technical systems.

They were fairly effective at building reports, but their reports generally lacked the financial analysis and business impact analysis of Incidents they were reporting on. Their reports instead focused on patterns of behavior and predictive analysis, which was helpful to the business in understanding the people problems they may or may not be facing, and were more valuable to the business than a technically focused Information Security report; but the lack of business impact suggested there may be a third mindset that should be leveraged in building a more comprehensive set of skills.

The final group of people built incredible reports and did a fair job of incident triage. These individuals were primarily focused on the economic impact of the program and defining further objectives that could be met in order to deliver more value to the business. These people were extremely valuable in communicating effectively with business stakeholders, but were, in general, the least technically skilled of the group.

It was clear to us that we had to separate the requisite activities of running an effective program into three distinct skill sets. Each of these skill sets are important to the overall success of a comprehensive IT Security program focused on Critical Information Assets, and each of them require a different skill set, and mindset, which dictated to us that no single person could fill all three roles. I have not encountered any evidence or met any individuals in the intervening years that would change my opinion on this analysis.

Cyber-Security Engineers

Much of the time when people think of Information Security professionals, they are, in fact envisioning Information Security Engineers or Cyber-Security Engineers. Throughout this book, I have been highlighting the fact that programs need more than technology, and similarly that Information Security teams need to be comprised of more than engineers. That said, engineers are vital to the success of the team. While they are not the only skill set that is required, the engineering skill set is crucial to the success of the program.

Think of the skill sets required to run an Information Security program in the same way as the skill sets required to build your house. You definitely need more than a carpenter to build a house, but trying to build a house without a carpenter would be very difficult. Similarly, engineers are required because many of the tools in the Information Security toolkit require a technical skill set to deploy appropriately.

So who are Information Security Engineers? They are often either Information Security majors or Network Engineers that have decided to focus their career path on security. They tend to have a technical skill set and are focused on the technical deployment of technologies in support of the program. They are primarily responsible for the Application Management portion of the program along with the technical aspects of Scope and Policy Governance.

Cyber-Security Analysts

Cyber-Security Analysts are often the most overlooked skill set in an effective Information Security program. In many cases, so-called analysts are really more engineers. True analysts are more focused on investigations than technology and are far more likely to have a criminal justice or similar background rather than Computer Science or Electrical Engineering. These people are responsible for investigations and behavioral analysis that is critical in order to combat advanced and evolving threats. I have had success finding these types of people outside the traditional Information Security channels looking in fields such as criminal justice and psychology. Simply put, this skill set is predicated on the mentality that looks for patterns of behavior and deviations from normal behavioral patterns.

Many technologies have been released lately that claim to perform behavioral analytics. True behavioral analytics requires an element of human analysis. While technologies may make it easier to highlight patterns of behavior that may be risky, qualitative analysis of human behavior generally requires another human to verify the results of the analysis. It is very difficult for a machine to determine intent based on a series of actions. It is easy for a machine to tell you *what* a person has done, but it is very difficult for technology to tell you *why* the same is happening.

Many engineers throughout my career have told me they can fulfill both the engineering and the analyst role. I have given many people an opportunity to do both, in a "hybrid" role. The fact is, it is a fundamentally different mindset that looks at technical challenges, which behave the same way when presented with the same set of circumstances, than it is to analyze human behavior, which can vary based on factors that are not necessarily perceptible such as feelings, attitudes, and moods. I have never met an engineer who can be an effective analyst, and I have also never met an analyst that can be a world-class engineer. My intent is not to disparage either skill set or mindset, but rather to identify them as fundamentally different.

Business Analysts/Consultants

This skill set is a traditional consultant skill set. These team members are responsible for interfacing with the business units to define requirements and delivering business intelligence in the form of reporting. They are responsible for managing from the business layer to the strategy layer on both sides of the model. Business Analysts and Consultants generally major in business skill sets like general business administration or finance, or are data scientists that have an interest in Information Security. These individuals act almost as interpreters between the Information Security team and the business itself. They are responsible for taking the metrics and key performance indicators from the security program and translating them into business metrics like ROI and performing cost-benefit analyses.

Business Analysts and Consultants are often overlooked in Information Security teams because they do not have a traditional Information Security skill set, but a good Business Analyst can be the difference between a chronically underfunded and understaffed security team and a team that has the necessary budget to accomplish its mission.

Team Management

The challenge in managing teams with diverse skill sets is that the teams need to be able to relate to their manager, and their manager needs to be able to relate to the team members. Empathy is a critical team manager value, and most of the time, the need for the manager to have education and/or experience with each of the job functions is important.

It is important to understand that managing and leading these diverse skill sets requires more than just understanding what each skill set is doing and how they contribute to the overall program. Effective management and leadership must also understand the career path for each skill set and how to train and incentivize the team properly. Increasingly, management and leadership is predicated on telling an effective story to the team members so they understand the role they play in the overall mission, and the importance of the mission to the company they work for as well as the world and economy as a whole.

According to the great American general Dwight D. Eisenhower, "Leadership is the art of getting someone to do something you want them to do, because they want to do it." Inspiring people to want to do something that you want them to do requires effective professional storytelling. If you ask someone to come into work and give their heart and soul to performing a menial task repetitively throughout an eight-hour shift, few people are going to be inspired to give that task their all. However, if you can paint the picture of why the task they are performing is vitally important to a cause greater than themselves and explain to them exactly how they fit into the puzzle, they are far more likely to apply themselves at a high level.

As the generations involved in the workforce shift, there will be an increased emphasis in leadership on inspiration. The growing generations in the workforce are less motivated by money and traditional benefits than previous generations, and far more motivated by the legacy their work will leave behind and being a part of something great and lasting. Teams with diverse skill sets can outperform teams with homogeneous skill sets, especially when good leadership and management is in place that can leverage unique skill sets to build effective teams. The role of management in next-generation Information Security programs is critical and cannot be overstated.

Incentivizing Behavior

When I was new to leadership, I was given a simple piece of advice that has become a central part of my career since receiving it. I was told to incentivize the behavior I want. This statement is beautiful in its simplicity, but very important in achieving results, yet often overlooked by management.

Security Operations Centers are no exception. Many times employees are incentivized in a Security Operations Center based on how quickly they close tickets or how many tickets they close. Building incentives on these metrics motivate individuals to go through the motions as quickly as possible, rather than driving the program to achieve results related to increasing the security posture of the program or to reduce the risk profile of the organization.

Building an effective program allows for risk to be quantified, and therefore for risk reduction to be measured. It is prudent, then to tie incentives for Security Operations Center employees to risk reduction goals. Doing so will ensure every member of the team is incentivized based on his or her contribution to the overall business goals of the program.

Fostering teamwork is also critical to success. Simply telling people they need to work together is ineffective. In order to foster a collaborative team environment, it is important to ensure at least a portion of incentive pay is tied to team performance rather than individual performance. Some employees or managers may find it unfair to incentivize team behavior rather than individual behavior. After all, what if a high-performing individual is on an under-performing team? What if under-performing individuals take advantage of this situation and others who pick up the slack are not rewarded? This argument makes sense, but in reality, there are very few people who are not reliant on the people around them for success. This is the nature of teams and even companies. A high-performing team will demand performance from each team member and hold each other accountable, which makes the team much easier to manage. Fostering an individualistic culture with individual incentives often will have the opposite effect. Information Security in the modern age is most definitely a team sport. Operating the programs, we have discussed throughout this book require a variety of skill sets operating in concert in order to be effective. In fact, a comprehensive Information Security program is very similar to mining for gold.

When I was working with the InteliSecure team to build an incentive program for my Security Operations Center staff, I wanted to ensure we were incentivizing the behavior we wanted. We knew the traditional Security Operations Center metrics would only incentivize transactional behavior, which was the antithesis of what our customers wanted and therefore ran counter to our interests. We were searching for better metrics when we ran across a show on the Discovery Channel called *Gold Rush*. The show followed different crews of gold miners as they went about the business of mining gold. Essentially, the process of mining for gold is relatively simple. Certain areas are selected for mining based on the likelihood that the dirt contains gold. The dirt is then transported to a sluice box, which is essentially a contraption that the dirt is put into and water is ran over with the intention of washing the dirt into a stream while the gold is captured in the box. There are two variables that contribute to the overall yield of gold for the crew: the quality of the pay dirt and the quality of the sluice box. We found this process to be very similar to building an Information Security program.

In an Information Security program, the process of building a sluice box properly with the proper angles to ensure that the gold is trapped and the dirt washes into the stream expediently is similar to architecting and deploying a system. The process of defining the rules for systems, which will subsequently raise violations of those rules to the attention of an analyst, is similar to the process of selecting what dirt will be mined. The process of actually running the dirt through the sluice box is similar to triaging events and investigating Incidents. All parts of the program in Information Security must work in concert in order to achieve effective risk reduction just like every portion of a team when mining for gold must do their job in order to maximize their yield. Therefore, like gold miners are incentivized based on how much gold they find, Information Security teams can also be effectively incentivized by how many Incidents they find and respond to that have significant impact to the business. Incentives of this kind will not only incentivize teamwork, but will also yield far better results than more traditional methods of incentivizing Security Operations Center employees.

The History of Software Development

The origins of software development draw a parallel to the current state of designing business processes. In the beginnings of software development, there were a variety of methods to develop software, but they all had essentially one goal in mind. The software was to perform a specific task or tasks and fulfill specific requirements. There was little attention paid at the beginnings of the process to security. Instead, after the software was finished, security holes would be found and subsequently patched in an endless cycle. There are still pieces of software that are developed in this way. Anyone familiar with Operating System security patches and patches for browsers are keenly aware of the reactive nature of software development.

However, throughout the evolution of software development, there have been applications and other pieces of software in which security has been identified as critical, and has been designed to be secure throughout the development process. These types of software are far more secure than their predecessors since they were designed to be secure, and security is a key function of the design, rather than an afterthought. It is not the intention of this section to explore the process of secure software development, but rather to highlight the fact that designing software to be secure from the outset yielded far more secure software. The current state of Information Security demands that businesses begin to consider security in their business processes. Very few business processes have been designed to account for security, and many are modified after the fact due to reactions to breaches or changing regulations. The results are very similar to the early days of software development, in that the business processes themselves are often changing and being "patched" as they are found to fall short with respect to security. The challenge for organizations moving forward into an uncertain cyber-security future is to determine whether they have an opportunity to commit to reevaluating key business processes and redesigning them with security in mind. I would argue it is prudent to do so, although I acknowledge it is no small task to do so.

Secure Business Process Design

There is no substitute for redesigning key business processes that interact with Critical Information Assets from the beginning with security in mind. It is often infeasible to do so, however, as most businesses do not have tolerance for all key business stakeholders to take the time to comprehensively redesign all of their processes. How then, do we move from a current state in which security is designed to augment business processes without materially changing them, to a state in which the process itself is secure? The answer lies in risk modeling. Effectively ranking business processes based on risk will require an organization to effectively quantify the risks that are present to their processes first, and performing a cost-benefit analysis to redesigning the process. On the cost side, the organization must quantify both the cost of having stakeholders perform the exercise along with any inefficiencies in the process that are introduced by designing the processes in a secure manner.

The above methodology is an effective way to approach secure business process design. The vast majority of organizations, sadly, will not reevaluate the security posture of their business processes until they experience a breach. In those cases, there will often be a need to evaluate the processes that are directly related to the breach as part of the post-incident analysis portion of the Incident Response plan. It is regrettable that it often requires irreparable harm to come to an organization in order for the organization to address systemic issues that exist with respect to security. It is the reactive nature of business and the force of business inertia that makes this a reality, however, not only in terms of security but in terms of general business processes and practices. Few organizations make meaningful reforms when things are going well; it generally takes a negative event in order to provoke meaningful change.

The process of designing business processes in a secure manner requires security to both have a seat at the table when the process is being designed, but also to help draft requirements for the process. For example, a legacy process to transfer information between two physical locations may have originally had requirements to perform the transfer as quickly as possible. A secure business process may require that information to be transferred from one location to another in an encrypted fashion, and to ensure that no one has access to the unencrypted information at any time without multifactor authentication. The former requirement would likely yield a faster transfer mechanism, but the latter requirement is far more likely to yield a reasonably fast transfer mechanism that is also secure.

There are many frameworks that exist to help organizations to design secure processes. Among them are the International Standards Organization (ISO) 27001 series and various similar frameworks. These frameworks establish a base set of controls that organizations should employ, a committee to operate the program, and a framework for documentation and communication throughout an organization. Frameworks can be very helpful in building security into organizations with little familiarity with security practices.

In order for any of these initiatives to be successful, there has to be an executive level commitment to the process. Security is a business problem, and executives that do not recognize that fundamental fact in the current climate have a relatively short shelf life. However, there is a profound difference between an understanding that security is everyone's responsibility, and a commitment to making security a part of everything the organization does. It is my strong opinion that the modern global economy requires the latter approach. Shifting the paradigm from one of business first and security as an afterthought to one of security as an inextricable part of conducting business responsibly in the new millennium is a fundamental shift in thinking that must occur for modern organizations to survive and thrive in the threat dynamic that exists in the world today.

Reactive vs. Proactive Security

One of the most important paradigms that must shift in the security space is the shift from comfort with response to a security incident after the fact to a posture in which Incidents can be prevented and mitigated before the threat manifests itself as harm to an organization. This shift must happen not only inside the organizations themselves and with the technology vendors, but also in the legal and regulatory climate to allow for offensive security measures.

The idea of offensive security is attractive on its surface, but admittedly there are significant ethical and moral challenges presented by predictive and offensive security measures. Proactive security in general also faces significant challenges. For example, if you stop the threat before it happens, how do you prove what the impact would have been or that it would have happened at all if your preventative measure was not in place? If you cannot demonstrate these things, how do we prove the Return on Investment (ROI) that is achieved by the preventative measure? The micro-economic impact of the solution would be difficult to quantify, and organizations would be forced to rely upon an imperfect macroeconomic calculation to baseline the industry and region they are in, to the extent those statistics are accurate and available, and determine if they are more or less exposed after they implement a measure. This is significantly challenging as businesses hesitate to invest significantly in people, process, and technology when they cannot calculate an anticipated and actual ROI.

Predictive security is the idea that past patterns of behavior are indicators of future behavior. This idea is not only popular with Information Security thinkers, but also dystopian authors who are looking into a cynical view of the future of law enforcement. The challenge is, how do you take punitive measures against someone who hasn't done anything yet? Just because a person has shown a behavior pattern that makes them significantly more likely to commit a certain act in the future does not mean that they will definitely perform that act. Human beings have free will that can allow them to change course just before crossing the threshold into an illegal or immoral act. To what extent should an organization be allowed to use predictive modeling and behavioral analysis, then, to reduce the risks presented by their employees or potential employees? This is the subject of fierce debate throughout the world. What is clear is that technology utilizing advanced analytics is beginning to give security professionals the data necessary to make predictive security decisions; the question is to what extent will they legally be able to deploy such methods to reduce their risk. There are significant privacy regulations globally that are designed to limit the data that can be collected on individuals as well as how that data can be used. The idea is to prevent predictive security modeling from limiting the earning potential of individuals who may match identified risky behavior patterns. These regulations can inhibit security programs to a significant degree, and in some cases, as a result, cause harm to the country's economy. It is an elusive balance to give organizations the tools they need to protect themselves while simultaneously giving people the freedom and privacy that they enjoyed prior to the evolution of technology to its current capabilities with respect to monitoring of communications and general electronic surveillance.

Offensive security is a different problem. Essentially, the central premise is if someone hacks me, can I hack them back? By "hacking back" I do not mean that the organization would steal from their attackers, but instead would take some retaliatory action that at least frustrated attackers, and possibly even caused harm to the systems they used to launch the attack, to the extent that those retaliatory attacks are legal. Further, the idea presented by Paul Asadoorian and John Strand at the 2012 RSA Conference is that statistics about attackers could be gathered and turned over to the proper authorities.[1] There are obvious nuances to this question, and like many others, it is not as simple as the high-level question may indicate. However, assuming an organization could clearly identify who they are being attacked by and they possess the capability to launch a counter strike that would not cause collateral damage to any third party, would they be within their rights to do so? Common sense says they should be, but there is very little legal precedent to suggest they would be legally protected should they do so. The issue is further complicated by the fact that these attacks are often perpetrated across traditional terrestrial borders.

What can an organization do then? If they are to turn over evidence to the authorities in their country, those authorities are unlikely to have jurisdiction over the perpetrators, so what good would that do? There are, at the time of this writing, few if any publicized agreements that would allow for prosecution and extradition between countries for these types of cases; the agreements that do exist deal primarily with neighboring countries and are not global in their reach, although those types of agreements may exist one day. The crux of the matter is the deterrent capability we are providing to organizations. As it currently stands, the attacker either reaps a financial windfall if successful, or has very little negative consequences if they fail. So long as those circumstances exist, cyber-crime is not only carries some of the highest potentials for benefits, but also carry some of the least negative consequences of any type of crime.

Building laws about offensive security will be important if we are to shift the cyber-crime paradigm. For example, if an organization were to sprinkle their data with "toxic data" or data that would cause harm to the attacker after a certain amount of time being outside of its intended environment, would that be acceptable? It would be similar to methods used by banks to deter bank robbers, but would it be legal if a file would physically destroy or infect an attacker's computer with ransomware? In order to implement any meaningful offensive security measures, governments and legislatures around the world will need to clarify the rules of engagement.

Regardless of whether organizations are allowed to defend themselves or nation-state militaries will be protecting their digital private and corporate citizens, it is easy to imagine a world in which there is a full-scale cyber-war between legitimate governments and businesses and the cyber-pirates and privateers we see as threat actors today that would rival the battles between sophisticated navies fielded by world powers and pirates of the seventeenth and eighteenth centuries. Similar to the seventeenth and eighteenth centuries, it is easy to imagine a scenario where the countries that allow organizations to protect themselves and also aggressively protect their digital corporate citizens will attract more businesses to their countries, thereby helping the economy and the quality of life in those countries. The global economy is changing, and partnerships between the public and private sector in various countries around the world may play a significant role in the wealth of nations in the new millennium.

---

[1] "What Is Offensive Security? – Definition from WhatIs.com. Accessed May 27, 2016. http://whatis.techtarget.com/definition/offensive-security.

Traditional Reactive Security Models

Security models at the time of this writing are largely reactive. Essentially, the metrics that security programs are measured by are metrics like Mean Time to Detection (MTTD) and Mean Time to Response (MTTR). These metrics imply that the best possible outcome is to shrink the amount of time it takes an organization to detect a breach or to respond to a breach, but what about taking steps to prevent a breach from happening in the first place? The legal, moral, and ethical challenges previously discussed make it difficult to implement proactive security models, but the idea of shifting from a reactive model to a proactive model is a worthwhile pursuit.

Traditional models are a good beginning to formulate a program, and as such, perfecting them until better options are available will help an organization be better positioned to implement a proactive security model. Particularly, minimizing false positives and determining risk levels for specific assets and users is critical to building a proactive program, as stopping things as they are happening or before they happen significantly raises the negative consequences associated with inappropriately interfering with authorized business processes. In order to prepare for the implementation of a proactive security model, it is imperative to ensure the business and the security teams are working seamlessly in concert to build and refine the program.

Adaptive Security

Adaptive security is an emerging and interesting concept that contains some aspects of proactive security without going so far as to present the challenges associated with a truly proactive program or technology. Essentially, adaptive security refers to programs and technologies that can adapt or change their responses based on shifting realities. There are a variety of vendors in the content- and context-aware security spaces that are striving to build adaptive security models into their products, with varied levels of success. There are essentially two types of adaptive security that are beginning to emerge: systematic adaptive security and user-centric adaptive security.

Systematic Adaptive Security

Systematic adaptive security builds response models based on system-generated events. For example, if a machine is determined to have a virus, a systematic adaptive security model would automatically program the system to isolate the machine off the network and shut down all methods of communication to that device as soon as the virus is discovered in an effort to limit the impact. This is not the only application of systematic adaptive security, but an example of how systems can work together to provide key pieces of information that can raise the risk profile of a machine or system, and treat that machine or system differently based on an escalating risk profile or mounting IoC.

The core tenet of systematic adaptive security is the idea that the risk profile is related to the system itself. This approach is familiar to more traditional bits, bytes, and signature-based technologies, but offers an approach that can be effective in implementing containment and eradication procedures in seconds or less rather than in hours or days as previously was the case when these trends had to be noticed and these changes had to be implemented manually. Systematic adaptive security can be very effective at identifying and protecting against external threats.

Identifying external threat actor groups based on tactics, techniques, and protocols offers the ability to build systematic adaptive security models to address external threats more appropriately than has been previously possible. For example, the system may be programmed to respond differently to organized criminal threat actors by terminating their access as quickly as possible, while nation-state actors may be observed for a longer period of time in order to discern how broad their reach is and what they are looking for. Gathering intelligence may be a more prudent response in one scenario over another based on the threat modeling exercises that have been performed. The key is not *what* you do with each group but the capability to respond to each threat *differently*.

User-Centric Adaptive Security

User-centric adaptive security tailors its adaptations based on user risk profiles rather than system risk profiles. These models can be extremely effective, but also have to be implemented with care as they can begin to infringe on user privacy. For example, most people would agree that users who are imminently going to work for a competitor may be more likely to take corporate secrets with them when they leave, but does that mean an organization has the right to monitor an employee's e-mail and web traffic for indicators like résumés attached to e-mail traffic or increased traffic to LinkedIn and use that as the basis for tightening security controls on that user? The legal answer to that question depends on where you live, but even if it would be legal to implement such a program, would it be ethical?

Regardless of the potential for abuse, user-centric adaptive security models offer intriguing possibilities that would allow an organization to build models in accordance with the different insider threat profiles and behavioral triggers and risk scores that would help classify user behavior into those categories as behavior patterns change. Systems can then be configured to treat people exhibiting malicious behavior patterns differently than users who match well-meaning insider behavior patterns. Building user risk profiles can help to minimize the impact of compromised people and also build different responses based on the profiles. For example, if a user is malicious, perhaps their actions are blocked and management is immediately notified, where if a well-meaning insider triggers a policy, maybe they are warned and asked if they would like to continue. If they choose to continue, the system may be configured to subsequently raise their risk rating. User-centric adaptive security models offer very good opportunities to address the insider threat in a more flexible manner than they are being addressed with current technologies and programs.

The "Genius of the 'AND'"

Jim Collins was the first to introduce the concept that there is tyranny inherent in the thought process that we must do one thing or another, and there is genius in the idea that we can instead do one thing and another. Looking for opportunities to do both is important. In the case of systematic adaptive security and user-centric adaptive security, the "Genius of the 'AND'" and would allow us to monitor both behavior patterns and system patterns and adapt our systematic security behaviors based on the aggregate of both sources of information. Doing so would allow programs to have unique response capabilities for each of the seven faces of data loss. That would represent a significant advancement toward the ultimate goal of security Critical Information Assets in a much better and more comprehensive fashion.

Behavioral Analytics

Behavioral Analytics is becoming a buzzword, which is regrettable because it is an important Information Security concept that is being marginalized by its overuse and sometimes misuse. True behavioral analytics is the art and science of utilizing human behavior factors to make good decisions with respect to how to treat users or systems. Behavioral analytics is at the core of user-centric adaptive security and is the focus of many emerging technologies, but comprehensive behavioral analytics, at the time of this writing, is still performed through an aggregate of technology capabilities and human qualitative analysis. Figure 8-1 illustrates the way three common technologies, Data Loss Prevention, Data Classification, and Security Incident and Event Management (SIEM) systems can be deployed in concert to help organizations quickly make qualitative decisions based on the information gathered by each of the products.

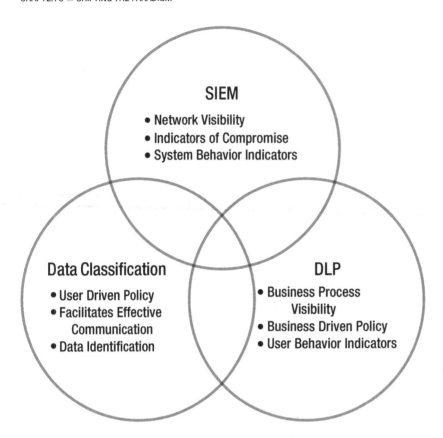

Figure 8-1. *Behavioral Analytics Using Current Technology*

The idea is that each of the technologies answers one of the three key questions that will help to determine the type of threat the organization is facing. Before discussing each of the questions, let us review the different threat actors in play that were discussed in depth in chapter 1 (External Actors) and chapter 6 (Internal Threats). First, there are four external threat groups for the purpose of this book: spies and nation-states, organized criminals, terrorists, and hacktivist groups. The three internal threat actors are malicious insiders, misguided or disgruntled employees, and well-meaning insiders.

The first question that must be answered, then, is whether the threat is internal or external. The ability of a SIEM system to take in feeds from a variety of security products to quickly surface Indicators of Compromise (IoC) and unusual system behavior in order to identify the origin of an attack. That simplifies the task significantly by eliminating close to half of the categories in either way. If the threat is external, the SIEM system can provide further insights into which of the categories the actors fall into based on tactics, techniques, and protocols. It is important to understand as well that the SIEM system is inclusive of the information coming in from the Data Loss Prevention system.

The second question that must be answered is what is the scope of the data that is at risk or actively being compromised? Is the transfer of that information in accordance with an authorized business process? These questions can be answered by the Data Loss Prevention system because it has the ability to monitor the content and context of transfers of data. This information can help to subclassify both internal and external threats. If the threat is determined to be internal, a third question must be answered.

The final question, for internal threats, that must be answered in order to make accurate behavioral determinations is the intent of the user. Data Classification systems in conjunction with SIEM systems can track the warnings and education provided to users prior to them taking a specific action recorded in Data Loss Prevention. If it is feasible that a user may not have known what they were doing is wrong, that is likely to yield a different response than if a user was educated, warned, and then continued to take a specific action refusing to heed those warnings.

The aggregate of the three technologies is extremely helpful in performing behavioral analysis, and therefore, in appropriately responding to threats. Future technologies that make it easier to answer these three questions will help organizations respond in a more expedient way and will also help lead the security industry down the path toward proactive security.

Workflow Automation

As I was writing this chapter, I had the good fortune to spend some time with two very good friends, and very intelligent men, Vahan Galachyan and Joe Romano, who are innovating in the workflow automation space. My conversation with these two highlighted the power of technology to support people and process through intelligent automation that can help to reduce opportunities for human error in the process. These types of technology integration represent appropriate uses of technology to fulfill its proper role in the people, process and technology triumvirate, which represents an important part of shifting the paradigm.

Much of my time is spent evangelizing the need for people and process to be established as part of the program, but this is not to diminish the importance of technology solutions. Tools are an essential part of building anything, and an Information Security program is no different. It is the practice of deploying technology as a stand-alone solution that I see as a major shortcoming of many programs. When technology is deployed properly, after people and process are taken into account, and in support of the same, technical solutions can be very powerful. Workflow automation is an example of utilizing technology effectively.

Automation at its core is seen as a replacement for people and process, and it is easy to see how this misconception is formed. After all, when automation is effectively implemented, there are often tasks that used to be performed by people that are suddenly performed utilizing automated tasks. However, in order for automation to be implemented effectively, the process has to be built and refined to be at its most efficient and has to be both repeatable and documented. Therefore, prior to becoming a candidate for automation, a process must be at least to level four of five on the capabilities maturity model. People are almost always required to implement the automation and are still involved in the process, although their role changes from performing menial tasks to providing oversight to the automated process to ensure it is working properly. Simply put, automation does not represent the triumph of technology over people and process as many think, but instead represents the seamless integration of people, process, and technology in which the aggregate of the three is more efficient and less burdensome for each.

Conclusion

There is a saying that says the first step to solving any problem is to admit you have one. Many people in the business community take one of two stances, both of which prevent improvement in their security posture. The first is the "ostrich approach." This is the approach in which business leaders stick their head in the proverbial sand. These are people that say things like "no one is dumb enough to click a link in an unknown email" or "no one would pay a ransom to an attacker" despite overwhelming evidence to the contrary. The second approach, which is on the opposite end of the spectrum, but equally destructive in my view is what I call "waving the white flag." This approach says "there is nothing we can do to protect ourselves," "the attackers will always be better than us," or simply "the situation is hopeless." Even if these statements are currently true, there are things that can be done to shift that paradigm!

The good news is leaders who decide to confront the Information Security problem head-on will quickly find that while there are no silver bullets, there are no shortage of success stories and ideas for improvement. It is my assumption that the majority of the people reading this book endeavor to solve problems, rather than pretending they don't exist or surrendering to them. The previous chapters have discussed many best practices and proven solutions that organizations can deploy today. The subsequent chapters will attempt to put the current situation in historical context and start the conversation with respect to how we can put the conditions in place on a large scale to make the cyber-world a significantly safer place to do business. It starts with the desire to change and the willingness to shift perspective.

CHAPTER 9

■ ■ ■

The Definition of Insanity

The definition of insanity is continuing to do the same thing over and over again, while expecting a different result.

—Albert Einstein

Albert Einstein's quote about insanity can be applied to a wide variety of industries and practices. However, inside of Information Security the sentiment is especially applicable to a maddening degree. I have given a number of speeches where people will push back on the content, some more forcefully than others, saying that "everyone already knows these things, they are basic best practices in Information Security." Yet, when I challenge those people and ask questions about the way they've *implemented* best practices in their environment, their lack of adoption of the principles they say are universally understood is appalling. The idea that these people know what they should be doing and continue to not do those things, all while railing against those who endeavor to provide them with methods to increase their success probability and adoption in the environment is negligent, in my view. Not knowing what to do is forgivable; knowing the right things to do and still not doing them is not. Some regulations have gone so far as to define such behavior as "willful neglect" and significantly increased the fines for organizations whose violations are deemed to fit that definition. The concept of corporate inertia, or the resistance to change inherent in organizations, is especially detrimental to Information Security programs. The threats are adapting and changing every day, yet their targets remain stagnant. As stated eloquently by Barrack Obama, and quoted in chapter 8, we must be the change we seek.

Building a comprehensive and successful Information Security program requires commitment to the program from the board and executive levels of an organization down, and must be done in a manner that is embraced by employees such that the program is successful from the bottom up. Successful programs may rely heavily on changing habits and business processes in order to implement the best practices that are widely known to be successful for decades, yet still fail to implement. Simple things like the Concept of Least Privilege, which states that users should be given access to the minimum amount of information that they need to successfully fulfill their job function, are rarely implemented. When these best practices are implemented, they are rarely implemented comprehensively to apply to all members of the organization. Separation of Duties, which states that a sole person should not be responsible for all parts of a process in order to reduce fraud, is rarely considered when job descriptions are written or when organizations are pressured to fulfill more responsibilities with fewer personnel. Password Management, which refers to the best practice of requiring strong passwords, and requiring that they be rotated frequently, is often not implemented to the level that it should be in order to balance security with usability. We are all asked to do more with less, and this business theme is unlikely to change. However, ensuring that we are not exposing our organizations to undue risk is a fiduciary responsibility for any member of management or leadership inside of an organization.

These changes will not be easy, and attackers from each of the threat actor groups detailed in chapter 1 around the world are banking on the fact that the majority of organizations either won't implement them, or will implement them poorly. Sadly, many organizations will not make a change, because the status quo is easy and change is hard. The problem we are facing in securing our most Critical Information Assets is a difficult challenge. Threat actor groups are adapting and changing constantly in a tireless effort to defeat our programs and compromise our Critical Information Assets. They are highly motivated, well-funded, smart, and adaptable. If we are to get ahead of our adversaries, and stay ahead of them as they adapt to our changing countermeasures, we must commit ourselves to doing so with the understanding that it will not be easy. U.S. President John F. Kennedy famously said, "We choose to go to the moon. We choose to go to the moon this decade and do the other things, not because they are easy, but because they are hard." Solving Information Security challenges that exist today and will continue to evolve will require a similar spirit of innovation in the face of overwhelming odds. However, we *can* solve this problem and we **must**.

Electric car manufacturer Tesla is an example of an organization that is attempting to build security into their designs from the outset when we examine their self-driving car initiative. Tesla is certainly not the only organization attempting to build a self-driving car, but they have spent more time and resources addressing the inherent threat of security vulnerabilities in self-driving cars. Tesla has gone so far as to invite hackers to try to compromise their systems so they can identify and repair vulnerabilities before they manifest themselves as attacks against Tesla's customers. Similar programs, often referred to as bug bounties, have become popular with other forward-thinking software developers as well. As we continue to advance in terms of technology, the stakes of Information Security continue to get higher. Ransomware that requires me to pay a ransom in order to restore access to my files is one thing, but ransomware that could hijack my car with both my child and me inside is a very different threat. I would be much more likely to pay that ransom when it literally becomes a life and death decision.

The first step is to stop the insanity! We must recognize the things that we continue to do, that we must change if we are to be successful. There is a famous saying that states "The first step in solving a problem is to admit you have one." Many security professionals are in denial. We must evaluate whether or not these problems exist in our organization honestly if we hope to solve the problems that exist. I have played a role in the construction of several hundred Information security programs for large and small organizations across the globe. Some of the core problems I have seen repeatedly will be explained in this chapter. First, let us draw a historical example to the situation in which we find ourselves.

Pickett's Charge

In the American Civil War, the Battle of Gettysburg is largely accepted by most historians as the pivotal battle in the conflict. Prior to Gettysburg, the Confederate Army was winning battles and gaining territory consistently, due, in my opinion, to superior tacticians in the Confederate Officers' corps. The Union had several advantages over the Confederate States in terms of overall manpower and industrial power, among other things, and was always likely to win a prolonged war of attrition. It was to the Confederate States' advantage to win the war quickly in order to ensure the Union Army was not able to overwhelm them with numbers, as the far more populated North drafted and trained soldiers at a much faster rate than the largely rural South. The Confederate Army suffered a defeat at the Battle of Gettysburg, and had massive casualties inflicted on them, which many historians point to as the turning point of the American Civil War. The Battle of Gettysburg was the last time the Confederate Army successfully invaded the North in the Civil War, in which they were defeated. In my opinion, the military blunder known as Pickett's Charge played a significant role in the final outcome of the war.

■ **Note** I spent time in the military and have spent a good portion of my life studying history, especially the history of warfare. I am intentionally simplifying the Civil War in order to use it as an example for the current state of Information Security without going too far in depth. There are many more factors that led to the tide of the war turning, and eventually resulting in a victory for the Union forces.

Confederate Major General George Pickett made the decision to attack a heavily fortified Union position on Cemetery Ridge. The position was high ground overlooking three-quarters of a mile of open field between the tree line and the base of the ridge. Most military theory would point to the fact that attacking a heavily fortified and elevated position, across an open field, was a very bad idea. The assault was misguided from the beginning.

In the face of overwhelming odds, General Pickett led a force of 15,000 Confederate soldiers on a direct assault on Cemetery Ridge. After facing withering rifle, musket, and cannon fire, the Confederate charge failed, and the Confederate Regiment under the command of General Pickett was forced to fall back. General Pickett was not deterred by his initial failure.

After failing on the initial charge, General Picket did not reevaluate his strategy or make any attempts to find a fundamental flaw in his approach. Instead, he ordered his men to charge Cemetery Ridge again, in the exact same manner, not once but twice. When the dust settled and the smoke cleared, the Confederate Army had inflicted very few casualties on the Union defenders of Cemetery Ridge, and General Picket's troops suffered 6,000 casualties. Pickett's misguided charges not only cost those men their lives on that day, but also materially contributed to the defeat of the Confederate States of America, forever altering United States, and consequently, global history.

Too many Information Security programs operate similarly to Pickett's Charge. As a community, we suffer breach after breach, related to many of the same programmatic shortcomings, yet many of those shortcomings persist, sometimes even inside of organizations that have been breached themselves. Rather than continuing to charge the proverbial Cemetery Ridge with no change in strategy, we must learn from our security shortcomings, or better yet, from the shortcomings of others, by studying the details of breaches and formulating strategies for how we could protect our own organization in similar circumstances.

■ **Note**   The above analogy is understandably imperfect, as kinetic warfare differs from cyber-security challenges in significant ways, but the need to reevaluate strategy after a failed attempt in either arena is important to ensure we do not embody Albert Einstein's definition of insanity.

Too often the response from organizations is to throw money or personnel at the problem. I will reiterate and reemphasize my points from previous chapters. It is perfectly acceptable to purchase a new application to fill a gap in a security program and to develop that program to maximum efficiency. It is also fine to hire additional resources to enhance capacity in an effort to grow and enhance a security program. My point is that, too often, these solutions are part of a knee-jerk reaction and are not part of an overall plan and means to an end goal. Often an increase in budget or manpower is *part* of the solution, but these measures will not help in cases where the **strategy** is fundamentally flawed or missing altogether.

It is important to remember that successfully building a compressive security program is not a one-time activity, but an effort to build and continuously improve upon the program that is built. As a result, studying breaches, whether they happened to our organization or another organization, is an important part of the process. When studying the details of a breach, either in our own organizations or in other organizations, it is important to determine the root cause of the breach. Was the breach due to a lack of resources? Sometimes even with unlimited resources, the program would not have surfaced the threat. In those cases, a fundamental shift in strategy and/or tactics is required. The Post-Incident activity portion of the Incident Response plan described in detail in chapter 5 is extremely important because it is that portion of the plan in which the organization identifies opportunities for improvement. Simply going through the motions will not produce the valuable changes to the program or business processes that are necessary in order to materially improve the security posture of the organization.

The first step in making any meaningful change is to admit there is a problem. Many times, I have sat inside of a room and had a security team tell me "everyone knows that" or "that can't happen to us" only to read a headline about the same company in the coming months, detailing as breach that was preventable had the team swallowed the pride enough to honestly evaluate their program. It is important to approach

Information Security with a measure of humility. The truth is there are adversaries that exist that can breach almost any organization given they have enough will and enough time. It is incumbent upon security teams to remain vigilant and adaptable. Another famous saying says, "pride comes before the fall," and I have personally witnessed a number of organizations that have been negatively impacted by hubris on the part of their security teams and/or leadership.

Planning to Fail

Benjamin Franklin famously said, "Failing to plan is planning to fail." Although there is increasing public awareness of Information Security challenges and large-scale data breaches, a shocking number of organizations do not have any plan whatsoever to protect themselves from these threats. According to research from the 2014 Ponemon cost of breach study, cited in Figure 9-1, 45%, or fewer than half, of organizations studies had any security strategy in place to protect information assets.

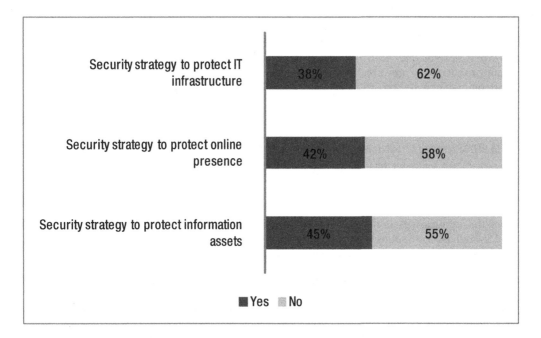

Figure 9-1. *Security Strategy Survey Source: "News & Updates." Ponemon Institute Releases 2014 Cost of Data Breach: Global Analysis. Accessed June 1, 2016.* `https://www.ponemon.org/blog/ponemon-institute-releases-2014-cost-of-data-breach-global-analysis`

Yet, when I present the need to protect Critical Information Assets to teams, there are people who would tell me that everyone knows that and I am wasting their time! Those same people are likely part of the 55% of organizations that have no plan. It is far easier to pretend to have a plan than to have to actually develop and implement it. Many organizations have a compliance program masquerading as a security program, and are desperate to protect the illusion that their program is effective. These organizations use "minimum regulatory compliance" as a fallback to prove that a requirement was met in order to minimize fault in case of a breach. Firstly, I want to warn anyone reading this book that the minimum government requirements are not sufficient for any serious security program. A comprehensive program should materially exceed any minimum regulations and will display plans for consistent and measured improvement. Secondly, my experiences with organizations who list compliance as their primary concern generally ignore security best practices, unless they happen to be mandatory. Instead, these organizations build a shell program for data protection and fail to adapt over time to new threats. I argue that a compliance-focused security program is not only incomplete but dangerous; while it might meet minimum governmental measures these programs lack consistent improvement and do not proactively update security measures. As a result, compliance programs, despite meeting minimum requirements, are open to claims of negligence for failure to implement reasonable controls that are capable of actively identifying and protecting from threats against an organization.

It is shocking that fewer than half of organizations have a plan at all, according to research by Ponemon summarized in Figure 9-2, especially because the question doesn't address the efficacy of the plan. It is fair to say that based on the research, many organizations are planning to fail by completely failing to plan with respect to Information Security. Why is that? I don't have a good answer to the question, but I know that there are several factors, including the historical lack of data security emphasis, the recent technological growth of computers and the Internet, and a lack of historical need to protect from nonphysical threats. It is my sincere hope that this book helps to increase the number of organization that build and execute a comprehensive Information Security program.

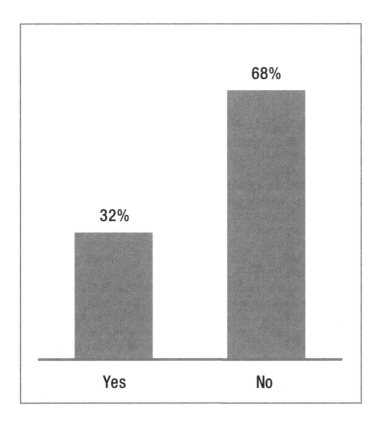

Figure 9-2. *Cyber-Insurance or Data Breach Detection Source: "News & Updates," Ponemon Institute Releases 2014 Cost of Data Breach: Global Analysis. Accessed June 1, 2016.* https://www.ponemon.org/blog/ponemon-institute-releases-2014-cost-of-data-breach-global-analysis

Worse yet is the fact that even fewer organizations have taken concrete steps to protect themselves. Many Information Security leaders debate whether organizations should have cyber-insurance, or some type of data breach protection, whether it be a program as outlined in this book, or simply a technology that is deployed. I would argue that every organization should have both to some extent, but the statistics referenced in Figure 9-2 show that fewer than one-third of organizations have *neither* data breach protection n**or** cyber-insurance.

Figure 9-2 is also cited from the 2014 Ponemon cost of a data breach survey and the figure is mind-boggling. The idea that so few organizations have either cyber-insurance or breach protection is difficult to fathom. Leon Panetta, former U.S. Secretary of Defense and Director of the U.S. Central Intelligence Agency, stated at the 2015 RSA Conference, "Organizations can either choose to deal with cyber threats through planning or they will be forced to deal with them through crisis." It is clear that many organizations will be forced to deal with threats through crisis if they do not commit to planning for how to protect themselves, and what they will do should their organizations be compromised.

It is clear from the aforementioned statistics and figures that the majority of organizations are not planning to protect their information assets, and do not have even basic protections in place. Anyone who claims that these types of protections are common knowledge and universally in place are either delusional or disingenuous. The lack of a comprehensive plan and protection strategy for cyber-threats specifically focused on Critical Information Assets is a problem that organizations must acknowledge and aggressively attempt to solve. The manner in which organizations choose to address these challenges is certainly important, but the **will** to address these challenges and the commitment to addressing them in a comprehensive way certainly must precede the discussions of *how* they should proceed.

Check Box Compliance

Chuck Bloomquist, cofounder of BEW Global, which subsequently became InteliSecure, and overall thought leader in the content analytics space, once told me that "There is no checkbox, and there is no easy button." When talking about Critical Information Asset security. The truth is, if it were easy to protect Critical Information Assets, everyone would do it, and regulations compelling organizations to do so would be irrelevant and unnecessary. It is not easy to do so, and as a result, many countries and industries have adopted a variety of regulations designed to protect consumers from the harm associated with having their information stolen. As a result, there is an entire cottage industry that has developed around complying with various regulations.

Complying with regulations is essential in many industries. The need to comply with regulations and the need to secure an organization's most Critical Assets are not mutually exclusive. It is true that many of the assets that are subject to regulations are also Critical Information Assets in need of the type of protection that a security program can provide. However, it is important to understand compliance is not security. Both are essential, especially in regulated industries, but conflating the two is one of the biggest mistakes security organizations make. In fact, as soon as a specific countermeasure is mandatory for an industry, it can be assumed that any sophisticated adversary that would attack that organization would have a plan to defeat that countermeasure. In Sun Tzu's *The Art of War*, the great military philosopher makes a point about the importance of deception, which is also applicable to Information Security. Sun Tzu said, "All warfare is based on deception. Hence, when we are able to attack, we must seem unable; when using our forces, we must appear inactive; when we are near, we must make the enemy believe we are far away; when far away, we must make him believe we are near."[1] Deception is also important when protecting Critical Information Assets from attackers.

Imagine, if you will, an American football team. If one team were to tell the opposition, prior to the play, which play they were running and who was going to have to ball, how successful would that team be? To put it in more international terms, if we were to extend the analogy to international football, which is known as soccer in North America, if a team were to dictate to the other team how their strikers were going to attack,

---

[1]Sun Tzu and S. B. Griffiths, *The Art of War. Place of Publication Not Identified* (Oxford: Oxford University Press, 1971).

or their strategy for placement of penalty kicks in a shootout, how successful would they be? Even ancient texts like Sun Tzu's "The Art of War" discuss the need for deception in combat, which can be extended in modern times to competition. The universal truth in all of these examples is the fact that in any form of competition or conflict, deception is a necessary advantage. Information Security is no different, a countermeasure exists for any measure that is taken by *either side*. Intelligence and counter-intelligence is important for both sides.

For the same reasons that we must study the adversary groups outlined in chapter 1, our adversaries seek to gain an understanding of what measures we have taken to secure our Critical Information Assets in an effort to defeat the protections we have put in place. Simply put, if an organization puts the minimum protections in place to comply with industry or regional regulations, that organization has essentially communicated to any potential attacker exactly what is in place. Put another way, any potential attacker who is targeting healthcare information in the United States is going to be aware of the Health Insurance Portability and Accountability Act (HIPAA) regulations and the protections dictated within. They will also almost universally have a plan to defeat those minimum protections.

■ **Important**   The sum of an organization's security program, then, is the measures that they have taken to secure Critical Information Assets that go *beyond* what is required from a compliance perspective.

Far too often, organizations lump Information Security and Compliance together, but they are fundamentally different functions, and often very different mentalities. Compliance refers to the organization's ability to execute the instructions of someone else, such as a government or industry council. Security is a struggle more closely related to an athletic competition or a military conflict. Compliance is a regulatory exercise that yields a binary result; an organization is either compliant or they are not. Security is a competition in which one side performs better than the other resulting in winners and losers proportional to the degree in which they were able to defeat their opponent's plans and goals. This is not to say that compliance is not important, only to say that compliance and security are fundamentally different. The goal of compliance is to pass audits, whereas the goal of security is to protect Critical Assets to the greatest extent possible.

Compliance can have a negative connotation for security professionals due to the fact that the two are often conflated, but compliance is not a bad thing. It is important, however, to clearly distinguish compliance from security and set different goals and assign separate budgets to each. Doing so will ensure that security measures are not taken in order to satisfy a compliance requirement, but are instead taken to strengthen the security posture of the organization. Similarly, it ensures compliance solutions are not hijacked by the security team, causing a delay in complying with necessary regulations.

The Ostrich Approach

Many organizations know that security is a concern, but choose to pretend there is no problem rather than to address the problem they have. I like to call this the ostrich approach as these types of organizations would rather stick their heads in the proverbial sand than address the issues facing their organization. This approach is far more prevalent than I like to admit, as many security teams acknowledge the shortcomings of their programs. Those shortcomings include lack of the proper people with the proper skills to address the problem, a lack of a proper program and processes to address the problems they have, or a lack of the appropriate technologies to help solve the problems that have been identified. Due to this approach, the idea of willful neglect and punitive damages have entered the regulatory environment as it relates to Information Security. Willful neglect refers to the idea that organizations that have been entrusted with data from the general public have a fiduciary duty to protect that data top a reasonable extent. Failure to do so that results in material harm to the public represents a violation of the public trust and therefore can result in punitive damages which can, in some cases, triple the amount of actual damages incurred. These changes in the regulatory environment are a predictable repudiation of the ostrich approach, which too many organizations have adopted. Some of those organizations have already been breached, resulting in real harm to the general public and the legitimate global economy.

Throughout my personal history inside the Information Security space, I have uncovered a multitude of problems for organizations that were previously unknown. Many organizations reacted in a responsible way, which was to gain an understanding of what was uncovered and starting to evaluate their options for how they could protect their organizations better in the future. However, some organizations chose to take the ostrich approach, in fact, some organizations have asked me to turn off my equipment and delete any trace of what I had discovered. In cases where the law did not dictate that I must report my findings, I did what was asked of me. In the current state of awareness with respect to Information Security, I do not believe the general public would accept such decisions from organizations, should information regarding those activities ever become public. These types of activities are bad enough when testing technologies, but the ostrich approach has even extended into production environments. I have actually had organizations in regulated industries ask me to only report regulatory violations I detected in their environments to them verbally and destroy all evidence of those violations. Obviously, there are legal, ethical, and moral implications with respect to requests like these, and a multitude of Non-Disclosure Agreements preclude me from making further comment on the issue, but suffice it to say that there are security teams that are far more concerned with covering findings up than they are with properly investing in order to reduce the likelihood those situations would exist. This is the ostrich approach at its worst.

Silos in Security

Imagine a chess game in which twelve people are each placed in an individual soundproof room. Eleven are on one team, and each have control of different pieces of the chess board. The other person controls all of the pieces on the other side of the board. Who would win the game? Obviously, the individual with control of the entire board would have a significant advantage over the eleven people that are disjointed and operating in silos. That visual example is very similar to the silos that exist in the majority of security programs. Attackers have a comprehensive view of the environment, but the defenders generally consist of siloed teams that do not communicate well, if at all. If you were to turn that example on its head, and allow the eleven players to communicate openly, it stands to reason the eleven players would be able to defeat the one, so long as the one was not a significantly more skilled chess player. This is the opportunity in front of security teams that are successful in breaking down silos. There is often significant talent performing different functions inside the environment, but when they do not communicate, the teams end up working against each other rather than collaboratively against a common adversary. It is not easy. As my grandfather always told me, if it were easy, everyone would do it.

Breaking down silos is easier said than done. Many people I speak to contend breaking down silos is an impossible task in large, bureaucratic organizations. I would concede that breaking down silos is difficult, but I would disagree that it is impossible. In order to break down silos, you must do two things; destroy barriers to communication, and create situations in which success can only be mutually achieved.

Destroying Barriers to Communication

The first task is to destroy barriers to communication. In order to do so, one must create a comprehensive strategy inclusive of people who value shared success more than individual accolades, processes that require input and expertise from disparate skill sets and teams, and technologies which facilitate knowledge sharing of information in all directions inside of an organization.

There is a natural tendency for people to not communicate. This tendency is counter-intuitive, as almost always, collaborative communication inside an organization leads to mutual benefit for both parties. It is not productive to opine on why these natural gaps exist. Instead, we should understand this dynamic and develop strategies to mitigate the threat it poses to our programs.

Mutually Assured Success

The concept that significantly contributed to the prevention of World War III during the Cold War between the United Soviet Socialist Republics (USSR) and the United States of America was the concept of Mutually Assured Destruction. The concept was that each country held enough nuclear capabilities to completely destroy the other, and if one attacked the other, regardless of who was the aggressor, they were both sure to perish completely. This scenario can be turned on its head in the Information Security space, or applied to any environment in which collaboration is key to overall success, when departments and silos that have traditionally been at odds can be shown scenarios in which they have mutually assured success. This idea hinges on the idea that these teams would be evaluated on criteria that would dictate that they are either both successful, or neither of them are. By removing scenarios in which one team can be successful without the other being successful, you are essentially making disparate teams a single team with shared goals and objectives, which happen to support the organizational mission and vision. This idea may seem utopian, but it is achievable for organizations willing to challenge the method in which they build and distribute goals.

Most departments and organizations measure performance against Key Performance Indicators (KPIs) and set goals that individuals and teams endeavor to achieve. Organizations seeking to build collaboration between departments can measure success and failures as well as set goals in which one department must involve another in order to promote building relationships and breaking down silos as part of each team's daily work. It is common for goals and KPIs to have an effect on raises and bonuses, which reinforces the previously discussed concept of incentivizing the behavior you want. Too often, organizations tell their employees that they want to foster a collaborative environment, yet their goals and performance metrics do not measure or reward collaborative activities, and worse, individuals inside the organization that act in a selfish manner, do not collaborate, engage in office politics, and build fiefdoms to consolidate power are rewarded with raises and promotions. Often, the organization is not consciously rewarding such behavior, but the people engaging in the behavior are very good at it. Therefore, the organization must aggressively target such behavior, punish it when they find it, and only reward behaviors that result in the mutually assured success of the organization in order to ensure individuals and teams are working collaboratively toward shared goals. Actions speak louder than words and employees observe the behaviors of people who are rewarded in an organization, and often emulate those behaviors.

Some business leaders philosophize that people are an organization's most valuable assets. Others qualify that statement to say that the right people are an organization's greatest asset. In my opinion, people working together to achieve a common goal are an unstoppable force, and people working against each other, thinking only of their own interests can quickly destroy the productivity and profitability of a department or an entire organization. Truly successful organizations reward individuals for accomplishing organizational objectives collaboratively with others in order to break down silos.

Technology Breaking Down Silos

Some organizations have silos deeply ingrained in their corporate culture that are fiercely defended. In those organizations, technologies can help share information across departments, even if the people inside those departments have no interest in doing so. Comprehensive analytics technologies and Security Incident and Event Management (SIEM) systems collect information from a variety of technology solutions in an environment and aggregate that data in a centralized repository of some kind. These repositories can provide a window into siloed portions of the organization.

At the time of this writing, there is a significant effort underway by many of the leading technology vendors to consolidate products in an effort to force collaboration between teams. The development of disparate products on a common platform can force disparate teams to work together while simultaneously allowing security teams to get better results with less manpower. These technology solutions endeavor to build solution packages rather than a collection of point products that do not share information across disparate platforms.

Red Herrings

A Red Herring is a term that originated in the early nineteenth century in London, and is credited to William Cobbett. A red herring is a salted and cured fish that Mr. Cobbett used to throw a hound off of a scent as a child, and the literary device refers to an object or idea that distracts someone from what is truly important.

The Information Security industry is full of Red Herrings as technology vendors continuously push new technologies and functionalities to the marketplace. Threats are sensationalized and buzzwords are created in order to create a market for the new product, but the problem is that many security professionals and teams are continuously moving from one shiny object to another while ignoring the basic tenets of security and far more prevalent threats they are yet to address. We will discuss some of the basics that should be universally implemented in the next section, but first, let us explore some of the recent Red Herrings that have served as distractions from important security countermeasures and best practices.

Example: Mobile Device Security

Mobile Devices are often brought up in meetings as something that need to be secured. Many security teams and security leaders are very concerned about what to do with mobile devices and how they are going to secure them. However, the data available suggests that very few breaches involve mobile devices, and while mobile device malware and exploits are certainly possible and could cause damage inside an environment, the threat exists primarily in the theoretical realm, at least at the time of this writing. According to the 2015 Verizon Data Breach Investigations Report, "0.03% of smartphones per week – out of tens of millions of devices on the Verizon network – were infected with 'higher-grade' malicious code." The truth of the matter is that mobile devices as an attack vector, at the time of this writing, are truly negligible. There are a variety of potential reasons for this. First, many phones are not connected to an organization's domain, which means that an attacker who compromises a phone would have access to all of the contents on that phone, but lateral movement would be difficult. Second, Mobile Operating Systems are being updated much more frequently than traditionally Operating Systems, which leads to a smaller window of time in which attackers can exploit vulnerabilities. Finally, there are still corporate systems that provide much more attractive targets than mobile devices due to the high concentration of information. Regardless, very few conversations or conferences about security do not contain conversations about mobile security.

There are now and will in the future be other examples of Red Herrings in Information Security industry. It is important to perform risk analysis and prioritize risks against Critical Assets when considering which technologies and programs to invest in. One size does not fit all and just because a product or program can protect against a real or perceived threat that can be sensationalized, does not mean that the specific threat should be of concern to a specific organization. Beware of Red Herrings that shift focus away from clear and present dangers and shifts resources to combating threats that do not represent significant risk.

Persistent Areas of Vulnerability

Amid the swirl of fear-driven technology purchases and Red Herrings that exist in the Information Security space, there are some consistent shortcomings that continue to plague security programs. Often, the challenges of security seem hopeless, especially with the growing talent gap for Information Security professionals and leaders. Many organizations find it extraordinarily challenging to find skilled professionals with the appropriate talent and experience to staff their teams. However, there are many simple best practices that can be implemented that could have a significant impact on the likelihood of a breach occurring.

As has been stated multiple times throughout this book, most of the more sophisticated threat actors can gain access to most environments if given enough time and resources. However, the silver lining in that dark cloud is that there are enough soft targets, or organizations with a relatively weak security posture, that even basic hardening measures may be enough to dissuade potential attackers since they could attack a different environment with less effort and still gain the types of information they seek.

With some exceptions, security programs are designed to increase the work factor, or time and resources it takes to compromise an environment, rather than making a network completely impervious to attack, which would require an exceptional amount of resources in terms of investment in both technology and personnel while making it slow, difficult, or impossible for authorized business processes to take place. Therefore, eliminating the most common attack surfaces are a good first step toward improving the security of an environment, and significantly increase an attacker's work factor should they launch an attack on the environment. Due to their effect on overall security as well as their relative low cost, the following examples, among others, should be implemented as quickly as possible by every organization. This is not to say other protections should not be put in place, as they certainly should, but the majority of breaches that I have encountered could have been mitigated in some way by addressing these recurring issues.

Single-Factor Authentication Servers

When I have an opportunity to speak to researchers and Incident Response professionals, the most common point of entry into an organization is single-factor authentication servers. Some researchers would narrow the scope to single-factor authentication Citrix servers, but most researchers I have spoken with agree that a single factor of authentication, which is normally a password, creates opportunities for attackers to use Social Engineering, malicious software on legitimate sites, and password skimming techniques to gain the passwords of users, especially privileged users, inside an organization. Multifactor authentication has become relatively easy and inexpensive to implement in organizations, and significantly increases the work factor associated with an attack on an environment.

There are three factors of authentication that can be used that are widely recognized among Information Security professionals. They are something you know, like a password or a passphrase; something you have, like a hardware token or a chip-enabled smart card; and something you are, like a fingerprint or a retinal scan. Multifactor authentication is the use of two or more of those three categories.

■ **Note** When implementing multifactor authentication, each factor must be from a different category of authentication as discussed in depth in chapter 6. The three possible factors of authentication are something you know, like a password; something you have, like a token; or something you are, like a fingerprint. Requiring a password and a passphrase is not multifactor authentication, but requiring a fingerprint as well as a password is multifactor authentication.

There are two primary considerations when selecting factors of authentication to implement: cost of implementation and likelihood of fraud. In general, the factor "something you know" is the cheapest to implement, but has the highest probability of fraud. The factor "something you are" is historically the most expensive to implement, but the most difficult to spoof. The factor "something you have" is generally in the middle. Each has its strengths and weaknesses, and has been described in detail in chapter 6.

The Future of Multifactor Authentication

Imagine a world where passwords no longer exist. In this world, dual-factor authentication is performed without something you know, or passwords being part of the equation. In this world, the most common method of authentication occurs through the cell phone you carry in your pocket, which is something you have, and the second factor of authentication is your thumbprint on that very same phone. In this world, it is much faster to authenticate as passwords no longer must be typed, and is far more secure because biometrics is part of every authentication. This world is certainly not as far away as many think, and is actually possible today with the technologies that exist.

That world becomes even further removed from the present as we start to look at identities confirmed through fingerprints or even DNA samples instead of Personally Identifiable Information (PII) such as Social Security Numbers (SSNs) in the United States, Social Insurance Numbers (SINs) in Canada, or United Kingdom Driver's License Numbers. In those scenarios, you would apply for a loan or government benefits with a fingerprint or DNA sample, which uniquely identifies an individual using something much more difficult to appropriate than a number assigned to a person at birth, or an alphanumeric number created based on a variety of attributes of a person's identity. These future concepts are certainly speculation, but could significantly reduce the prevalence of cyber-crime from a different angle. Rather than protecting the information, it is making the verification methods much stronger to ensure simply knowing what other people know would be insufficient to perpetrate large-scale fraud.

Regardless of the mechanism, it is clear that stronger protections of a person's identity are necessary as we move into the future. The status quo that allows a person's credit and identity to be coopted based on a cyber-attack is unacceptable and should be universally accepted as such by the general public. However, until it is, it is incumbent upon organizations who harbor such powerful information to protect such information in accordance with the principles put forth in this book.

Social Engineering

Social Engineering is the art and science of convincing a person to do something that is not in their or their organization's interest by tricking or coercing them to do so. Convincing someone to hold a door open for you, as an unauthorized user, by having your hands full is a form of Social Engineering. Calling a user and pretending to be part of their IT department and asking for their password is another form. Phishing, or trying to gain access to a user's credentials via e-mail, over the phone, or other means, is another form. The examples of Social Engineering are endless. It is an attack on an individual user's knowledge and it is very difficult to defend against.

One of the difficulties presented by Social Engineering is the fact that many users that have access to valuable information do not count Information Security among their primary responsibilities. It is easy to condemn an individual user, but as was stated in chapter 6, many Information Security professionals do not have knowledge of basic finance tasks, just like many users in the finance department do not have an in-depth knowledge of Information Security principles. It is, however, important to educate and continuously remind users of their individual responsibilities in protecting information inside of an organization.

Many proactive organizations perform Social Engineering attacks against their own users, either internally or through contracting with third parties, in an effort to identify users who may be vulnerable to attack and to educate those users prior to the attack causing harm to the organization. These types of exercises help to protect the organization from the first step in many attacks, which is Social Engineering. However, most organizations are vulnerable to sophisticated attackers. This is a problem that is not easily solved, as sophisticated attackers are very good at Social Engineering. There is no easy solution to this problem. Combating it requires a program that reinforces Information Security principles consistently and evolves as the attackers evolve their tactics, techniques, and protocols. Information Security is everyone's responsibility. There is no part of an Information Security program that depends on that fact more than working to prevent users from becoming victims of Social Engineering.

Back to Basics

There are core Information Security concepts that are foundational to the Certified Information Security Systems Professional (CISSP) exam and the Certified Information Security Auditor (CISA) exam, but while most organizations have CISSP- and CISA-certified individuals on their teams, many of these concepts are poorly implemented, if implemented at all. In the subsequent sections, we will explore each of these concepts along with an example of a publicized breach that either occurred or was exasperated by a failure to properly implement a basic concept.

Many people believe these concepts are universally implemented because the concepts are widely known. Such beliefs are naive as there is a sizable gap between widely known and widely applied concepts, inside of Information Security as well as in general. When joining a new organization, many employees and executives assume some basic protections are in place, but those assumptions are dangerous. It is important to examine all people, processes, and technologies in place as part of a security program when one is taking over responsibility or accountability for that program. Often, the act of asking questions or looking at the program with a fresh perspective can highlight shortcomings of the program that were always maintained as part of the status quo.

Concept of Least Privilege and Need to Know

The Concept of Least Privilege states that an individual employee should have access to the minimum amount of systems and data that are necessary for performance of his or her duties. This is often coupled with "Need to Know," which requires that an employee demonstrate why they need access to a certain system or piece of information before the access is granted. These concepts are widely implemented in military and government sectors, generally accomplished by classification levels and corresponding clearance levels that determine whether or not an individual has the proper clearance or authorization to access a specific building, system, or piece of information. Most governments globally have implemented an effective Least Privilege and Need to Know system.

The private sector, however, rarely implements Concept of Least Privilege and Need to Know with such discipline. In my experience, few private organizations outside of the Government Contractor space have processes as part of their security program to request access to a system or piece of information, and a process for that request to be reviewed, granted or denied, and periodically reevaluated. Even in the very few organizations that do implement Least Privilege for the majority of employees, there are often exceptions that introduce significant gaps into the program and introduce risk to the organization.

One example of overly permissive credentials that is prevalent in a wide variety of organizations is system administrators in the IT department. Many organizations to not separate system access from data access, which is a major problem. For example, many system administrators need full access to *systems*. That *does not* necessarily mean they need access to every piece of information stored on that system, but most organizations do not separate those rights, which means that administrator users have access to all of the data inside the organization, even though they do not have a Need to Know for that information.

eBay Breach

One example of the damage that can be caused by the failure to implement the Concept of Least Privilege properly is the breach suffered in 2014 by eBay, which is a popular online auction site and retailer. eBay suffered a breach in which 15 million of their customers' information was accessed. As part of the Incident Response, it was discovered that the breach originated from a single set of compromised employee credentials. Regardless of how that employee was compromised, what could that person's role possibly be that would require access to the information of 145 million people? It is impossible for that person to use the information they were given access to even if they wanted to.

Privileged Access Management

One solution to the challenges presented by overly permissive administrator accounts is Privileged Access Management (PAM). PAM allows elevated access to be granted to users for specific reasons, to perform specific functions, and within certain time frames. Simply because a user may *sometimes* need elevated access to perform a job function, does not necessarily mean that they *always* need the elevated level of access.

Another benefit of PAM Management is the implication that because the time frame that a user utilizes his or her elevated access can be controlled, then change control can be enforced with this technical control. Further, Need to Know can be established and audited as part of the change control process as Need to Know can become a required element of the Change Request, which is submitted prior to elevated access being granted to a user for the performance of a specific task.

Separation of Duties and Job Rotation

Separation of Duties is a concept that can be somewhat related to Concept of Least Privilege, but it is more concerned with preventing fraud than it is with restricting access to data. Separation of Duties essentially states that no one person should have responsibilities that allow him or her to complete an entire process without requiring others to perform a part of the process. Implementing Separation of Duties controls are not only beneficial for security reasons, but is also highly advisable as a means of double-checking work and identifying errors.

Job Rotation is another concept that is related to Separation of Duties in that it is designed to reduce fraudulent activity. The idea is that if you change who is responsible for what, any collusion taking place would be quickly identified as the scheme would be broken. Job rotation is a difficult best practice to implement as many knowledge workers are highly specialized, but in industries that are prone to fraud, which have a more generalized skill set, like financial services, may benefit from rotating responsibilities on a periodic basis. Note that Job Rotation does not mean that the change has to be permanent or even long-term. Job Rotation can be accomplished by moving an employee for one month and allowing another to provide review and ancillary duties for the given process if long-term replacement is not an available option.

Societe Generale Breach

Societe Generale is a French Financial Services firm that participates in a variety of financial services activities from traditional banking to a variety of trading activities. According to allegations from the company, in 2008, Societe Generale trader Jérôme Kerviel was allegedly granted access to systems to perform activities directly related to his job function. He also allegedly had access to a second system that allowed him to approve his own trades, which were allegedly fraudulent.

If the allegations are true, the ability to both initiate and approve trades is a clear violation of Separation of Duties, which would have created the conditions necessary to allow Mr. Kerviel to perpetrate an allegedly massive fraud. According to available research on the incident, the trading loss associated with the failure to properly implement Separation of Duties was estimated at 4.9 billion Euros, or roughly 7 billion dollars, given the exchange rate at the time.[2]

There are a variety of technical controls that can monitor and enforce Separation of Duties controls. Some solutions and platforms even require two different people to log in simultaneously in order to perform certain activities. Other systems require the approver to log in separately from the requestor in order to ensure that fraud is more difficult to perpetrate. Regardless of how it is implemented, Separation of Duties can be an important safeguard to help prevent significant losses due to fraudulent activities or other insider threats.

---

[2]https://www.novell.com/docrep/documents/wsxar92soq/Consulting%20Mag,%20Eliminating%20SOD%20Violations%20White%20Paper_en.pdf.

Vulnerability Scanning and Patching

I often tell security teams that people are scanning their systems for vulnerabilities daily, and if they are not also doing so, they are at a significant disadvantage. The truth is, it is neither difficult nor expensive to scan an organization for well-known vulnerabilities, whether you are a part of that organization or not. IT is also neither difficult nor expensive for an attacker to compromise a well-known vulnerability using commoditized malware. Therefore, knowing what vulnerabilities exist inside systems is critical for an organization to protect that system.

Knowing a vulnerability exists is not enough; it is also important to ensure the vulnerabilities are patched, when patches are available. In situations in which a patch is either not yet available for a system, or the function of the system precludes it from being patched, special protections should be built to ensure that server is not compromised using the well-known vulnerability. These countermeasures can include external security products like Intrusion Detections Systems and Intrusion Prevention Systems (IDS/IPS), or more vigilant monitoring of the systems with alerting through an SIEM system. As discussed in chapter 1, many attackers are operating with a cost-benefit analysis in mind. For those groups, it is of material importance whether they can exploit an organization using commodity malware as opposed to an attack that would require more resources and more time, such as a zero-day attack or a Social Engineering campaign of some kind.

Community Health Systems Breach

In April of 2014, a flaw in Open SSL, nicknamed Heartbleed, was announced publicly. The story led the nightly news on many national and international news broadcasts, and graced the front page of many newspapers around the world. In the aftermath of the Target breach, cyber-security stories were gaining ever-increasing visibility in the news media. In the days and weeks after the announcement of the vulnerability, patches were available for most systems to address the threat.

In August of 2014, Community Health Systems, which is the second-largest hospital system in the United States, consisting of 207 hospitals spanning 29 states, announced that they had suffered a large data breach as a result of the Heartbleed bug. How could this happen after several months of patches being available? Four and one-half million people were affected by the breach, and many of those affected joined in a class action lawsuit, looking for answers as well as compensation.

I do not have inside information about what happened to Community Health Systems, but there are only two possible reasons this breach was able to occur. First, Community Health Systems could have not been scanning their infrastructure for vulnerabilities, in which case they may have assumed all their systems were patched, but with no way to verify, mistakenly did not patch some of the servers. Second, they may have scanned for the vulnerabilities, identified the vulnerabilities, and not patched them for some reason. There are legitimate reasons to not patch systems, but in cases where systems cannot be patched, it is prudent to take countermeasures to ensure those servers are not exposed to the Internet. Regardless of the root cause, the damage was massive, and the breach appears to have been avoidable. This is a great example of why it is important to ensure that systems are scanned for vulnerabilities and those vulnerabilities are addressed through a mature vulnerability management program.

Engaging the Business

Throughout this book, and frankly every conversation I have with organizations around the globe, there is an undertone, or central theme, about the need to engage the business in conversations in order to build a comprehensive Information Security program. It is important to state this again explicitly. If you take one thing from this book, please understand that you **must** engage business leaders if you hope to build a program that will be of value and protect the organization. If a security organization is doing security for security's sake, they are simply overhead. In order to provide value to the business, the program and the business activities are inextricably linked.

When I present this concept to Information Security professionals and conferences there are times where I am met with curiosity about how to engage the business effectively, which is detailed in chapter 4. There are other times, however, where I am met with the feeling that "of course we have to engage the business, tell me something I don't know." However, there has yet to be a single person who has adopted that attitude who could provide me with a cohesive methodology for how they engage the business. The truth is, the most difficult thing for most security programs is bridging the gap between security and business operations.

The single biggest failure of Information Security departments is the ability to engage and communicate with the business. The importance in doing so cannot be overstated, and the failure to do so invariably leads to the failure of the program, in my opinion.

CHAPTER 10

Deja Vu

Everything that is old is new, and everything that's new is old.

—Stephanie Mills

Since the Target breach of 2013, there have been a relentless stream of highly publicized cyber-attacks against and vulnerabilities in systems, applications, organizations, processes, and even people. Many times, the victim organizations release statements designed to make it appear as if nothing could have stopped the attacks from happening. The combination of these attacks and the claims that there was no possible defense for those attacks make it easy for organizations to see the situation as hopeless, especially for the nontechnical executive community. Many of the vulnerabilities and methods for exploiting them are highly technical in nature and the attackers' relative skill makes it seem as if organizations are facing impossible odds. However, most breaches or attacks, in retrospect, yield a change in process or program that could've prevented the breach entirely, or limited the damage caused by the attack. Many of the claims that defense is impossible are designed to escape liability on the part of the victim organization; and we, as people and a business community, have faced similar odds before and found a way to prevail.

There was a time when conventional wisdom said that bank and stagecoach robberies were destined to be a part of daily life in America forever. The situation was very similar to the cyber-crime conditions that exist today. However, very few people in the United States today walk into a bank with a legitimate concern that it will be robbed while they are there, and very few banking customers have been negatively impacted by a robbery. When exploring the current situation in which we find ourselves, it is important to remember that every big problem seems impossible, until it is solved. We can choose to take a defeatist attitude and resign ourselves to the fact that cyber-attacks and breaches are inevitable, or we can be part of the solution seeking every possible avenue to defeat these threats and make it more difficult for them to be successful.

■ **Note** The Wild West example is not the only one that is relevant and parallel. There is a similar parallel that can be drawn with fourteenth-century pirates making global commerce and international shipping a dangerous endeavor. One of the solutions to that problem gave rise to stock markets. Others set precedents for how the public sector and private sector in a country could partner to help make the world a safer place for business. We will use the Wild West example in this chapter, but other examples make the same point.

Just as the Wild West in the nineteenth century, solving the problems that exist in the virtual world will require a comprehensive effort between security professionals, technology companies, law enforcement, and the government to create and enforce laws that are effective at stemming the tide of this type of crime. The difference is that we are now living in a globally connected world, which means that any solution will require global cooperation between governments for the benefit of the overall global economy. Such cooperation is definitely unprecedented, but certainly not impossible.

The Wild West

Twentieth-century bank robber "Slick" Willie Sutton was once asked why he kept robbing banks. He simply replied "because that's where the money is." In the modern world, this is the same reason why global cyber-crime syndicates keep attacking organizations over the Internet. The Old West in the United states in the nineteenth century was a largely lawless and dangerous place. As more settlers migrated to the American West in short of opportunities and cheap land, enterprising criminals took advantage of the largely unregulated and unsettled territories, robbing banks, stagecoaches, and trains as law enforcement struggled to keep up with Westward Expansion. It was partially the lack of established frameworks for identifying crime and prosecuting criminals, especially across state lines, which created an environment that was profitable for criminals and difficult for law enforcement professionals to regulate. This is why the 1800s American West got the nickname the "Wild West." Do these conditions sound familiar?

The current situation in the parallel electronic universe that spans the globe and takes no notice of terrestrial borders is similar to the Western territories in the United States in the nineteenth century in some important ways. First, it is a very dangerous place that is flush with cash as fortunes are gained and lost at a much faster rate than they were in the traditional physical world. Enterprising criminals have found ways to take advantage of the speed in which information and capital can be transferred as well as the global connectivity, resulting in people and organizations having vast sums of money and information of value stolen from them at an alarming rate. Further, it is very difficult to police and patrol these online sessions and criminals can lurk in theoretical shadows and hide in little known corners of the Internet, such as the Dark Web, just as criminals in the 1800s could lurk in the shadows and less crowded frontier towns to evade capture, arrest, or general law enforcement attention.

The online presence of financial institutions is a relatively soft target and a lucrative mark just as stagecoaches moving between frontier towns in the 1800s provided an appealing target for roving gangs of bank robbers and other outlaws. In fact, the challenges faced in the American West are not dissimilar from the silk road that brought wealthy merchants to Asia from Europe or the highwaymen that robbed wealthy travelers between towns in the Middle Ages within the boundaries of the European continent. The common theme is that any time there is a frontier or expansion of civilization, there are tremendous opportunities for creating wealth through legitimate means, and tremendous opportunities to transfer wealth through illicit means. In fact, throughout history, any time there were new and exciting ways for people to legitimately create or expand wealth, proportional opportunities for illicit wealth creation generally exist, generally to the detriment of the expanding legitimate economy. It could be said that new ways of doing business directly correlate to new ways of profiting from crime, while the crimes, such as theft and piracy, remain as time-honored traditions in human society. Few people would look at the emerging globally connected marketplace and do not see a frontier that is rapidly changing and still largely being explored. The major difference in the digital frontier is that in other frontiers throughout history, what would exist did exist: it just had yet to be discovered. The digital world is seemingly infinitely expanding and is unlikely to slow down in the foreseeable future. Things a person does not know about today may not have existed yesterday since creation in the digital world is not limited by the same factors as limits creation in the physical world. Laws and regulations designed specifically for this frontier have begun to emerge in order to regulate this new marketplace and to prevent criminal activity from causing damage to legitimate business. Examples of these laws and regulations include global privacy laws, safe harbor regulations, and agreements between individual countries regarding cross-border prosecution of crimes. Additionally, laws that already exist in the physical world are being extended to cover the digital world as well. Examples of this include the ability to file charges of vandalism for defacing a web site in some countries, or the ability to file charges for bullying on social media platforms like Facebook.

The problem with laws and regulations is that they are not created quickly, and have difficulty keeping up with a rapidly changing marketplace. It will require smart and adaptable teams inside of individual organizations in order to fill the gaps.

The correlation between the Wild West and the current state of the globally connected world known as the World Wide Web is strong, and just as modern-day California is a relatively safe place to visit, it is my strong belief that there will eventually be a time where the Internet is not rife with crime and danger. Many things will need to change in order to make that true, and places like the Dark Web will likely always be dangerous, just like any dark alley in any major city in the world is still dangerous.

Just like there was much work to do in the Old West to turn it into a safe and civilized place, the Information Security industry has a lot of work to do today to make the digital world a safer place to do business. While our work will be difficult, it is crucial to the global economy, and it is not impossible.

Evolving the Approach

Lawmen and sheriffs in the western United States in the Post-Civil War period found themselves in a precarious position in dealing with a rash of bank robberies and stagecoach robberies plaguing frontier towns. They were outgunned and severely outnumbered. Further, the laws regarding the methods they could and could not use to fight these crimes were not clearly defined. The line between the law and criminals was very thin and blurry. In fact, many of the people who became lawmen in the Wild West were former criminals and generally used questionable methods to keep the peace in that time and place.

This situation should seem familiar to any Information Security professional in modern times. There are far more bad guys than good guys, and the bad guys don't have to play by the rules, whereas the good guys do. Further, there are many situations in which the bad guys who are caught are offered the opportunity to switch sides in exchange for lighter sentences. Since the rules are evolving, the good guys are at a further handicap as yesterday's countermeasure may be illegal tomorrow, which leads to a hesitance to implement it. To make matters worse, the digital world is digitally connected, and borders do not slow down cyber-criminals. Conversely, every country has different regulations affecting Information Security teams that range from minor impediments to effective programs to proverbial handcuffs that preclude an organization from taking necessary steps to protect themselves. Since these regulations are inconsistent, to be generous, from country to country, as well as constantly evolving, the situation facing security organizations seems dire. I, for one, find solace in the fact that the situation facing a late nineteenth-century sheriff was no less daunting, and had life and death implications for the individual, which we do not face in the digital world.

Lessons from History

George Santayana famously said, "those who cannot remember the past are doomed to repeat it." The fact that there are parallels between bank robbers in the Wild West and the cyber-crime epidemic that we see today is interesting, but only relevant in the lessons from history that can be learned from the correlation. There were many things that were done to make the bank robbing epidemic that affected Westward Expansion during the nineteenth century a relic of the past. Some of those steps were specific to that problem and that time, but it may be possible to replicate some of them in order to address what we are currently facing.

Perhaps the most important lesson from history as it is related to cyber-crime is that while the situation appears dire and hopeless, as it must have to bank employees in the nineteenth-century American West, we *can* and we *must* defeat this threat. Doing so will not be easy. It will require a concerted effort and a partnership between private companies, who are currently rivals, governments and the private sector, and innovation and a spirit of cooperation among security companies and Information Security professionals across the globe. First, we should examine the methods that largely eradicated the prevalence of bank robbery as a common crime with a high success rate over a period of roughly one hundred years of incremental progress and evolving countermeasures against an evolving threat.

Creation of the Federal Bureau of Investigation – 1908

The creation of the Federal Bureau of Investigation (FBI) in the United States in 1908 by Attorney General of the United States Charles Bonaparte was formed in partnership with U.S. President Theodore Roosevelt.[1] The formation of the Bureau represented a significant change to the way that laws were enforced in the United States, and was highly controversial. Prior to the FBI being formed, many times criminals could escape prosecution or apprehension by crossing state or county lines. The FBI created a nationwide law enforcement apparatus that forced traditional outlaws to change. It is not a coincidence that the transition between the Wild West outlaw and the more organized criminals of the 1920s and 1930s in the United States coincided with the creation of the FBI.

The problem we face today is not constrained by borders, which makes it far more difficult for us to combat. However, prior to the American Civil War, the United States was more of a loose collection of states than a cohesive federal government. In fact, the situation prior to the creation of the FBI and the current situation, where attacks normally originate in one sovereign country and target another, is more similar to the situation in the United States prior to the formation of the FBI than most would realize. The main difference, however, was the U.S. Constitution, which provided a mechanism for regulating how the individual states work together. There is no similar governing document that governs how countries work together to combat threats to international commerce in the global economy.

The first step in enabling a similar type of cross-border law enforcement agency is some type of agreement or treaty for the express purpose of fighting global cyber-crime. Just like the creation of the FBI was highly controversial in the United States of America, this type of treaty will be highly controversial around the world. It will be especially controversial in countries where cyber-crime is prevalent and represents opportunity to those who benefit economically or politically through cyber-crime. However, this type of agreement is critical in order to be able to prosecute criminals across borders, or at least an agreement for the host countries to prosecute these crimes themselves on behalf of international plaintiffs. An ideal scenario would be a global extradition agreement, but that is highly unlikely. The next best thing, in my mind, is to allow prosecutors from the victim country to bring charges against a cyber-criminal in his or her own country. It is far more likely that a more limited treaty is the best the global community could hope for, but it is important because as long as there is very little threat of prosecution and "hacking back" or cyber counterattacks are illegal, there are few negative consequences that serve to dissuade cyber-criminals.

Having a mechanism in which cyber-criminals can be prosecuted across country lines is important, but it is only the first step in re-creating the success that the United States FBI had in vastly reducing the prevalence of bank robberies. An organization with the theoretical capability to replicate the success of the United States' FBI for much of the developed world currently exists in the form of the United Nations. New resolutions would be required and current treaties would need to be expanded in order to cover the digital world, but it would be much easier to implement those types of reforms inside the United Nations than it would be to charter an entirely new organization. There must also be an investigatory body that has jurisdiction over multiple countries or at least a partnership between task forces belonging to different countries in order to track down criminal syndicates that may move between countries and certainly perform cross-border attacks. If the world chose to leverage the United Nations for this function, these cases could be heard in the International Court in The Hague.

Slowing down organized criminals with a global task force will be controversial and very difficult. It would require a very popular and effective world leader with vast amounts of political capital. More realistically, it would require a number of world leaders working in concert over the course of decades making incremental progress toward those goals. Unfortunately, it would require far more crime and harm to individuals and economies in order to provide sufficient political will for such an undertaking.

---

[1]FBI, 2010. Accessed April 19, 2016. https://www.fbi.gov/about-us/history/brief-history.

Even more controversial and difficult would be having a similar task force designed to combat state-sponsored attacks. It has been historically the role of the military of the target country or its Intelligence apparatus to defend the government from state-sponsored cyber-espionage. However, what happens when the state-sponsored attacks are made on private citizens and corporations? How does that change when the target corporation is multinational? Is it not the traditional role of the military to protect their citizens from harm? If militaries are protecting themselves from cyber-attacks, shouldn't they be protecting their citizens and companies from these types of attacks just as they would should it be an attack with traditional weapons? This is presenting a gray area in which most private companies do not know the extent of their government's capabilities, which is held as a state secret in most cases, but the government has some type of obligation to protect their citizenry. Ultimately, a global task force designed to combat state-sponsored cyber-attacks is unlikely, as it is likely that every country has an active offensive capability. Instead, it will require a public-private partnership as will be detailed in chapter 12.

The Federal Deposit Insurance Corporation (FDIC) – 1933

The Federal Deposit Insurance Corporation (FDIC) that was created in 1933 had very little to do with crime or bank robbery, and far more to do with the Great Depression and restoring public confidence in the banking system as a safe place for citizens to keep their money. The FDIC was created by congress during the presidency of Franklin Delano Roosevelt to combat bank insolvency. The FDIC currently provides insurance to member banks up to $250,000 for each depositor.[2]

The FDIC does not explicitly cover bank robbery; however, regulations require banks to hold supplemental insurance known as a "banker's blanket bond." Between these blanket bonds and the FDIC, customers of the bank are protected against harm coming to the bank. Many people mistakenly believe this is all part of the FDIC, but regardless, the various insurance protections offered to consumers means that there is very little that could happen to a bank that would negatively impact its customers. Similar insurances and guarantees exist throughout the world in order to make sure that consumers are insulated from criminal activity.

The insurance that insulates customers from bank robbery has been replicated in the cyber-world. The Payment Card Industry (PCI) council and card-issuing banks insulate customers from the effect of retail breaches involving credit cards. The industry has taken steps to cancel and replace cards within minutes when they are reported stolen and to detect anomalous behavior in spending patterns and temporarily suspend accounts until the spending can be confirmed by the cardholder. For example, I recently received a text message while standing at the checkout counter at a grocery store while on vacation requiring that I approve my expense prior to the transaction being processed. All of these steps taken in conjunction with each other have limited the amount of gain criminals get from stealing credit card numbers while nearly eliminating harm to the consumer. These types of improvements should be implemented whenever possible.

A similar idea for national identification numbers like U.S. Social Security Numbers (SSNs), Canadian Social Insurance Numbers (SINs), and similar numbers used to identify people throughout the world is necessary and will be outlined in chapter 12.

Anti-Bank Robbing Technology

There were a variety of technology innovations throughout the years that, along with changes in process and people, in the form of law enforcement changes and changes to legal statutes, helped to stem the tide of bank robberies in the United States. From outlaws in the Wild West to the Organized Criminals that plagued major cities in America throughout most of the twentieth century, banks were under a sophisticated and evolving threat, similar to the threat faced by Information Security teams today. The world's timeline has

---

[2]"The History of the FDIC | Investopedia," Investopedia, 2008. Accessed April 19, 2016. http://www.investopedia.com/articles/economics/09/fdic-history.asp.

accelerated with the advances in technology today, but the journey in defeating the current threats is likely to be similar, if not taking place over nearly as many decades. We will need advancements in people in the form of Information Security professionals, process in the form of security programs, and partnerships with governments and law enforcement, as well as technology.

Throughout the next section we will explore technologies that helped diminish bank robbery as a lucrative crime with a high success rate, and draw parallels to similar technologies that could theoretically be deployed in support of the cause of Information Security. It is important for us to learn the lessons of history, and find opportunities to draw parallels from successes of the past, while applying parallel solutions to current problems.

Armed Security Guards

Armed security guards are as old as civilization itself, protecting rulers and places where assets of value have been stored throughout the annals of history. To be fair, armed security guards are not really a technology innovation so much as a change in how business at banks was done, but the presence of armed guards inside banks is a significant development that bears exploration. In response to an increase of bank robberies in the Wild West, armed security guards began to be stationed inside of banks in the western United States and the former Confederate States of America after the Civil War.

Armed guards certainly increase the chance of violence should there be an actual event, as the armed guards are not likely to stand idly by or be pacified peacefully. That said, some criminals will be dissuaded by their presence, and choose not to commit the crime at all. Armed security does change the type of criminal that is likely to attack a bank as well. If someone is going to continue bank robbery as a primary source of income when armed security guards are prevalent, must be willing and able to commit violence as part of their activity. As a result, the growing number of banks employing armed guards led to a decrease in robberies, but an increase in the likelihood that someone would be shot and killed in the course of the robberies that continued to exist.

In the cyber-security landscape, the threat of death or serious injury does not exist, but having vigilant security teams, which are the equivalent of armed guards in cyberspace, is likely to dissuade a casual or unsophisticated attacker. However, this is not always true because offensive security, or "hacking back" is not a current option to those operating on the right side of the law. This stipulation would be similar to not allowing police officers or armed security guards to shoot back at criminals who were shooting at them. Not only would this put officers and guards in great danger, but it would also significantly diminish the deterrent those individuals provide. Therefore, there is little detriment for an unsuccessful attacker. Other than wasted time, there is little negative impact for a failed attack. Further, the lessons learned gained make it relatively easy for amateur attackers to gain skills and experience with little threat of consequence, especially when they are operating across terrestrial borders.

Any time you are facing an adversary, it is necessary to ensure that, at a minimum, the good guys are given a level playing field. In my opinion, there must be some effort made to allow counterattacks in a responsible fashion. It is very difficult for a defending organization to operate with handcuffs on. That said, collateral damage and cases of mistaken identity must be minimized to every possible extent. These concerns exist in the physical world as well, but those problems are exasperated by technologies that allow attackers to hide their identity and impersonate other people.

Exploding Dye Packs – 1965

Exploding dye packs were invented in Georgia in 1965 as a device to aid law enforcement in apprehending criminals and reducing the likelihood that a criminal would escape undetected. Even if the criminals were to escape, the dye packs would destroy the money they had stolen and render it useless. At the time of this writing, the majority of banks currently employ exploding dye packs to dissuade robbers from robbing banks, and helping to apprehend them or rendering their haul worthless should they still choose to do so.

Essentially, the dye packs work on a wireless transmitter. The bags of money each have a dye pack inside. So long as the dye pack was within a certain distance of a transmitter, it would not explode. Once it was removed from the premises, and therefore lost its signal to the transmitter, it would explode, destroying the cash, and marking the suspects.[3]

There was a time while I was involved in the music industry where there were certain music distributors who were creating a "poison pill" in their music files. Essentially, if you legally purchased a music download, you really received a music file imbedded with a virus and a second, imperceptible file that acted as an antidote for that virus. Should you subsequently share the music illegally, however, you would only share the raw music file with the virus and not the antidote, which would result in a form of ransomware requiring the user who illegally received the file to pay for it or have negative consequences that ranged from erasing data on the hard drive to reporting the user and the location of the computer to the proper authorities. In many places, this type of technology was not allowed, but the idea is compelling, and could offer an opportunity to dissuade modern criminals in the same way that dye packs have dissuaded bank robberies.

Data that renders the entire system worthless should it be stolen is deemed to be heavy handed by many world governments. What if, instead, the data itself was rendered unusable without causing harm to the system? The idea goes as follows: the data has a poison pill inside of it that will scramble its contents and render it worthless if it misses a certain number of consecutive check-ins. To my knowledge, this technology does not exist today, but is something, similar to exploding dye packs, which could make the stolen data unusable should it be stolen. Similar technologies that allow for encrypted files to be shared and access to the files subsequently revoked do exist. Using these types of technologies for a different application, like the one outlined above, is within the realm of possibility utilizing technology that exists today.

Security Cameras – 1968

In New York State in 1968 security cameras made their debut as a method for fighting crime. Suddenly, criminals had to be concerned that their activities were being recorded. Obviously, having recordings of crimes in progress aided law enforcement in arresting suspects and perpetrators of crime and increased their conviction rate as they had footage of the crime taking place.

Ultimately, many businesses that could not afford a real video monitoring system deployed dummy cameras or fake monitoring systems that offered an effective deterrent to would-be criminals. The idea that every move a criminal made could be watched and recorded gave birth to a new era of paranoia for criminal elements, which limited their ability to freely conduct their illicit activities. Of course, there is a balance between security and privacy, one which continues around the world today with respect to security cámeras. The idea that someone is recording our every move in modern life is a reality that most members of the general public do not want to acknowledge. However, it is generally accepted today that anything that a person does in the public square will not be protected from monitoring or recording.[4]

In the digital world, similar technology exists that can track everything a user does on a system, down to where he or she clicks on a screen and what characters are typed into each application. A similar struggle between security and privacy also exists while governments around the world seek to find the balance that allows them to protect the privacy of their citizens in cyberspace while also providing a safe environment for their corporate citizens to do business. As was eventually agreed to with respect to video surveillance, it is my belief that countries that do not allow companies to protect themselves will suffer economic harm as companies seek to do business in countries where they are afforded more opportunities to protect themselves. Ultimately, there will be very little thoughts of privacy as a right in cyberspace as monitoring becomes ubiquitous. Should we choose privacy over security as a global community, we will continue to be plagued with the cyber-crime epidemic we face today.

---

[3]"Dye Packs Foil Bank Robbers' Clean Getaways." Tribunedigital-sunsentinel. 1989. Accessed April 19, 2016. http://articles.sun-sentinel.com/1989-11-19/news/8902100716_1_dye-packs-bank-robbers-robbery.
[4]"The History of Video Security Cameras [Infographic]." Video Security and CCTV Surveillance Blog –. Accessed April 19, 2016. http://www.supercircuits.com/resources/blog/the-history-of-video-security-cameras.

Silent Alarms

Silent alarms are alarms that alert authorities to a robbery without alerting the robbers that an alarm is going off. This does not give the criminals time to react prior to the arrival of law enforcement authorities. It also does not give criminals an opportunity to abort the robbery before it begins in earnest when they realize there are countermeasures in place. As a result, criminals do not know if silent alarms are in place in other banks, and therefore gives them pause before robbing the bank, or makes them spend less time during a robbery, knowing that authorities could be on the way without their knowledge. A final benefit is that silent alarms greatly increase the likelihood that the perpetrator of the crime is apprehended, which prevents future crimes from being perpetrated by that suspect, and has an impact on that suspect's criminal network.

Resisting the urge to deploy technology responses as part of a security program acts similarly to a silent alarm. In chapter 4 we explored the Becton Dickinson case, in which there was an effort as part of the attacker to probe the system to determine what defenses may be in place. Had alarms triggered that were perceptible to the end user, the user would have either aborted the theft, or, more likely, tried other methods of exfiltrating the data until he found one that did not trigger an alarm. Instead, only the proper authorities, in this case a cyber-security analyst, were alerted to the suspicious activity. The thief was being watched closely as a result of his reconnaissance actions, but he was not alerted to the increased scrutiny. Only when he actually started exfiltrating large volumes of data was the trap sprung and the suspect apprehended.

It is often stated in Information Security circles that programs only catch the unsophisticated or unskilled criminals. However, based on public record in the Becton Dickinson theft case, this same individual had perpetrated the same scheme successfully at least one other organization. This fact suggests that the thief was at least sophisticated and intelligent enough to successfully steal sensitive and valuable information related to future products from at least one Fortune 500 company. The silent alarm approach is effective both against bank robbery as well as against digital theft.

Motion Sensors

Motion sensors are deployed to detect motion where there should be none. These sensors are deployed to prevent robberies while the bank is not open for business. The principle of motion sensors is essentially to detect deviations from the baseline. The system ignores motion during business hours, since motion during business hours should be taking place. However, after hours, there should be no motion inside the bank, especially near the vault. Therefore, detecting motion after hours can set off alarms. This approach was successful in thwarting after-hours attacks from safecrackers, who specialized in the ability to break into safes and vaults without proper authority.

Today, context analytics systems such as System Incident and Event Management (SIEM) systems, like the offerings from LogRhythm, Intel Security, and IBM; next-generation endpoint security products like Bit 9 and Carbon Black; or network-based systems like Trip Wire or FirEye that establish baselines of behavior and detect deviations from that baseline are the modern equivalent of motion sensor technology. Normal systematic and user behaviors are analyzed from a quantitative perspective to establish behavioral patterns. Modern-day safecrackers, in the form of skilled threat actors, are very good at disabling alarms on systems and breaking into those systems. However, while experts at circumventing protections, those actors must still traverse the network and cause systems to behave in an abnormal manner in order to get an abnormal result, such as exfiltrating data to an unauthorized destination. There truly is no way around this. Some actors have specialized in "low and slow" attacks that are designed to stay under the radar by doing very little of the exploit at a time, but those attacks are still deviations from normal behavior on a system or system, a user account or accounts, or a combination of these.

Motion sensor technology, as well as its modern equivalent in the form of context analytics tools, are effective against external threats – especially when those threats are attacking a system or data repository outside of normal business hours, which is often the case in order to help attackers evade the primary time frame where they know systems are being monitored by security teams or a Security Operations Center. Even though many Security Operations Centers are manned on a 24/7 basis, the off hours shifts are often less skilled analysts, or lack certain capabilities that are possessed by the analysts or teams that work the regular business hours. True 24/7 monitoring requires congruent skill sets around the clock, which leads to a very expensive proposition. Often, the expense of such an operation can be shared between several companies in a Managed Services model, which is a popular method of providing the necessary personnel with the proper skill sets to operate an effective security program.

The Evolution of an Outlaw

There is an outlaw for every time: from pirates on the high seas, to highwaymen on the roads of Middle Ages Europe. From bank robbers in the 1800s and Organized Crime syndicated known as the Mafia in the early 1900s to gang members in inner cities in the late twentieth century and digital crime syndicates of today, criminals throughout history have taken different forms and utilized tactics that are in line with the times in order to stay one step ahead of law enforcement. In reaction to these changing criminal profiles, law enforcement and security professionals have consistently developed methods to make specific criminal acts far less successful and damaging to the overall economy.

Crime is as old as civilization itself. As long as there have been societies, there have been elements inside of that society willing to violate societal norms in order to gain an advantage over their fellow citizens. The idea of building a global strategy to combat cyber-crime is not to eliminate crime completely, but to make the criminals less successful and mitigate the damage they cause to legitimate business. There is a saying that says "only the dead have seen the end of war." I would argue that the saying could be applied to crime as well saying only the dead have seen the end of crime. It is incumbent upon us as an industry to reduce the efficacy of crime in an effort to decrease its prevalence.

Nineteenth-Century Outlaws

Nineteenth-century outlaws in the Wild West period consisted largely of men that were trained to ride horses and fight as part of the American Civil War. Many young men moved west after the war, and those without money or skills outside of martial skills gained in wartime, turned to crime as a means of making a living.

▓ **Note**   This is not to say that all outlaws were ex-military as skills such as shooting and riding horseback were not uncommon, only to say that many veterans, especially Confederate ones, who could not find work after the war turned toward crime or law enforcement as a way to support themselves or their families.

Famous outlaws like Jesse James and Billy the Kid inhabited this era, which primarily ranged between the end of the American Civil War in 1865 and just after the turn of the century, and specifically concentrated in the western United States, which was expanding rapidly and did not have the infrastructure in place to govern and police the area comprehensively.

The Gold Rush also helped to exasperate the problem as some prospectors were generating vast sums of wealth very quickly, and that wealth needed to be stored and transferred across the plains and deserts of the largely lawless area. This provided an appealing target for those who had skills related to riding horses and shooting guns, and not a lot of economic opportunity in front of them.

While gangs did form in the Wild West, criminals had yet to form large or wide-ranging Organized Crime networks and generally operated in small groups. The lack of widespread telecommunications also meant that word did not travel very quickly in the nineteenth century, compared to modern standards, which allowed criminals to move from town to town with little ability for law enforcement to stay ahead of them. Further, law enforcement at this time was not nearly as organized as it has become today with local law enforcement being the primary method of policing and investigation.

Twentieth-Century Outlaws

There were a variety of factors that made Wild West-style bank robberies less effective throughout the years. Among them were the expansion of the railroad, which allowed far more people convenient access to the western United States and also connected the Industrial northeast with the west. Also, there was increased settling and development that accompanied easier modes of travel into these formerly remote areas. Further, the growth of communication systems made it easier for towns and states to communicate with each other.

In the 1920s and 1930s the prohibition period gave rise to a new type of criminal, often referred to as "public enemies," a term coined by FBI Director J. Edgar Hoover, which was far more sophisticated and organized than Wild West outlaws. The need to build a criminal network to distribute and sell illegal alcohol created what is now known as Organized Crime. These criminal enterprises had no intention of limiting themselves to a single crime or source of income either.[5]

Bank robbers like Pretty Boy Floyd, Baby Face Nelson, and John Dillinger were part of these highly Organized Crime syndicates that prevented significant challenges to law enforcement and the financial services community. The success rate and overall lucrative nature of this era of criminals represented explosive growth, but was relatively short-lived. The technologies discussed previously in this chapter were introduced, and with the introduction of each of these technologies, the prospect of getting away with robbing banks waned, and the crimes themselves became less lucrative. As a result, the number of bank robberies steadily declined over the decades and financial institutions have operated in a relatively safe environment, until the advent of the Internet.

It is important to remember that we are using bank robbery as the primary example in this chapter, but it is far from the only type of crime that was prevalent during these time periods, as the Italian Mafia was at its peak during this time frame as well. The central point is that criminals have not changed, the primary change is how those individuals with skill, determination, and a disregard for the law choose to circumvent the law for their own gain.

Outlaws in the New Millennium

The business of crime has become much less onerous and dangerous in its latest evolution. There was a time where criminals had to go to where the assets they wanted to steal were located, and risk immediate arrest, death, or dismemberment in the course of their crime. Modern criminals can attempt to rob thousands of banks while wearing pajamas and sipping coffee in the comfort of their own home. To be fair, being a criminal requires far more skill and dedication to the craft than it used to, but the element of danger has been significantly diminished.

Socioeconomic Contributions

There is a large-scale transfer of wealth that is occurring between developed nations and less-fortunate nations that is being facilitated by cyber-crime. Cyber-crime is big business and is often the most lucrative option for skilled young people in many countries. Further, many state-sponsored cyber-attacks have similar motives. The transfer of wealth is important, because a hyper-connected world allows for the transfer of wealth through illicit means from more prosperous countries or regions to those that are less fortunate. Until now, crime rarely transferred wealth from one economy to another, but rather transferred wealth inside of a macroeconomy.

---

[5]"History of Bank Robberies," Crime Library. Accessed April 19, 2016. http://www.crimemuseum.org/crime-library/history-of-bank-robberies.

In the United States and most of Europe, Information Security is a relatively lucrative business. There is negative unemployment, and many professionals with even average skills find themselves with the flexibility to live wherever they'd like while making a good salary for their efforts. In many places around the world, there is a dearth of such opportunity. In such environments, many of the most skilled people with respect to cyber-security are cyber-criminals and members of state-sponsored teams of hackers, depending on which region is being referenced. It is important to understand that our adversaries are often the best and brightest minds in a country and not the dregs of society that are often envisioned when criminals are mentioned.

These highly skilled individuals generally join groups or enclaves to share information and collaborate to share information, exploits, and tactics. In many ways, these hacker conglomerates are very similar to Organized Crime around the world, and bear great resemblance to the Public Enemy era of the 1930s. Criminal organizations are sometimes the most lucrative career path in certain parts of the world. One such area is known as "Hackerville" where cyber-crime is not only the biggest industry, but some would argue the only industry providing good economic opportunity and upward mobility.

Hackerville

There is a small town in Romania, located a few hours outside Bucharest, which is the modern equivalent of a lawless frontier town. It is called Râmnicu Vâlcea and as soon as you arrive, it is clear that this town is fueled by something different than the rest of the Romanian countryside. Surrounded by relatively poor villages, Râmnicu Vâlcea is flush with luxury items like European sports cars and fine clothing.

For those familiar with Italian Mafia dons in the United States, cities like Chicago and New York City in the twentieth century would readily recognize the scene. A part of town, or in this case an entire town, which has very little legitimate economic opportunity, is suddenly seemingly flush with cash. Everyone in the neighborhood or town knows where the money is coming from, but it is no one's interest for the illicit activity to stop.

Romania is not a particularly wealthy country, with a Gross Domestic Product (GDP) per capita of $9,499 in 2013,[6] which, for reference compares to a per capita GDP of roughly $53,000 in the United States and roughly $42,000 in the United Kingdom as a point of reference.[7] However, according to the World Bank, Romania has one of the highest growth rates in the world, approaching 4%, driven largely by an increase in internal demand. An increase in internal demand is generally preceded by an infusion of cash from external sources, and with no known natural resources boom or globally popular export market, Râmnicu Vâlcea may offer clues into what is driving this rapid growth in Romanian spending.

For any town to become a haven for criminals, the citizens must be complicit. Many people in Râmnicu Vâlcea are keenly aware of cyber-crime and who the criminals are, but they are bound to a code of silence that prevents them from alerting the authorities. The code of silence in Romania is called "Omerta," which is the same code of silence that precluded Mafia members and citizens in Italian American neighborhoods from speaking to authorities during the "Public Enemy" era of bank robbery previously discussed in this chapter. In fact, if you were to explore any location and time in history that became a haven for criminals, you will likely find that a code of silence among the criminals and the citizens they live among is required and critical to the success of the criminal enterprise. There are many variations of the saying, but essentially an old saying says that the world will always have evil people, but evil only thrives when good people choose to do nothing about the evil that surrounds them.

---

[6]"World Development Indicators, Google Public Data Explorer. Accessed May 2, 2016. `https://www.google.com/publicdata/explore?ds=d5bncppjof8f9_`.

[7]"World Development Indicators," Google Public Data Explorer. Accessed May 2, 2016. `https://www.google.com/publicdata/explore?ds=d5bncppjof8f9_`.

Romania was a communist country until the Romanian revolution of 1989. While under communist control, Romania had little access to information, and there were very few imported products, especially cars, visible in the towns. Technology and media was tightly controlled, which largely isolated the population. The Romanian people quickly reversed this trend after the revolution, and they suddenly had access to information and systems throughout the globally connected world. By 1998, access to the Internet had become widespread throughout Romania, and by 2002 online cyber-crime was relatively widespread.

Romanian hackers started with relatively primitive methods of attacks, which consisted largely of either scams that used Social Engineering tactics to convince naive customers to voluntarily disclose their information, and attacks against accounts that were predicated on successfully guessing passwords that were not secure. In those days, guesses such as "Password" or "123456" were able to compromise a disturbing number of systems.

The attacks and the attackers have become significantly more sophisticated over the years, but the cyber-criminals in Râmnicu Vâlcea still generally fall into two categories: scammers who are not necessarily technically savvy, but specialize in perpetrating scams against naive or unsuspecting victims; and hackers, which possess technical skills.

The scammers have had to evolve with the times as well as the hackers. While the hackers have had to evade increasingly vigilant security teams and increasingly effective countermeasures, scammers have had to deal with a more skeptical public and the reputation that they have built for themselves. At this point, very few people in the developed world are likely to send money to Romania, due to the prevalence of cyber-crime there. Therefore, the scammers have had to develop an international operation in which they have employees stationed in more trusted countries around Europe so they can pick up transfers and funnel the money back to the scammers in Râmnicu Vâlcea. This has turned the once relatively poor town of 120,000 into an international hub for cyber-crime.

There are various ways that people with the skills to become hackers or scammers and the moral disposition to do so can earn a living in Râmnicu Vâlcea. Many join Organized Criminal organizations or go into business for themselves. Still others have become a sort of digital mercenaries who offer their skills and exploits for hire to organizations or individuals who would like to target a person or organization. In Râmnicu Vâlcea, skills in technology or interpersonal skills are likely to result in a relatively high earnings potential, as is the case in many places. However, in Râmnicu Vâlcea, the most lucrative opportunities for skilled individuals are on the illicit side of the Internet.

The point of telling the story of Hackerville is not to scare people, or to condemn the people of Râmnicu Vâlcea. The importance of the story is to understand the conditions that created Râmnicu Vâlcea and to start to eliminate those conditions to prevent the next Hackerville from popping up if and when the Romanian authorities are able to reign in the cyber-criminal activity in Râmnicu Vâlcea. In any environment with access to the Internet that offers better opportunities for technologically skilled individuals in illicit business than exist in legitimate business, and pair those economic conditions with a strong code of silence, cyber-crime will take root. If left unchecked, the prevalence of that crime will continue to grow until it is targeted and eliminated.

Conclusion

American twentieth-century author Ian Caldwell once wrote, "I write about modern people who share a deep sense of connection to the mysteries of the past. I find that I understand myself and my world better when I'm able to peer into history as a mirror." We must hold up the mirror of history to the problems of today in order to understand them in context and draw parallels that can help us in this struggle. The situation may feel helpless at times, but if we stand before the historical mirror we may find an eighteenth-century version of ourselves concerned about rampant crime occurring on the American frontier. As we lament the global nature of the problem and despair about places like "Hackerville" in Romania, the mirror shows us a portrait of people just like us concerned about crimes that cross state borders and places like Dodge City. The mirror can give us ideas; context; and most importantly, hope.

The challenges we face today have evolved, without a doubt, but they are not new. Since the beginning of human civilization, there have been people who endeavor to steal from others. The "white hat" security professionals of today are akin to the "white knights" in the Middle Ages. People with skills in combat, swords, and lances in the Middle Ages – keyboards and command-line interfaces now – have protected the innocent from harm throughout human history. The correlation between today and the American West is very strong. The terms "white hat" and "black hat" even find their origins in a television show about the frontier days in the American West called *The Lone Ranger* in reference to the good guys wearing white cowboy hats while the bad guys all wore black ones.

This is not to say that all of the answers are commonly known; they are not. However, the indomitable spirit of the free economy can and will overcome all threats, including the current threats we are facing. The remainder of this book is dedicated to ideas for how the private sector can work among themselves in chapter 11 to help to solve the problems we face, and in chapter 12 we will raise some ideas for how public-private partnerships can be effective in reducing harm to the global economy. This problem we face is difficult and multifaceted. The adversaries we face are smart and adaptable. Regardless, we can prevail, we must prevail, and we shall prevail.

CHAPTER 11

The Information Security Community

Don't underestimate the power of your vision to change the world. Whether that world is your office, your community, an industry or a global movement, you need to have a core belief that what you contribute can fundamentally change the paradigm or way of thinking about problems.

—Leroy Hood

Private industry has long been taught that they should keep everything secret from their competition in order to retain competitive advantage. In many cases, protecting those secrets is the overall goal of the Information Security program. However, there are times where industries and need to band together to share intelligence in an effort to combat a problem. Currently, individuals are dealing with Information Security threats on a personal level, corporate level, and industry level; governments around the world are overseeing the carnage from a detached perspective, rarely stepping in to help their constituents help themselves in a meaningful way. In terms of Information Security, like-minded leaders from organizations and governments are beginning to work together in order to share information about successful and unsuccessful cyber-attacks in an effort to strengthen the community. These types of efforts should be commended and expanded.

Note   The role of governments is explored in chapter 12. The content of this chapter is focused on what organizations and industries can do without government participation.

As discussed in chapters 1 and 10, threat actors often communicate with each other, share tactics, techniques and protocols that have been successful, as well as buy and sell exploits to be used repeatedly. This is scary to think about, but when you consider this tactic, it becomes apparent that if private companies shared information in a similar way, they could limit the efficacy of repeated and recycled attacks, which would have an impact on the overall success rate of cyber-crime. Additionally, companies like Tesla, Microsoft, and others are using bug bounties, as mentioned in chapter 10, in order to compensate the hacker community to report bugs and vulnerabilities directly to them instead of using the vulnerabilities against them. Similar programs serving entire industry verticals, and not just software manufacturers and producers of products, could be very helpful in identifying security vulnerabilities before they result in breaches. In order to defeat a community of criminals that are pooling knowledge in order to hone their craft, we must also share knowledge across the Information Security space to the extent that the information shared does not expose our organizations to undue risk and without publishing information that could cause a loss of

© Jeremy Wittkop 2016
J. Wittkop, *Building a Comprehensive IT Security Program*, DOI 10.1007/978-1-4842-2053-5_11

brand reputation. It is also important to find ways to seize the initiative, including things like bug bounties or vulnerability bounties that allow organizations the opportunity to search for, and potentially close, security holes before they result in disaster.

The risks associated with sharing information with partners and competitors alike through vertical-specific Information Security groups must be addressed, but must not be used as an excuse to not participate in such information exchanges. Individual organizations should protect themselves to the best of their ability, and may use their track record of protecting client information as a competitive advantage in both the business-to-business and business-to-consumer markets. However, learning from the successes and failures of others is in the best interest of the entire industry and of the global economy as a whole. Building the public trust in industries and institutions when it comes to Information Security is important in building consumer confidence and enabling the free exchange of currency in exchange for goods and services. Publicly seizing the initiative and having the capability to identify and close security loopholes before they are exploited is not only prudent, but can also improve customer confidence significantly if messaged to the marketplace properly.

Sharing Information

In order to combat the threats that are constantly evolving, members of the Information Security community must freely share information so we may learn from each other's mistakes. It is philosophically difficult for companies in the same vertical to share information because those organizations are competitors, but failing to do so increases the likelihood that attackers will be able to replicate attacks across different organizations in an industry with a high level of success. We have seen attackers do so across the retail industry in the fast few years using similar attacks to breach Target, Neiman Marcus, and Home Depot in relatively short order.

There was a time when outsourcing security services, especially to Managed Security Services Providers (MSSPs) focused on securing and monitoring the most Critical Information Assets inside an organization was also unheard of. When I first started with what was then BEW Global, a large part of my role was to help organizations shift their thinking in a way that would allow them to see the benefits of having a dedicated team of security experts monitoring and managing their systems as something that outweighed the risk of outsourcing those services. Over the years, it has become far more mainstream to outsource such services; and if the industry commits to communication, over time, it is likely that we can successfully shift our collective mindset with respect to communication as it relates to security. There are active members of the community, including Blue Cross Blue Shield of New Jersey, which are working to foster these types of communication in their industries.

Sophisticated attackers share information about what is successful and what is not after attacks and even share exploits and zero-day attacks across frameworks they have developed in order to stay ahead of countermeasures that organizations are implementing. In order to combat these types of threats, we, as a community, must find ways to share information about attacks, both attempted and successful. Ideally, we will go one step further and find ways to go on the offensive and seize the initiative that are both legally and morally acceptable. Where that line is drawn is yet to be seen, but it is relatively uncontroversial that we can probe our own defenses in order to find and fix our weaknesses before attackers do.

We must find ways to protect ourselves and create a safe environment to share information. Some organizations have begun to do so, especially in the health care sector. Information sharing in health care often starts with a conference or a neutral party. One example is the Healthcare Information and Management Systems Society (HIMSS) at the local chapter and national chapter level. Using HIMSS as a vehicle, organizations have begun to discuss successes and failures related to Information Security.

Health records are very sensitive pieces of information to many individuals. They also exist for anyone who has ever received some type of medical care. The idea that health records are stored with Personally Identifiable Information fully in tact is concerning to many, including myself. One potential solution that is in use in some places is tokenization that allows for patient identities to be replaced by something that is meaningless outside of the health care provider. This is something that is helpful but does not go nearly as far as it should. One possible solution is to use multifactor authentication to access the sensitive portions of a patient record. For example, requiring a fingerprint to decrypt a patient's information could be very helpful for situations in which the intended recipient is the patient themselves. There would need to be alternate arrangements to facilitate crucial functions outside of provider-patient communication like billing and referrals, but these types of ideas should be discussed in all industries that deal in Personally Identifiable Information or financial services.

Other organizations have begun to develop forums for Information Security among their partners and service providers. These endeavors are a good beginning for sharing information across industries, but there is a need to expand these conversations and replicate them across industries. In order to truly be a community seeking to defend ourselves from evolving threats, we must commit to share information, while protecting sensitive information. It is critical that any information that is shared is scrubbed, anonymized, and only shared in compliance with confidentiality agreements. We must commit to first do no harm as we endeavor to improve our programs and our communities.

The Elderwood Framework

I had an opportunity to speak at a cyber-security summit right after a gentleman by the name of Jon DiMaggio, who is a member of Symantec's Security Technology and Response (STAR) team, which is responsible for investigating breaches and threat actors around the world. Specifically, they track sophisticated threat actors that have attacked multiple organizations in an effort to study their patterns, examine what they are targeting, and hopefully find ways to defeat them.

DiMaggio gave a presentation about a group of attackers that have been responsible for recent health care breaches that Symantec refers to as Black Vine. The content of the presentation was fascinating as Jon took the audience, myself included, through the history of the organization that he and his team were able to piece together and the evolution of what they were trying to find and why. While the entire story is compelling and relevant to the overall Information Security conversation, the portion of the story that is particularly relevant to the point I am trying to make is the fact that they were sponsored and funded by the Chinese government, and they were using a framework to share exploits and notes with other groups sponsored by the Chinese government that were conducting attacks against other organizations in search of different types of information.

The framework is known as the Elderwood Framework to Symantec, and it is essentially a mechanism in which teams of attackers in the field can share exploits and tactics along with notes as to which tactics were successful and unsuccessful against specific targets and verticals. This level of sophistication is scary, but also illustrates an interesting point. Your adversaries are sharing information with other threat actors about how they can best defeat your defenses and countermeasures; shouldn't you be sharing information with your peers in the industry about what the attackers are doing, and how we could combat it?

Creating a Framework for Sharing Information

Creating a framework to share security, breach, incident, and vulnerability information between organizations is not an easy task or undertaking but it could significantly increase the security profile of all of its participants. A framework could be a technology framework that shares anonymized information across a channel and provides a feed to member organizations, as exists to some extent in the financial services industry, or a group that meets on a recurring basis to share information during a meeting as is starting to emerge in certain pockets of the health insurance industry. Regardless of the vehicle of sharing information, the fact the information is being freely shared is an important precursor to widespread success throughout an industry or sector. There are other activities such as innovation, executive commitment to security, proactive business process enhancements, and many other topics discussed in previous chapters of this book that will deliver quality results for individual organizations; but the ability to share information across organizations and learn lessons from each other's successes and failures can vastly accelerate the overall security posture of a group of organizations, without each organization having to learn those lessons the hard way.

Creating the framework may require significant effort and investment, depending on what type of framework is being built, but sharing information about attacks brings benefits that clearly outweigh the costs, in my view. Frameworks could also be created by regulatory bodies in order to advance the security of the organizations they regulate. For example, the Payment Card Industry (PCI) Council could create a framework in which information was shared electronically about breaches involving credit card information, or the Department of Health and Human Services (HHS) could provide information about breaches involving health care information. Currently, information is available detailing things like which organization was breached and how many records were lost, which serves to inform consumers on the relative security of the companies they do business with, but does little to help other organizations to avoid similar attacks. It would be much more valuable to add information about *how* an attack happened rather than simply providing information about what happened and when. To the extent that it is possible, researchers trying to contribute information or hypotheses about *why* things are happening could also be helpful.

Some may think that why something is happening may be obvious. After all, if someone is attacking a hospital and accessing patient records, aren't they obviously targeting Protected Health Information? Not necessarily. The research into the case of the Anthem breach indicates that while Personally Identifiable Information sitting on the same server as Protected Health Information, only the Personally Identifiable Information appears to have been stolen. Why are they attacking a health care organization to gain access to personal information records? Theories abound, but the majority of them revolve around the fact that health insurers also have information about who an employer is for an individual, which may be valuable to the attacker, especially if the employer might be the U.S. government.

■ **Note**   There are rumors from credible sources that the target of the Anthem breach was specifically information related to U.S. government employees for the purpose of identifying spies and other individuals inside the U.S. government who may be using false identities to enter other countries.

The underlying point is, those attackers may attack any organization that keeps records on employment information, meaning the threat actor profile may not be concentrated on health care at all. This is an example of the reason establishing motive is important in order to appropriately apply lessons learned from attacks.

Industry Alerting

Each industry has different concerns and is attacked in different ways. However, similar attacks are commonly deployed against different organizations within the same industry. It would be most helpful to create a mechanism to share information about attacks throughout an industry, which would likely be implemented as part of a framework as previously discussed. Once the framework is built, a mechanism to alert or update its membership is also important in order to utilize the information gained to increase the group's protection profile before a second group member is attacked. Essentially, it would be an alarm system, or early warning system that would limit the effect a single successful exploit could have.

■ **Note**   There are circles of thought that are against sharing information with competitors inside of an industry or sector. The thinking is that if their competitors are less secure than them, they are less likely to get breached as attackers are more likely to target their less-secure competitor. There is some validity to that theory, but since attackers often have the ability to weaponize an exploit and launch it against several targets simultaneously, that line of thinking may be headed toward obsolescence. Some organizations are finding that working with their competitors and noncompetitive entities inside their industries and sectors yield better results.

There are examples of places that are doing this well today. It is not my intent to present this idea as novel, but rather to highlight areas of success in hopes that the success can be replicated across different industry verticals, and be expanded inside the industries that are already doing well. Most of the examples I have are anecdotal, and are the result of my conversations with security teams inside of organizations, although information on some of them can be found on the Internet. Due to agreements I have made with the organizations who have shared this information with me, I am unable to publish the details of the organizations, but I can say they often take the form of threat intelligence feeds that update all of the participating organizations' security software if one is compromised. Some of the industries that have these types of arrangements are health care and financial services, although they do not include all members of the industry.

All of the examples have one thing in common: They all started somewhere. K. C. Sherwood once wrote, "The hardest part is getting started." This is especially true when we look at problems that seem large or endeavor to create organizations or groups that seem impossible. Perfectionism is sometimes the enemy of action. It is important to understand that something does not have to be perfect before it can be implemented. So long as it is better than what existed previously, it can be implemented and approved upon over time. An industry group could start as simply as an agreement between two security teams to call each other if they see something strange happening. Don't become overwhelmed by the idea of pulling an entire industry together. Rather, look for opportunities to collaborate with people you know and ask them to invite people they know to the collaboration group. Before you know it, the group could be relatively large and sharing intelligence!

The Role of Security Vendors

Security vendors should certainly play a role in providing information to their customers and to the community about the attacks they are seeing. We see them doing so through the annual threat reports they release based on research that they have gathered. They are also beginning to provide mechanisms to share information with their customers about attacks affecting each other, in an anonymous fashion. These vendors play an increasingly important role and may, at some point, be the ones who actually create the technology frameworks that enable the communication of information.

At the time of this writing, companies like Intel Security, Symantec, Forcepoint, FireEye, and Palo Alto have enough of a presence where between them, they are likely deployed in the majority of organizations globally. These vendors have the ability to gather information about attacks globally and share that information in the form of security feeds and notifications to their customers.

The future role of security vendors may be to find ways to provide feeds to customers of other vendors in order to enable the customer to have a wider scope of information provided to them. This is philosophically difficult as well, because many of these organizations are fierce competitors with each other, but doing so would be very beneficial to the community as a whole, I would opine that it will happen eventually, if such plans are not already in the works.

Sometimes security vendors that are directly competing are unlikely to share information with each other. In those cases, vendors should seek out entities delivering noncompetitive security products in order to form a partnership. Regardless of the rules around who partners with whom, partnerships will be of benefit to the cause of security as a whole.

Protecting Participants

The types of information that must be shared in order to advance the cause of security and allow other organizations to learn from one organization's mistakes could cause embarrassment or financial harm should that information be leaked. There are legal agreements that are designed to protect organizations from the inappropriate disclosure of information that would be shared between parties and they should be in place prior to information being shared. Additionally, there are pieces of information that should not be shared in a group setting, so each participating organization should go through a review prior to sharing information to the group to ensure they are not violating the privacy or their employees, partners, or customers and they are not violating any legal regulations.

Privacy and Legal Review

Prior to sharing anything in a group setting, the organization should conduct a privacy and legal review to ensure nothing that is being shared violates any privacy restrictions or any legal requirements. The participants of the group should share the content they wish to present with the privacy and legal teams in order to identify if there are any portions of the content that should not be shared.

After reviewing the initial content, the privacy and legal teams should identify questions that are likely to be asked and provide guidance to the attendees of the meeting of which questions they should and should not answer and how much detail they are authorized to provide.

Some people would argue that restricting the free sharing of information violates the intended purpose of the group. However, if members of the group are sharing information that they should not, the members are likely to be forbidden from participating in future sessions, which is an existential threat to the group itself. There is a balance that can be found that allows an organization to share information that is beneficial to other group members in terms of bolstering their security posture or addressing vulnerabilities before they are exploited that does not compromise legal agreements or private information. In some cases, anonymizing the data is enough to protect the privacy of the subject of that data without undermining the value of the information.

The Rise of the Platform

Far too often, Information Security has become a parade of products and vendors. Various research cites different numbers, but essentially the research suggests the average enterprise organization has close to twenty-five security vendors providing products as part of their Information Security program. Worse, those products often do not communicate with each other. I attend the RSA conference in San Francisco each year, and if you were to walk the floor of the RSA conference, you would see hundreds, if not thousands, or vendors displaying their cyber-security technology. How can we, as a community, make sense of all those different products?

There is definitely a role for start-up organizations in any industry. New companies often provide a different way of doing things or a unique capability that did not exist prior to the existence of the company. This is an overwhelmingly positive contribution to the marketplace. However, the segregation of every feature into an individual product is not good for the consumer, either from a financial perspective or from an ongoing management perspective.

The answer to the problem is beginning to emerge in the security industry, and it is the platform. Some vendors are creating platforms that would require a customer to buy all their products in order to reap the benefits, but the popularity of those types of platforms is waning. What the industry needs, which is starting to emerge, is a platform that enables not only the platform vendor's products, but also products on the open market. These platforms will enable start-ups and established Information Security brands to coexist and each provide value to the community at large.

A separate strategy is also starting to emerge in which the platform is, itself, a stand-alone product. These platforms then integrate with the point solutions to provide a centralized management and reporting interface that allows the security teams to treat the disparate products as a single comprehensive platform solution. This approach offers a good bridge between the traditional point-product driven marketplace and the future marketplace that will consist of platforms or products that can integrate onto not only a single console, but also can share information across a centralized information repository.

Regardless of the delivery mechanism, the need for all security information to be housed in a single place and the capable of very fast correlation across platforms and products provided by different security vendors is clear. This was the original idea that drove the popularity of System Incident and Event Management (SIEM) tools. However, deeper correlation and more rich information than is currently supported by these types of tools is necessary. SIEM systems may also fill this void as some of them start to morph into true Security Intelligence Platforms, but the central premise remains the same. There are too many operational and security benefits associated with managing and monitoring all devices through a platform to be ignored. Some of those benefits are outlined briefly below.

Rich Correlation

There are a variety of security products that are designed for a variety of purposes. While each has its own focus, correlating events between them can have an immense amount of value for an organization. For example, a web gateway is designed to prevent malicious software from being downloaded from the Internet and to prevent users from visiting web sites that are deemed to be dangerous or inappropriate by the organization.

Data Loss Prevention systems are designed to monitor the content of transfers of data through a variety of means, including the Internet, in order to identify and stop the leakage of data from an environment. What happens when a user is found to be downloading lists of customers to an external USB device? That action is likely against corporate policy, but is it malicious, or is that user just trying to circumvent the system in order to work from home over the weekend? How can we know?

The web gateway has information about that person's browsing history, which may offer important clues into that person's intent. To date, the majority of successful Data Loss Prevention programs would include mechanisms for manually searching for those clues before recommending an action for organizational leadership to take. If all of the information from both systems is on a single platform, however, the platform could automatically provide such a correlation and provide a risk score to the incident itself, giving it a contextual priority, rather than a traditional priority for that system, which is a priority based on the volume of sensitive data.

These two systems were simply used as an example, but there are countless security systems that gather information in the performance of their primary use case that could be helpful to the mission of another technology. Such correlation offers a true advantage to the platform approach.

Ease of Operational Management

Another benefit to a platform is to limit the number of interfaces that an Information Security team member has to learn. There is a large and growing cyber-security skills gap. According to the Information Systems Audit and Control Association (ISACA), there will be a shortage of two million cyber-security professionals worldwide by 2019.[1] The real impact of this shortage is that it takes organizations a long time to hire resources, and often, the resources they do hire are leaving for better-paying opportunities an average of six to eighteen months after joining an organization. That gap means that once acquired, cyber-security professionals must be able to be trained very quickly, and should the need arise to replace them, that their replacements can also be trained quickly. This dynamic increases the value of having a platform to consolidate disparate products.

Depending on who you ask, the average enterprise organization owns products from somewhere between twenty and forty security vendors. Even when an organization has multiple products from a single vendor, those products often have different interfaces for each, meaning a cyber-security professional would have to learn each interface required by his or her job function before he or she could be effective. Consolidating all of those products onto a platform, or a few platforms, is ideal to ensure new employees can be trained and effective as quickly as possible.

---

[1]"Cybersecurity Skills Gap," Cybersecurity Skills Gap. Accessed June 2, 2016.
http://www.isaca.org/cyber/PublishingImages/Cybersecurity-Skills-Gap-1500.jpg.

Further, even after an employee is trained, there is significant time savings associated with managing systems through a platform. There is a cost in terms of resource allocation each time an employee logs into a system. If the employee can perform all of his or her work through a single platform, significant savings in terms of resource time can be realized.

Monitoring and Auditing

Another impact of the cyber-security skills gap is the fact that many times organizations can simply not find resources with the level of experience they need within the budget that they are given to hire said resources. As a result, there are concerns about problems being caused by inexperienced staff members.

Many platforms feature the capability to monitor users and audit what they are doing. The results of this monitoring and auditing can be used to trace back the source of a problem or for training team members in the future.

Access Control

Another positive impact of a platform is the ability to control who may access what resources, and how they may access them. As discussed throughout this book, multifactor authentication is vital in helping to secure systems. Building multifactor authentication controls can be time consuming, however, and the amount of time it takes is multiplied by the number of systems it must be implemented for. Consolidating access to systems through a platform also reduces the amount of effort that must be spent in order to implement multifactor authentication.

Platform Conclusion

As outlined above, there are a variety of benefits to deploying a platform to assist in managing disparate technologies. Organizations will soon have a variety of choices with respect to where to get a platform, but the idea of having a security platform is gaining popularity.

■ **Caution** There are some drawbacks, or concerns with platforms as well. The more data is centralized and consolidated, the more attractive of a target it becomes. It is easier, in my opinion, to secure a single platform rather than several point products, but security of a platform is of greater concern due to the volume and density of the information it houses. Another concern with consolidation is that it can run counter to the best practice of defense n depth. It is still recommended to have triggers or secondary systems outside of a homogenous platform in order to detect exploits in weaknesses or vulnerabilities in the platform.

The End-User Paradigm

It is often said that the individual end user is the weakest link in a security program, which is often true. Conversely, the end user is also the first line of defense for any security program. A truly successful security program will find opportunities to leverage their user population as their first line of defense and support them in areas where they may be weak due to the fact that human beings are fallible and prone to mistakes. The first step toward shifting this paradigm is to find ways to include users as part of the solution rather than looking at them as part of the problem, or worse yet, the entirety of the problem.

Respect the End User

As discussed in chapter 6, there is a need for Information Security teams and the end-user community to have a mutual respect that allows them to each provide value to the organization and the program. It is important to understand that the security team will never know as much about individual pieces of the data as the people who create it and work with it on a daily basis. For example, I was approached by an engineer when I was designing a program who was upset that he and other end users were not as involved in the program as they thought they should be. He essentially told me, "you know that design diagrams are important, but if I were to show you two different design diagrams, would you be able to tell me which had been filed with United States Patent and Trademark Office and was publically available at the United States Library of Congress, and which was yet to be patented, and therefore very sensitive? Well, I could."

Let's forget for a moment that he asked a rhetorical question and answered his own question before I had an opportunity to get a word in edgewise. The fact is, he is right. The security team and business unit leaders must focus on what is important to the entire organization while simultaneously building a mechanism that can facilitate the protection of data driven by the end user. At the time of this writing, such goals are accomplished by fully integrated Data Loss Prevention and Data Classification systems.

Dunning–Kruger Effect

A study by Cornell University discovered a cognitive bias that showed a direct correlation between overconfidence and ignorance. This is confirmation of one of my favorite quotes from Albert Einstein in which he said, "The more I learn, the more I realize I don't know." Essentially, those who think they know everything are the most ignorant among us. Beware of anyone who pretends to know everything about something as deep, complex, and perpetually changing as Information Security.

Dunning and Kruger administered a test to students and then, at the conclusion of the test, asked them how they thought they did on a percentile scale. The people who performed best on the test tended to underestimate their percentile because they believed most people were as smart as they were. Those who scored in the 80th percentile were often scoring themselves in the 50th percentile. While they did not think they did poorly, they possessed the humility to cause them to believe their good performance was not extraordinary. Those who scored the lowest, scored themselves the highest. Many of those that tested in the 10th percentile, for example, scored themselves in the 80th percentile or better. It is believed that the reason why is that they did not possess enough knowledge to understand what they didn't know. This effect permeates the Information Security space and can be observed throughout the world. Essentially, every answer should inspire more questions. Therefore, the more you learn, the more unanswered questions you will have.

I have encountered many people that I would say fall into the category of extreme ignorance as revealed by the Dunning–Kruger Effect. It is easy to spot these people in Information Security, as they speak in absolutes. They will say things like "everyone knows that" or "attacks always begin in a certain way." There are no absolutes in Information Security. The most difficult part of people suffering from the Dunning–Kruger Effect is that they truly believe they are correct, and you will not be able to convince them otherwise. If you find yourself in a conversation with this type of person, do your best to distance yourself from them. Their ignorance is dangerous.

Humility is important in any aspect of business, in my opinion. In order to improve, one must first accept that he or she is not perfect, and does not have all the answers. Therefore, arrogance is the enemy of intelligence and innovation. Further, leaders that exhibit humility are much more successful with their subordinates. In my career, I have always asked my team to be personally humble, while taking pride in the overall organization. As a rule, I still believe this is the best approach.

Being humble does not mean that a person cannot be forceful; it simply means that they keep an open mind and listen to divergent viewpoints. Often, leaders will be charged with making a decision and committing to a direction. The humble leader simple listens to a variety of differing perspectives and takes them into account before making a decision and acting on it. Humility should not be seen as the enemy of action.

Building Internal Bridges

Too often, Information Security initiatives and teams are cultivated in a vacuum and not seen as part of the larger business. This is a problem for a variety of reasons outlined earlier in this book. However, it is incumbent upon those initiatives to be inclusive. I started giving a speaking engagement titled "How to Build an Inclusive Security Program" in 2016. The reason I did so is to attempt to educate those building programs about the value of including vast perspectives and experiences into the program.

Historically, security teams have been secretive, preferring to do their work behind closed doors. Many security professionals do not want anyone to know what monitoring is in place or what security measures are being taken for fear that users will circumvent those measures if they are aware of them. These fears aren't unfounded, but there are ways to balance the need for some degree of obscurity with respect to the program, and the need to include various teams in its formation. It is important that this balance is found in each organization, and one size will not fit all with respect to what the balance actually is.

One area of contention that I have personally began to address is the dynamic of privacy professionals and security professionals. There is a natural adversarial relationship between the two groups because complete security would mandate that there is no privacy, and complete privacy would mandate that there is no security. However, there are elements of common ground. For example, a well-built and effective security program could help protect employee and customer privacy by preventing the intentional or unintentional inappropriate disclosure of information. Additionally, there are ways in which security programs can be built to comply with local and international privacy laws and corporate privacy standards, while still providing protection to the organization. These compromises and balances must be found in order for the security program to work harmoniously inside of an organization.

Conclusion

There are undoubtedly other solutions that would help us improve our security posture as a community of legitimate businesses. The idea of this chapter is not to build an exhaustive all-encompassing list, but to start to stimulate thought and provoke a discussion. How can we work better together to make the cyberworld safer for all of its inhabitants? What types of things make sense for us to collaborate on and where do we draw the line? The answers to these questions will differ between individuals and companies and certainly between countries regions, industries, and sectors. However, where common ground can be found, there is value in collaboration. We should seek that common ground and encourage that collaboration, especially since we know sophisticated threat actor groups are doing so.

CHAPTER 12

■ ■ ■

Partnering with Governments

One of the main lessons I have learned during my five years as Secretary-General is that broad partnerships are the key to solving broad challenges. When governments, the United Nations, businesses, philanthropies and civil society work hand-in-hand, we can achieve great things.

—Ban Ki-moon (Former United Nations Secretary-General)

Few would argue that the cyber-security challenge facing organizations throughout the world is not broad. The former Secretary General states that such broad problems require broad solutions, and I believe that generality specifically applies to the challenges we are facing. If we are to make the cyberworld a safer place to do business, it will require partnerships between citizens and their government, but will also require some level of broad cooperation globally that is uncommon at best and unprecedented at worst.

The central premise of partnering with governments in order to advance the interests of the citizenry is not only an appealing concept, but the very reason that governments exist, according to many famous thinkers throughout history. The reality of partnering with governments, however, has been much more complicated. At the time of this writing, there was a major case in the United States that highlighted both the need for public and private partnership as well as the inherent challenges that governments face as they have earned the suspicion of their populace due to their propensity to indiscriminately gather information on their population when technology presents the opportunity to do so.

Apple and San Bernardino

The February 2016 case of Apple versus the Federal Bureau of Investigation (FBI) revolved around two individuals in San Bernardino, California, who perpetrated a mass shooting, and at the center of the controversy is Apple. Essentially, the U.S. FBI was trying to gather information about the deceased shooters and gather as much information as possible about the attack and any other actors that may have provided material support to the two perpetrators. On its surface, the case seems relatively simple. The vast majority of people in the United States favor providing reasonable support to their government in order to prevent subsequent attacks on the civilian populace and to bring criminals to justice. It is the definition of reasonable support, however, that is at issue in this and many other cases involving government demands to bypass security technologies on demand.

Apple's central argument revolves around the premise that there is currently not a method to bypass their devices' native encryption and creating such a method would not only provide aid to legitimate parties in the government who have obtained a warrant, but also would provide an opportunity for illegitimate actors to also use the same methods to steal information from the population. The underlying distrust on the part of many private citizens extends to the fact that within hours of the U.S. federal government's demand from Apple for one specific case, several state and local governments had already released statements indicating their desire for similar capabilities to aid in the investigations of other crimes.

Unfortunately for ultimate clarity in the United States as it relates to the obligation of private companies to destroy their own security mechanisms to benefit criminal investigations, the U.S. FBI was able to contract with a company that successfully broke into the phone, eliminating the need for litigation in the matter. The case was slated to also set an international precedent with respect to similar questions around the world. Should governments around the world be allowed to compel businesses to compromise security measures designed to protect their users around the world in order to aid in an ongoing investigation? If so, where is the line of crimes or investigations that are serious enough to compel a private company to do so? Is it limited to terrorism? What about murder? At this point, we, as a community, will have to wait until the next time a world government has occasion to compel a private company to do something similar in order to get an answer to the larger question.

Governments around the world have a long-standing history of gathering as much information as they possibly can, sometimes in full view of the general populace, and sometimes in a more clandestine fashion. There have been several high-profile news stories that have proven these massive data collection programs exist throughout the world. In order to make the digital world a safer place to do business, partnerships between the public and private sectors in developed nations must be built, cultivated, and continuously strengthened. However, there is a central issue of trust between the government and the population that must be addressed in order for any public-private partnership to exist in any meaningful way.

Gas Station Sushi

There is a running joke in the United States of America in which people name ridiculous things they trust more than their central government. One popular example is someone who may say "I trust sushi from the gas station more than I trust the United States Federal Government, or certain individuals within the government, with my information." The U.S. government, in many cases, has earned this reputation. There have been many high-profile secret programs designed to gather massive amounts of information on U.S. citizens with and without proper congressional authorization, and sometimes, seemingly with a questionable legal basis. There are other instances where the government has pressured companies like Facebook, Verizon, Google, and others that have large volumes of information about citizens, to share that information with the government without the consent of the affected public. There have also been many scandals involving the improper handling of U.S. secrets. The combination of the two categories of news gives many in the United States pause with respect to sharing more intimate information with the government. On the other side, the government seems to be reluctant to share information with the citizenry. Such reluctance has been evidenced by resistance to Freedom of Information Act (FOIA) disclosures that have been redacted to the point where the information becomes useless. The intent of the act is to provide transparency on government activities to members of the public, but many would question whether that aim has been achieved in any meaningful way.

This problem and perception is not limited to the United States either. Many private citizens have an adversarial relationship with their governments and have a deep-seated distrust for government attempts to collect information about them. Consequently, government initiatives are viewed through the lens of skepticism, often for good reason. In order for a government partnership with the private sector to be effective, the government must conduct their programs in a truly transparent fashion. Even if they do, there will be members of the community that will be slow to embrace government assistance with respect to securing their sensitive information.

People around the world have many reasons to distrust their government. However, there are many times in which the same federal apparatus that they fear provides crucial assistance in helping to secure organizational critical assets. We discussed one example of the FBI's role in the Becton Dickinson and Company case in chapter 4. There must be a level of trust rebuilt between the public and private sector in order for organizations to begin to cooperate to protect information. There is a common interest that unites the public and private sector in protecting information, however, as cyber-crime can have macroeconomic consequences that can affect not only private citizens, but has the potential to impact larger economic statistics as well. It may be uncomfortable at times, but it is necessary if we are to advance the cause of safety and security in an increasingly connected world.

A Question of Trust

Everything that we are going to discuss in this chapter requires building trust between the government and the governed in the affected area. None of these ideas will be effective if the government does not trust its citizenry to some extent and vice versa. U.S. President Ronald Reagan once said, "Trust but verify." That type of attitude is acceptable in this context so long as trust can be established.

Trust is not a one-way street. First, governments around the world must be more transparent about what information they are collecting, how they are collecting it, and what they intend to do with the information once it is collected. This does not apply to espionage activity, as it would be naive to believe that clandestine information collection will ever cease, but those activities should not be used to monitor the government's own citizens. So long as it is, there is an adversarial relationship between the government and its populace, which is not the intent of any productive system of government. The government and the citizens should be partners with the government acting as a service provider for its citizenry. Partnerships are founded on mutual trust and respect. Without trust, there can be no partnership.

Second, citizens must trust their government to an extent, trust but verify is an acceptable approach, in order to build a productive partnership. Also, citizens must understand that their personal information is vulnerable and most individual citizens are powerless to protect it. How many organizations have you given your Personally Identifiable Information (PII) to in the course of your lifetime? For most of us the number is in the thousands or tens of thousands. Governments often punish people for losing your information, but does that make your information any less lost? Building mechanisms to help private citizens recover from the loss of their information is key in any of these discussions.

The Role of Government and the Private Sector

Before discussing individual partnerships or opportunities to partner, it is important to discuss the proper role of government. This is a subject of debate, but there are a few generalizations that I think are relatively noncontroversial. I make these generalizations fully aware that cultural attitudes in different parts of the world vary, and that individuals inside those regions also hold significant differences of opinion. I have a natural suspicion of those who wield power, so I am not advocating that individuals and organizations relinquish privacy in the name of security. However, there are certain functions that are naturally suited to a government apparatus with respect to Information Security.

First, the government is a natural place to aggregate information related to attacks on its citizens. In the United States, many more people report cyber-crime to the FBI than they did in the past. That is a positive step forward. More needs to be reported. Organizations should report tactics, techniques, and protocols (TTPs) in use by attackers as well as how they gained access, how they traversed the system, elevated access, and ultimately exfiltrated data. This information is important in the investigative efforts of the government.

There is an important distinction between providing detailed information about how attacks took place and providing information about individuals. The former is imperative, the latter should be avoided. This type of cooperation is why there must be trust and transparency in the process. Anyone providing information to the government should be very transparent with respect to what they are and are not providing. If the public discovers transfers being made in secret, there is likely to be a significant backlash.

Finally, there is an opportunity for the government to press attackers into service when they are caught. There is a precedent for this in the United States that could be replicated globally. Essentially, when someone is caught, they are offered a significantly reduced sentence in exchange for their cooperation. This cooperation is then used to help organizations protect themselves from other attackers utilizing similar tactics.

Partnerships That Work

Increasing the overall security posture of organizations around the globe will, in my opinion, require far more partnerships between private organizations and governments around the world. However, there are partnerships that exist, which offer good examples of what can be accomplished when public and private sectors work together. Each of these examples has had a material impact on security. While more must certainly be done, we should endeavor to build on our successes.

It is important to understand that there are partnerships between public and private attackers in the cyber-security space. The attacker landscape is populated with state-owned teams, state-sponsored teams, and completely independent criminals. There is also evidence that there are communications and commerce related to exploits that are shared between these groups at times if both parties can benefit. For example, there is evidence that state-sponsored and other sophisticated groups sell their zero-day exploits to less-sophisticated groups that lack the ability to build such exploits on their own, once they have been used. Those exploits are then used repetitively in the time between when the exploit is known and a countermeasure exists and the time that the countermeasure is widely deployed.

In order to combat such cooperation between sophisticated and well-funded groups and more common cyber-criminals, defenders will need access to information from their governments' military and intelligence organizations. To be clear, this access can be in the form of helping to feed intelligence to systems in order to detect and mitigate threats rather than being communicated in a verbal or written form. Secret military and intelligence information should remain so, but to the extent the information can be leveraged to assist in the security of private companies without compromising military secrets, those opportunities should be capitalized upon. Below I will explain how this type of cooperation is beginning to emerge, but maturing and expanding upon these opportunities is crucial to reduce the efficacy of cyber-attacks. We will explore some of the public-private partnerships that are currently in place that I have been exposed to in the coming sections.

■ **Note**   Due to the fact that I have spent my entire career based in the United States, most of the examples I have are examples that I have been exposed to in the United States. The intent is not to suggest that similar examples do not exist in other parts of the world. I am simply using what I am familiar with for my examples.

InfraGard

In 1996, the Cleveland Field Office of the U.S. FBI asked some of the cyber-security professionals in Northern Ohio to assist the Bureau in determining how to better protect public and private Information Technology (IT) Infrastructure.[1] The federal government understood that there was much information to be gained from private cyber-security teams, and those teams understood that the FBI had information that they would never have access to. Combining intelligence gathered by the federal government with the real-world experiences of private organizations was a valuable partnership for both sides.

InfraGard was officially authorized in 1998 with Presidential Decision Directive 63, signed by President Bill Clinton. Since then, InfraGard chapters have been formed in large cities throughout the United States. I have personally participated in a variety of InfraGard events throughout the country and have found value in hearing insights from members of the FBI, military cyber-warfare teams, and high-ranking intelligence officials.

---

[1]"InfraGard History," InfraGard. Accessed May 17, 2016. `https://www.infragard.org/CFAjRMAWzORWLy%25252FOHF` `CSxODyvXzq7l3BivnobcQKrbg%25253D!`

InfraGard works because it allows private organizations to share information with an organization that they trust, in this case the U.S. FBI. The FBI then anonymizes the information and shares it with other members of the community that may benefit from this information. For example, if a utility company is hit with a certain type of attack that represents a threat to critical infrastructure, the FBI can anonymize that information, investigate it, and provide information to other utility companies about what happened in the attack and how they can protect themselves from similar attacks and similar actors. There are also meetings where guest speakers from the government share information with the member community or organizations. Information ranges from attack profiles that are being observed to ways they can work closely with the appropriate government authorities in case of emergency. At times, subject matter experts serve as guest speakers to educate the membership on relevant topics and trends in the industry. The members of InfraGard benefit from gaining valuable insights from government agencies, and the government agencies benefit from helping to advance their goal of protecting critical infrastructure and also protecting the economic interests of the United States from cyber-crime directed and individual organizations. Most people that I have spoken with that have participated in InfraGard find it extremely valuable.

InfraGard works in the United States, and these successes could easily be replicated in other countries. The majority of countries have both an intelligence apparatus as well as a division of the military responsible for cyber-security or cyber-warfare. Private organizations in those countries also have a volume of information related to the threats they are facing. My recommendation would be that each country form something similar to InfraGard, and that each organization participate in InfraGard or its equivalent. This partnership has proven to be beneficial to all parties where it has been implemented.

Defense Industrial Base

In the United States, the Defense Industrial Base is inclusive of all organizations that are providers of equipment, information, or personnel that are relied upon by the U.S. military for the National Defense. This seems like a targeted list of companies, but it includes over 100,000 organizations.[2]

As part of the Defense Industrial Base, there is a sector-specific plan put together by the U.S. government that details the risk framework and the Risk Treatment Plan that is put in place to protect these critical organizations to ensure they are armed with the information they need to protect themselves and continue to provide services that are critical to the National Defense.

■ **Note** There is a blog[3] that has been brought to my attention during the review of this section that references the Defense Industrial Base (DIB) shrinking in importance and influence. In my opinion, articles like this are misleading. The amount of money spent on defense in the United States is not shrinking in any meaningful way. It fluctuates depending on wartime or peacetime, but overall, the United States spends more on its military than any other country in the world. Basically, what the blog is citing is the fact that the largest defense contractors are shrinking. There are several contributing factors including the Department of Defense's commitment work with small business where possible, and the fact that many companies who also serve the commercial sector are winning government contracts. As a result, the largest DIB participants are shrinking, but the members of the DIB are growing. This is to prevent the military apparatus from disproportionately depending on a few companies. I think that makes the DIB and the sector-specific plan from the Department of Defense more important instead of less.

---

[2]"Homeland Security," Defense Industrial Base Sector. Accessed May 17, 2016.
https://www.dhs.gov/defense-industrial-base-sector.
[3]"The Incredible Shrinking Defense Industrial Base," *SIGNAL Magazine*, 2015. Accessed June 3, 2016.
http://www.afcea.org/content/?q=Blog-incredible-shrinking-defense-industrial-base.

In the United States, each sector that is considered critical infrastructure, such as the power grid, the Defense Industrial Base, the Financial Sector, Water Supply, etc., has a sector-specific risk plan that is assigned to an overseeing government agency For example, the DIB is sponsored by the Department of Defense and the power companies are sponsored by the Department of Energy. This is a mechanism in which information relevant to each sector can be shared with the companies that make up the critical capability. This mechanism allows personnel with clearances inside the government to evaluate classification levels to determine if certain relevant information can be shared outside the government.

These types of partnerships likely exist in other countries, but in my opinion, should be expanded to cover all sectors that are important to the economy, and not just the critical infrastructure. This would open up this type of information sharing to virtually every organization in the world. Ultimately, nothing is more critical than a nation's economy since a failing economy will eventually cause the collapse of any government if the economic downturn is severe and persistent enough. Therefore, cyber-crime and industrial espionage could theoretically be an existential threat to economies should the problem become widespread and persistent enough to affect a specific countries' Gross Domestic Product (GDP) in a negative fashion.

National Cybersecurity Center

Currently, there is a significant partnership in its early stages in the United States called the National Cybersecurity Intelligence Center (NCIC). Members of the Military, Defense, and private cyber-security experts are in the planning phases to build an institution that will act as a think tank and intelligence sharing center for small- to medium-sized businesses that do not possess the resources to conduct research into cyber-threats.

The Center is not designed to replace the cyber-security apparatuses that are in place in larger organizations that have a cyber-security budget, but is designed to provide a minimum level of knowledge and protection in the form of best practices to organizations that cannot afford the staff or the consulting necessary to build a comprehensive cyber-security program.

The Center is also making an attempt to fill, to some extent, the cyber-security talent gap. There is a significant shortfall of qualified candidates to fill the cyber-security jobs that exist, and the gap is projected to grow for the foreseeable future. The Colorado Technology Association "estimates businesses and government agencies in the state today need 4,000–6,000 workers with expertise in computer networking and cybersecurity," and that is just in Colorado. That problem persists in other states and countries as well.[4]

■ **Note**   It is possible that these types of initiatives are happening in other places throughout the world, since my proximity to the facility has driven my awareness of the project.

These types of initiatives are vital to advancing the cause of securing organizations and raising the barriers to entry for attackers. Establishing a baseline of protection that is aided by government intelligence from military and traditional intelligence agencies is a great idea, and it is a good example of a way that governments can provide services and protection to their corporate citizens.

---

[4]"National Cybersecurity Center Could Become 'Huge Economic Driver' for Colorado Springs," *Colorado Springs Gazette.* Accessed May 17, 2016. http://m.gazette.com/national-cybersecurity-center-could-become-huge-economic-driver-for-colorado-springs/article/1567957.

National Vulnerability Database

In the United States, there is a National Vulnerability Database, which is a method of sharing information about vulnerabilities that are identified in common computing platforms and systems. According to the government web site, "NVD is the U.S. government repository of standards based vulnerability management data represented using the Security Content Automation Protocol (SCAP). This data enables automation of vulnerability management, security measurement, and compliance. NVD includes databases of security checklists, security-related software flaws, misconfigurations, product names, and impact metrics."[5]

This database is a valuable resource to ensure that known vulnerabilities cannot continue to be exploited after they have been effectively used. This can be very helpful in protecting against unsophisticated attack groups as they are often repeating attacks that others have discovered and used successfully. It is important to have such information available to the general public. This is similar to other crime sectors in which information is shared throughout the world on the nightly news or through "Most Wanted" lists. The intent is to inform the public of vulnerabilities so they may tune their systems to protect them from those types of attacks.

CREST

CREST is a nonprofit organization in the United Kingdom that is loosely affiliated with government standards and best practices. CREST is helping to fill a gap globally in certifying penetration testers and incident response services. There are respected certifications like Certified Ethical Hacker (CEH) that are offered by other organizations other than CREST, but CREST endeavors to provide a much higher level of assurance to those who have exceeded the average skill level of their peers. These types of certification bodies that are continuing to build frameworks for assuring the skills of individuals are not often purely government entities, but are quasi-government organizations drawing dues from their membership and acting as governing bodies. CREST is far from the only such organization, but is an example of an organization forming to meet the evolving needs of the overall marketplace.

Regulations

Putting regulations in this list is personally controversial for me, because many regulations have done more harm than good in the Information Security space. That said, there are regulations that have worked well around the world to help protect organizations and consumers. There are also regulations, normally related to employee privacy, which make it significantly more difficult to protect Critical Information Assets in the country.

The core of the controversy related to employee privacy is related to ownership. Do I own what I create at work or does it belong to my employer, or even my government? Most countries would say an employee's work product belongs to their employer, since the employer is compensating the employee for his or her labor at the time he or she is creating the work product. In countries where everyone is employed by the government, that means their work product is government owned, and in societies where individual corporations employ people, the corporation generally owns the work product. In my view, this means that anything the employee creates as part of their employment should be subject to monitoring. However, many countries, especially in Europe, do not agree. European countries often have provisions in place to prevent organizations from monitoring their employees' "personal communications." The central problem with that idea is that if the employee mistakenly believes their work product belongs to them, even when their employment agreements explicitly state otherwise, they may consider copying their work product to home systems for future use constitutes a personal communication. This presents a problem for organizations who seek to protect the Intellectual Property they commission.

---

[5]"Homeland Security," Defense Industrial Base Sector. Accessed May 17, 2016.
https://www.dhs.gov/defense-industrial-base-sector.

In North America, the attitude is that if you wish to communicate in a private and personal manner, those communications should be conducted on a privately owned device, which the organization does not monitor. The prevailing attitude in Europe, however, is that employees have a right to privacy, even when using corporate assets. As a result, there is a mandate that any monitoring of employee communications include provisions to allow for discriminate monitoring that excludes personal communications or anything that could be potentially personal.

Other countries wish to apply probable cause protections for employees. Essentially, an organization would need probable cause that an individual is behaving maliciously to monitor an individual. In the United States, identifying that someone is looking for a job is cause enough to monitor their activity, for example, but in many countries it is not sufficient. The problem is, if you cannot monitor an employee, in what way could you establish probable cause? How do you know if that employee looking for another job is taking corporate information with them? Often, people who intend to act maliciously toward their organization will intentionally ensure they do not arouse suspicion outside of their electronic activity.

Regardless of my opinions on the matter, privacy regulations are not likely to disappear in the foreseeable future. As a result, security programs must be designed to account for and comply with these regulations. The key to building a security program in such an environment is finding ways to be compliant with local laws while still protecting their property. This is a difficult problem to solve, but one to which many times a solution can be found if each country is approached with legal counsel independently.

There are also regulations that have been very helpful in increasing the security posture of individual organizations. Compliance is not security, as we have discussed throughout this book, but requiring compliance requires organizations to build teams that can then be extended beyond compliance and into more effective security measures. Twenty years ago, very few organizations had IT Security departments, but currently most organizations do. Certainly, the growing global threats played a major role, but regulations have likely contributed as well. Oftentimes, compliance will mandate that an organization have a specific security capability. While the efficacy of that capability is not mandated, security teams could leverage the mandatory investment to improve the security profile of their organization.

What Should Be the Role of Government?

The proper role of government in terms of Information Security will likely be different in different regions around the globe. Each region has its own culture and attitudes toward the proper role of government, which are steeped in history and often deeply ingrained into the national identity of the country and the psyche of the citizenry. One size will not fit all, but all countries will need some level of support from their governments in order to protect themselves, especially when trying to protect from sophisticated state-sponsored threats.

During my time working in InteliSecure's Managed Services department, we have found cases of governments around the world infecting consumer services like search engines to install malware on users' computers. The malware then transfers corporate information to the government in the background. These types of activities position the government as a security adversary rather than an ally to private business and exasperate the issue of trust we discussed earlier in this chapter.

The problem with the cyber-threat landscape is that it has significantly blurred the line between an individual's responsibility to protect him- or herself, and the responsibility the central government has to defend its citizens. In a connected world, it is very difficult to determine the origin of an attack until the attack is over. Even then, the origin of the attack that is determined is often a hypothesis rather than a definitive answer. Another problem is that in traditional situations, the weaponry used by militaries is significantly more sophisticated than what a common criminal has access to. For example, private businesses may take precautions against armed robbery with a handgun, but very few, if any, have protections for if they were attacked by a Main Battle Tank. In the cyber-battlefield, most criminal organizations have access to similar exploits as nation-states would have, or even secondhand exploits utilized by a nation-state and then resold to the cyber-criminal or terrorist community. The cyber-battlefield is one big gray area, which makes it difficult for governments to find their proper role with respect to where they should intervene, and what level of protection is appropriate to assume the organization will employ. Effective roles and responsibilities are yet to be determined, which adds to the uncertainty. However, what is clear is that voluntary public-private partnerships have the potential to solve some of the problems we face as a business community while the landscape is being defined around the world.

Effective Public Partner Partnership Opportunities

Clarity is key with respect to what types of countermeasures and counterattacks are acceptable on the part of legitimate business. There are a variety of countermeasures that organizations would like to deploy that are described below. Each government should provide clarity with respect to what is and is not acceptable as soon as possible in order to give defenders guidelines with respect to how far they can go. Ultimately, there must be consequences when attackers get caught in order to discourage future attacks. Unfortunately, today there are very few.

Counterattacks and Hacking Back

Many organizations that have a robust security program have begun to ask for a counterattack capability in which they can cause harm to attackers when those attackers can be positively identified. This is a very difficult political question, and due to the fact that attacks happen between countries and regions in most cases, it is a geopolitical question as well. The central premise is that if someone attacks my network, why can I not counterattack them?

The idea is compelling and seems appealing, but as is often the case, the devil is in the details. The first concern is positive identification. How can you be sure that your investigation into the origin of the attack is accurate? Many attacks feature deception as part of the attack. How do we know we are counterattacking the right people without causing collateral damage? Essentially, you have private organizations conducting cyber-warfare activities under that scenario, and engaging in what may be considered an act of war.

The central problem, though, is very few of these attackers are prosecuted through legal channels, and there have to be some consequences to an attacker if we hope to dissuade future attacks. Essentially, private organizations are frustrated that they are targets, with little protection. Many of these organizations are keen to develop offensive capabilities.

While it is unlikely that these types of counterattacks will ever be allowed, as it would likely result in chaos, the sentiment needs to be addressed. Most global governments have an offensive capability. What if private organizations were empowered to turn over their forensic evidence in the event of an attack, and the military or intelligence apparatus that possesses the country's offensive capability attacks the attackers on behalf of their citizens? This is a strange thing to even discuss, but these are the questions that begin to be raised in a globally connected world.

One idea is to financially penalize world governments who allow attacks to be launched from their borders. The United States, for example, contributes money and aid to a large number of countries around the world. Establishing baselines of how countries should behave in the cyberworld and enforcing those baselines through financial means could be an effective way to motivate those countries to prosecute crimes that are launched against organizations in other countries within their borders.

Militaries and Corporations Working Together

It is often the responsibility of the military to protect organizations from kinetic threats against their property such as traditional spies or bombing campaigns, to use an extreme example. Does that extend to the cyberworld? In my opinion, it should, meaning that state-sponsored attacks on corporations, whether designed to steal information or destroy systems or infrastructure should be considered an attack on national interests in which retaliation by a military apparatus is considered appropriate. This does not absolve the organization of the responsibility to protect themselves to the extent that protection is feasible. It simply means that when state-sponsored or terrorist cyber-attacks are identified, there is a mechanism for organizations to report the attacks along with the evidence of said attacks to government authorities so the military cyber-warfare apparatus may degrade or destroy the attackers' capability to inflict further harm to their citizens. These types of decisions obviously have geopolitical ramifications, but the idea that a country can sponsor attacks on private organizations in the sovereign territory of another nation without consequence is a perception that must change.

Corporations in pretty much every country globally pay taxes in exchange for services like protection as well as infrastructure such as roads, and increasingly, Internet access. Countries around the world compete for corporate headquarters both on the taxes and other costs of doing business as well as the services they provide. It is my opinion that if one country or several countries dedicated resources to aggressively defending corporations headquartered in their countries and targeting threat actors that launch attacks inside their borders could likely attract organizations to their countries.

The cyberworld is different than the traditional world in many ways, but the basic human and corporate desires to feel safe and be able to conduct business without having things of value stolen from them persist. Law enforcement and militaries are a significant part of the services that are offered by governments to their corporate and human citizens. Similar protections should be extended to the digital world, in my opinion.

You Are Not a Number!

There was a time when numbers as a means of lifelong identification were practical and there were few alternatives to this type of identification. During the time of the creation of many of these forms of identification, it was realistic for a person to be granted a single number and keep that number secret to them over the course of their lives. The combination of their name, their birthdate, and this number was generally enough to uniquely identify a person.

Those days are gone and those rules do not apply in a hyper-connected world. Having something like a number that is essentially something you know, the most easily compromised factor of authentication, give a thief the opportunity to steal a person's entire identity simply by stealing the number and possibly some other personal characteristics is dangerous and, in my view, irresponsible. Identity theft is a major problem globally with many micro-economic and macro-economic consequences for individuals and countries.

There are likely many ways that I have not thought of that could solve the problems associated with having a single number that is easily stolen identify a person for life. My suggestion is to either use multifactor authentication to identify individuals, or to create a mechanism that would allow a person to get a new identification number should theirs become compromised similar to how credit cards can be reissued should they be compromised.

Regardless of the methodology employed, it is important for governments to address the issue that exists as an increasing percentage of identities has been compromised. If the method for identifying people is not reformed, we will eventually reach a saturation point in which enough of a majority of people have compromised identities, where the identifications are worthless. I have already seen a significant shift in my lifetime. I was born in the United States, so I was issued a Social Security Number at birth. When I was a child, my Social Security Number was taken as definitive proof of my identity. At this point, it is a single piece of information, among many others, that is required for me to identify myself. The changes I am suggesting will not significantly increase the burden on the individual for identification, but will strengthen the identification significantly.

Multifactor Authentication for Identities

Most people have become accustomed to multifactor authentication to access systems at work, wouldn't it make sense that it would require more than a single factor of authentication to apply for long-term debt or enter into a contract that could affect a person's credit rating and subsequently their ability to borrow in the future? Many times, these types of transactions require multiple pieces of information, like your name, birthdate, mother's maiden name, high school mascot, etc. The problem is all of these things are something you know, which is a single factor of authentication. As discussed in chapter 4, technology has progressed to the point that we could add a factor of authentication, like something you have or something you are in order to further identify an individual.

Such a scenario would require either world governments to build infrastructure to identify people, or to turn over the management of identities to a third party, possibly a credit reporting agency. Privatizing identities would be a politically controversial move and is unlikely to happen any time soon, but governments building infrastructure to either issue a token to identify an individual or to register something they already have to identify them is an increasingly realistic possibility.

For example, if the government gave everyone a hardware token to identify themselves, and any time they wanted to apply for credit, government benefits, or anything else that required them to identify themselves, they would essentially provide both factors of authentication to a government portal, which would then issue a one-time use token that, combined with the person's name and birthdate would authorize a single transaction that the lender or bank could verify with the government agency. This scenario would be far more difficult for people to compromise and would certainly have some tangible impact on the prevalence of identity theft. This type of proposal is likely to be highly controversial. The truth is, the public must shift their way of thinking with respect to security and identifying themselves for these changes to ever be implemented. However, there is real harm caused to the public by identity theft and these measures could help to mitigate that risk. It will take a charismatic leader to explain this to the general public, but doing so would be a worthwhile endeavor.

Nonpersistent Identities

The credit card industry provides a good example of how nonpersistent numbers can be used effectively to reduce the effect of cyber-crime. When a cyber-criminal steals a credit card number, the number is not persistent, and can be deactivated within moments of it being reported stolen or observed to be displaying an anomalous behavior pattern.

A similar methodology could be applied to identification numbers to make them much safer. There would certainly need to be more administration than currently exists, but, in my mind, the benefits outweigh the increased administrative overhead. In this scenario, if your identification number was stolen, a new one would be issued to you and the old one would be deactivated very quickly.

Such a system would require far more possibilities and number combinations in order to facilitate the additional capacity. This could be accomplished by increasing the number of digits, which would make the number more difficult to remember, or the numbers could be made alphanumeric, which would provide more than enough possible combinations to satisfy the expanded requirements without changing the length of the numbers, which are between nine and ten digits in most countries currently.

There would also need to be a system in place that would automatically update creditors when a number was changed. This would require a significant partnership between the credit reporting agencies and the government agency that handled the identities. The process would essentially be when an identity is updated, the database is updated and changes are pushed to credit reporting agencies daily. The credit reporting agencies would then have a mechanism to notify the creditors associated with that person in some batch fashion. There may be other ideas for how to accomplish this that would be easier to administer, but that is one way that such a process could be implemented leveraging people, process, and technology.

Conclusion

The proper role of government and the extent to which partnerships should exist between the public and private sectors is likely to be the subject of debate for years to come. However, what is not likely to be up for debate is that there is some role for governments to assist in helping to defend their private and corporate citizens from harm in the digital arena. It is important for members of both sectors globally to continuously raise opportunities and ideas for effective collaboration.

Similar to the situation faced in the nineteenth- and twentieth-century American West, we face a time of expanding capabilities that offer unprecedented opportunities for people all over the globe to prosper in ways that were previously difficult if not impossible. The idea that ideas and information can be transferred throughout the world at the speed of light is exciting and compelling. However, with that increased connectivity that can be a force for good, comes danger. Throughout history, any period of rapid expansion of prosperity brings with it new threats. This digital age is no different. Ethan Woodson, cyber-security expert at American Family Insurance, once told me, "The good thing about the internet is everything is on the internet. The problem with the internet is that everything is on the internet." The idea is simple but it sums up the problems we are facing.

The challenges we are facing today are neither surprising nor impossible to overcome. History teaches us many lessons on the subject, including the fact that eventually, we will overcome the challenges we face as a people. We will find ways to protect information in a globally connected world. We will find ways to dissuade criminals and bring them to justice. We will make the digital world a safer place to do business. It is my firm belief that following the principles outlined in this book, which build on best practices that are widely known, but unfortunately, not universally implemented in the Information Security space, will offer a solid foundation for individual organizations to solve the problems they face. Undoubtedly, we will need to continue to build on these principles. The overriding message of this book is hope. We can solve these challenges, and we must, therefore we will. As we always have.

Index

Get the eBook for only $5!

Why limit yourself?

Now you can take the weightless companion with you wherever you go and access your content on your PC, phone, tablet, or reader.

Since you've purchased this print book, we're happy to offer you the eBook in all 3 formats for just $5.

Convenient and fully searchable, the PDF version enables you to easily find and copy code—or perform examples by quickly toggling between instructions and applications. The MOBI format is ideal for your Kindle, while the ePUB can be utilized on a variety of mobile devices.

To learn more, go to www.apress.com/companion or contact support@apress.com.